CW01019911

The Autobiography of a Yogi

The
Autobiography
of a
Yogi

Paramhansa Yogananda

MAIN STREET

MAIN STREET

THE AUTOBIOGRAPHY OF A YOGI

This edition Copyright © 2013, Main Street

First MAIN STREET Paperback Edition, 2013

ISBN 978-81-216-1879-3

Published by
MAIN STREET
An imprint of Hind Pocket Books
E-14, Sector-11, Noida-201301

Design and layout: SCANSET
J-40, Jorbagh Lane, New Delhi-110003

Printed at Sai Printo Pack Pvt. Ltd., New Delhi-110020

PRINTED IN INDIA

13/13/07/01/20/SCANSET/SRK/SPP/SPP/NP-/NP-

Contents

1
My Parents and Early Life

The characteristic features of Indian culture have long been a search for ultimate verities and the concomitant disciple-guru relationship. My own path led me to a Christlike sage whose beautiful life was chiseled for the ages. He was one of the great masters who are India's sole remaining wealth. Emerging in every generation, they have bulwarked their land against the fate of Babylon and Egypt.

I find my earliest memories covering the anachronistic features of a previous incarnation. Clear recollections came to me of a distant life, a yogi amidst the Himalayan snows. These glimpses of the past, by some dimensionless link, also afforded me a glimpse of the future.

The helpless humiliations of infancy are not banished from my mind. I was resentfully conscious of not being able to walk or express myself freely. Prayerful surges arose within me as I realized my bodily impotence. Psychological ferment and my unresponsive body brought me to many obstinate crying-spells. I recall the general family bewilderment at my distress. Happier memories, too, crowd in on me: my mother's caresses, and my first attempts at lisping phrase and toddling step. These early triumphs, usually forgotten quickly, are yet a natural basis of self-confidence.

Although odd, clear memories of infancy are not extremely rare. During travels in numerous lands, I have listened to early recollections from the lips of veracious men and women.

I was born in the last decade of the nineteenth century, and passed my first eight years at Gorakhpur in the United Provinces of India. We were eight children: four boys and four girls. I, Mukunda Lal Ghosh, was the second son and the fourth child.

Father and Mother were Bengalis, of the KSHATRIYA caste. Both were blessed with saintly nature. Father, Bhagabati Charan Ghosh, was an outstanding mathematician and logician. But Mother was a queen of hearts, and taught us only through love.

A daily gesture of respect to Father was given by Mother's dressing us carefully in the afternoons to welcome him home from the office. His position was similar to that of a vice-president, in the Bengal-Nagpur Railway, one of India's large companies. His work involved traveling, and our family lived in several cities during my childhood.

Mother held an open hand toward the needy. Father was also kindly disposed, but his respect for law and order extended to the budget. One fortnight Mother spent, in feeding the poor, more than Father's monthly income.

Father was a strict disciplinarian to his children in their early years, but his attitude toward himself was truly Spartan. He never visited the theater, for instance, but sought his recreation in various spiritual practices and in reading the BHAGAVAD GITA. Shunning all luxuries, he would cling to one old pair of shoes until they were useless. His sons bought automobiles after they came into popular use, but Father was always content with the trolley car for his daily ride to the office.

Early in their married life, my parents became disciples of a great master, Lahiri Mahasaya of Benares. This contact strengthened Father's naturally ascetical temperament.

Father first met Lahiri Mahasaya through Abinash Babu, an employee in the Gorakhpur office of the Bengal-Nagpur Railway. Abinash instructed my young ears with engrossing tales of many Indian saints. He invariably concluded with a tribute to the superior glories of his own guru.

"Did you ever hear of the extraordinary circumstances under which your father became a disciple of Lahiri Mahasaya?"

It was on a lazy summer afternoon, as Abinash and I sat together in the compound of my home, that he put this intriguing question. I shook my head with a smile of anticipation.

"Years ago, before you were born, I asked your father to give me a week's leave from my Gorakhpur duties in order to visit my guru in Benares. Your father ridiculed my plan.

"'Are you going to become a religious fanatic?' he inquired. 'Concentrate on your office work if you want to forge ahead.'

"Sadly walking home along a woodland path that day, I met your father in a palanquin. He dismissed his servants and conveyance, and fell into step beside me. Seeking to console me, he pointed out the advantages of striving for worldly success. But I heard him listlessly. My heart was repeating: 'Lahiri Mahasaya! I cannot live without seeing you!'

"Our path took us to the edge of a tranquil field, where the rays of the late afternoon sun were still crowning the tall ripple of the wild grass. We paused in admiration. There in the field, only a few yards from us, the form of my great guru suddenly appeared!

"'Bhagabati, you are too hard on your employee!' His

voice was resonant in our astounded ears. He vanished as mysteriously as he had come. On my knees I was exclaiming, 'Lahiri Mahasaya! Lahiri Mahasaya!' Your father was motionless with stupefaction for a few moments.

"'Abinash, not only do I give YOU leave, but I give MYSELF leave to start for Benares tomorrow. I must know this great Lahiri Mahasaya, who is able to materialize himself at will in order to intercede for you! I will take my wife and ask this master to initiate us in his spiritual path. Will you guide us to him?'

"The next evening your parents and I entrained for Benares. We took a horse cart the following day, and then had to walk through narrow lanes to my guru's secluded home. Entering his little parlor, we bowed before the master, enlocked in his habitual lotus posture. He blinked his piercing eyes and leveled them on your father.

"'Bhagabati, you are too hard on your employee!' His words were the same as those he had used two days before in the Gorakhpur field. He added, 'I am glad that you have allowed Abinash to visit me, and that you and your wife have accompanied him.'

"To their joy, he initiated your parents in the spiritual practice of KRIYA YOGA. Your father and I, as brother disciples, have been close friends since the memorable day of the vision. Lahiri Mahasaya took a definite interest in your own birth. Your life shall surely be linked with his own: the master's blessing never fails."

Lahiri Mahasaya left this world shortly after I had entered it. His picture, in an ornate frame, always graced our family altar in the various cities to which Father was transferred by his office.

His picture had a surpassing influence over my life. As I grew, the thought of the master grew with me. In meditation I would often see his photographic image emerge from its small frame and, taking a living form, sit before me. When I attempted to touch the feet of his luminous body, it would change and again become the picture. As childhood slipped into boyhood, I found Lahiri Mahasaya transformed in my mind from a little image, cribbed in a frame, to a living, enlightening presence. I frequently prayed to him in moments of trial or confusion, finding within me his solacing direction.

I was blessed about the age of eight with a wonderful healing through the photograph of Lahiri Mahasaya. This experience gave intensification to my love. While at our family estate in Ichapur, Bengal, I was stricken with Asiatic cholera. My life was despaired of; the doctors could do nothing. At my bedside, Mother frantically motioned me to look at Lahiri Mahasaya's picture on the wall above my head.

"Bow to him mentally!" She knew I was too feeble even to lift my hands in salutation. "If you really show your devotion and inwardly kneel before him, your life will be spared!"

I gazed at his photograph and saw there a blinding light, enveloping my body and the entire room. My nausea and other uncontrollable symptoms disappeared; I was well. Shortly after my healing through the potency of the guru's picture, I had an influential spiritual vision. Sitting on my bed one morning, I fell into a deep reverie.

"What is behind the darkness of closed eyes?" This probing thought came powerfully into my mind. An immense flash of light at once manifested to my inward gaze. Divine shapes of saints, sitting in meditation posture in mountain caves, formed like miniature cinema pictures on the large screen of radiance within my forehead.

"Who are you?" I spoke aloud.

"We are the Himalayan yogis." The celestial response is difficult to describe; my heart was thrilled.

"Ah, I long to go to the Himalayas and become like you!" The vision vanished, but the silvery beams expanded in ever-widening circles to infinity.

"What is this wondrous glow?"

"I am Iswara. I am Light." The voice was as murmuring clouds.

"I want to be one with Thee!"

Out of the slow dwindling of my divine ecstasy, I salvaged a permanent legacy of inspiration to seek God. "He is eternal, ever-new Joy!" This memory persisted long after the day of rapture.

Our family moved to Lahore in the Punjab. There I acquired a picture of the Divine Mother in the form of the Goddess Kali. It sanctified a small informal shrine on the balcony of our home. An unequivocal conviction came over me that fulfillment would crown any of my prayers uttered in that sacred spot. Standing there with Uma one day, I watched two kites flying over the roofs of the buildings on the opposite side of the very narrow lane.

"Why are you so quiet?" Uma pushed me playfully.

"I am just thinking how wonderful it is that Divine Mother gives me whatever I ask."

"I suppose She would give you those two kites!" My sister laughed derisively.

"Why not?" I began silent prayers for their possession.

Matches are played in India with kites whose strings are covered with glue and ground glass. Each player attempts to sever the string of his opponent. A freed kite sails over the roofs; there is great fun in catching it. Inasmuch as Uma and I were on the balcony, it seemed impossible that any loosed kite could come into our hands; its string would naturally dangle over the roofs.

The players across the lane began their match. One string was cut; immediately the kite floated in my direction. It was stationary for a moment, through sudden abatement of breeze, which sufficed to firmly entangle the string with a cactus plant on top of the opposite house. A perfect loop was formed for my seizure. I handed the prize to Uma. I continued my prayers for another kite. And lo! The kite was in my grasp.

"Indeed, Divine Mother listens to you! This is all too uncanny for me!" Sister bolted away like a frightened fawn.

2

My Mother's Death and the Mystic Amulet

My mother's greatest desire was the marriage of my elder brother. "Ah, when I behold the face of Ananta's wife, I shall find heaven on this earth!" I frequently heard Mother express in these words her strong Indian sentiment for family continuity.

I was about eleven years old at the time of Ananta's betrothal. Mother was in Calcutta, joyously supervising the wedding preparations. Father and I alone remained at our home in Bareilly in northern India, whence Father had been transferred after two years at Lahore.

Mother was welcoming numerous relatives, daily arriving in Calcutta from distant homes. She lodged them comfortably in a large, newly acquired house at 50 Amherst Street. Everything was in readiness – the banquet delicacies, the gay throne on which Brother was to be carried to the home of the bride-to-be, the rows of colorful lights, the mammoth cardboard elephants and camels, the English, Scottish and Indian orchestras, the professional entertainers, the priests for the ancient rituals.

Father and I, in gala spirits, were planning to join the

family in time for the ceremony. Shortly before the great day, however, I had an ominous vision.

It was in Bareilly on a midnight. As I slept beside Father on the piazza of our bungalow, I was awakened by a peculiar flutter of the mosquito netting over the bed. The flimsy curtains parted and I saw the beloved form of my mother.

"Awaken your father!" Her voice was only a whisper. "Take the first available train, at four o'clock this morning. Rush to Calcutta if you would see me!" The wraith-like figure vanished.

"Father, Father! Mother is dying!" The terror in my tone aroused him instantly. I sobbed out the fatal tidings.

"Never mind that hallucination of yours." Father gave his characteristic negation to a new situation. "Your mother is in excellent health. If we get any bad news, we shall leave tomorrow."

"You shall never forgive yourself for not starting now!" Anguish caused me to add bitterly, "Nor shall I ever forgive you!"

The melancholy morning came with explicit words: "Mother dangerously ill; marriage postponed; come at once."

Father and I left distractedly. Already bereft, I felt, of my mother, I could not endure a world suddenly barren to the bone. I loved Mother as my dearest friend on earth.

When we reached our Calcutta home, it was only to confront the stunning mystery of death. I collapsed into an almost lifeless state. Years passed before any reconciliation entered my heart.

Father and I returned to Bareilly soon after the crematory rites for the well-beloved. One day, one of my cousins, fresh from a period of travel in the holy hills, visited us in Bareilly.

I listened eagerly to his tales about the high mountain abode of yogis and swamis.

And I fled that afternoon toward Nainital in the Himalayan foothills. Ananta gave determined chase; I was forced to return sadly to Bareilly. My heart wept for the lost Mothers, human and divine.

Fourteen months after Mother's passing, I learned that she had left me a momentous message. Ananta was present at her deathbed and had recorded her words. One evening he summoned me to his side.

"Mukunda, I have been reluctant to give you strange tidings." Ananta's tone held a note of resignation. "My fear was to inflame your desire to leave home. But in any case you are bristling with divine ardor. When I captured you recently on your way to the Himalayas, I came to a definite resolve. I must not further postpone the fulfillment of my solemn promise." My brother handed me a small box, and delivered Mother's message.

"Let these words be my final blessing, my beloved son Mukunda!" Mother had said. "The hour is here when I must relate a number of phenomenal events following your birth. I first knew your destined path when you were but a babe in my arms. I carried you then to the home of my guru in Benares. Almost hidden behind a throng of disciples, I could barely see Lahiri Mahasaya as he sat in deep meditation.

"While I patted you, I was praying that the great guru take notice and bestow a blessing. As my silent devotional demand grew in intensity, he opened his eyes and beckoned me to approach. The others made a way for me; I bowed at the sacred feet. My master seated you on his lap, placing his hand on your forehead by way of spiritually baptizing you.

"'Little mother, thy son will be a yogi. As a spiritual engine, he will carry many souls to God's kingdom.'

"In this way, dear son, I came to know that your road lies far from worldly ambitions. The most singular event in my life brought further confirmation – an event which now impels my deathbed message.

"It was an interview with a sage in the Punjab. While our family was living in Lahore, one morning the servant came precipitantly into my room.

"'Mistress, a strange SADHU is here. He insists that he "see the mother of Mukunda."'

"I went at once to greet the visitor. Bowing at his feet, I sensed that before me was a true man of God.

"'Mother,' he said, 'the great masters wish you to know that your stay on earth will not be long. Your next illness shall prove to be your last.' There was a silence, during which I felt no alarm but only a vibration of great peace. Finally he addressed me again:

"'You are to be the custodian of a certain silver amulet. I will not give it to you today; to demonstrate the truth in my words, the talisman shall materialize in your hands tomorrow as you meditate. On your deathbed, you must instruct your eldest son Ananta to keep the amulet for one year and then to hand it over to your second son. Mukunda will understand the meaning of the talisman from the great ones. He should receive it about the time he is ready to renounce all worldly hopes and start his vital search for God.'

"I bowed before the saint in great reverence. And he departed with a blessing. The next evening, as I sat with folded hands in meditation, a silver amulet materialized between my palms, even as the SADHU had promised. I have jealously guarded it for more than two years, and now leave it in Ananta's keeping. Do not grieve for me, as I shall have been ushered by my great guru into the arms of the Infinite. Farewell, my child; the Cosmic Mother will protect you."

A blaze of illumination came over me with possession of the amulet. I understood that it came from teachers of past lives, who were invisibly guiding my steps.

3

The Saint with Two Bodies: Swami Pranabananda

"Father, if I promise to return home without coercion, may I take a sight-seeing trip to Benares?"

My keen love of travel was seldom hindered by Father. He permitted me, even as a mere boy, to visit many cities and pilgrimage spots. Father promised to give my request due consideration. The next day he summoned me and held out a round-trip pass from Bareilly to Benares, a number of rupee notes, and two letters.

"I have a business matter to propose to a Benares friend, Kedar Nath Babu. Unfortunately I have lost his address. But I believe you will be able to get this letter to him through our common friend, Swami Pranabananda. The swami, my brother disciple, has attained an exalted spiritual stature. You will benefit by his company; this second note will serve as your introduction."

Father's eyes twinkled as he added, "Mind, no more flights from home!"

I set forth with the zest of my twelve years. Reaching Benares, I proceeded immediately to the swami's residence. The front door was open; I made my way to a long, hall-like room on the second floor. A rather stout man, wearing only a loin-cloth, was seated in lotus posture on a slightly raised platform. A beatific smile played about his lips. To dispel my thought that I had intruded, he greeted me as an old friend.

I knelt and touched his feet.

"Are you Swami Pranabananda?"

He nodded. "Are you Bhagabati's son?" His words were out before I had had time to get Father's letter from my pocket. In astonishment, I handed him the note of introduction, which now seemed superfluous.

"Of course I will locate Kedar Nath Babu for you." The saint again surprised me by his clairvoyance. He glanced at the letter, and made a few affectionate references to my parent.

Abruptly terminating our conversation, the saint became gravely motionless. A sphinxlike air enveloped him. At first his eyes sparkled, as if observing something of interest, then grew dull. I felt abashed at his pauciloquy; he had not yet told me how I could meet Father's friend.

"Little sir, don't get worried. The man you wish to see will be with you in half an hour." The yogi was reading my mind.

Again he fell into inscrutable silence. My watch informed me that thirty minutes had elapsed.

The swami aroused himself. "I think Kedar Nath Babu is nearing the door."

I heard somebody coming up the stairs. An amazed incomprehension arose suddenly; my thoughts raced in confusion: "How is it possible that Father's friend has been summoned to this place without the help of a messenger? The swami has spoken to no one but myself since my arrival!"

Abruptly I quitted the room and descended the steps. Halfway down I met a thin, fair-skinned man of medium height. He appeared to be in a hurry.

"Are you Kedar Nath Babu?" Excitement colored my voice.

"Yes. Are you not Bhagabati's son who has been waiting here to meet me?" He smiled in friendly fashion.

"Sir, how do you happen to come here?"

"Everything is mysterious today! Less than an hour ago I had just finished my bath in the Ganges when Swami Pranabananda approached me. I have no idea how he knew I was there at that time.

"'Bhagabati's son is waiting for you in my apartment,' he said. 'Will you come with me?' I gladly agreed. As we proceeded hand in hand, the swami in his wooden sandals was strangely able to outpace me, though I wore these stout walking shoes.

"'How long will it take you to reach my place?' Pranabanandaji suddenly halted to ask me this question.

"'About half an hour.'

"'I have something else to do at present.' He gave me an enigmatical glance. 'I must leave you behind. You can join me in my house, where Bhagabati's son and I will be awaiting you.'

"Before I could remonstrate, he dashed swiftly past me and disappeared in the crowd. I walked here as fast as possible."

This explanation only increased my bewilderment. I inquired how long he had known the swami.

"We met a few times last year, but not recently. I was very glad to see him again today at the bathing GHAT."

"I cannot believe my ears! Am I losing my mind? Did you meet him in a vision, or did you actually see him, touch his hand, and hear the sound of his feet?"

"I don't know what you're driving at!" He flushed angrily. "I am not lying to you. Can't you understand that only through the swami could I have known you were waiting at this place for me?"

"Why, that man, Swami Pranabananda, has not left my sight a moment since I first came about an hour ago." I blurted out the whole story.

His eyes opened widely. "Are we living in this material age, or are we dreaming? I never expected to witness such a miracle in my life! I thought this swami was just an ordinary man, and now I find he can materialize an extra body and work through it!" Together we entered the saint's room.

As the visitor bowed before him, the saint turned to me with a quizzical smile.

"Why are you stupefied at all this? The subtle unity of the phenomenal world is not hidden from true yogis. I instantly see and converse with my disciples in distant Calcutta. They can similarly transcend at will every obstacle of gross matter."

It was probably in an effort to stir spiritual ardor in my young breast that the swami had condescended to tell me of his powers of astral radio and television. But instead of enthusiasm, I experienced only an awe-stricken fear. Inasmuch as I was destined to undertake my divine search through one particular guru – Sri Yukteswar, whom I had not yet met – I felt no inclination to accept Pranabananda as my teacher.

The master sought to banish my disquietude by bestowing a soul-awakening gaze, and by some inspiring words about his guru.

Saying this, Swami Pranabananda retired into one of his long silences. As I was taking leave, touching his feet reverently, he gave me his blessing:

"Your life belongs to the path of renunciation and yoga. I shall see you again, with your father, later on." The years brought fulfillment to both these predictions.

4
My Interrupted Flight toward the Himalayas

"Leave your classroom on some trifling pretext, and engage a hackney carriage. Stop in the lane where no one in my house can see you."

These were my final instructions to Amar Mitter, a high school friend who planned to accompany me to the Himalayas. We had chosen the following day for our flight. The amulet, like spiritual yeast, was silently at work within me. Amidst the Himalayan snows, I hoped to find the master whose face often appeared to me in visions. The family was living now in Calcutta, where Father had been permanently transferred.

The memorable morning arrived with inauspicious rain. Hearing the wheels of Amar's carriage in the road, I hastily tied together a blanket, a pair of sandals, Lahiri Mahasaya's picture, a copy of the BHAGAVAD GITA, a string of prayer beads, and two loincloths. This bundle I threw from my third-story window. And I ran down the steps.

Retrieving my bundle, I joined Amar with conspiratorial caution. On the way to the station, we stopped for my cousin, Jotin Ghosh, whom I called Jatinda. He was a new convert, longing for a guru in the Himalayas.

At the station we bought tickets to Burdwan, where we planned to transfer for Hardwar in the Himalayan foothills.

"Let the money be divided in three portions." Jatinda broke a long silence with this suggestion. "Each of us should buy his own ticket at Burdwan. Thus no one at the station will surmise that we are running away together."

I unsuspectingly agreed. At dusk our train stopped at Burdwan. Jatinda entered the ticket office; Amar and I sat on the platform. We waited fifteen minutes, then made unavailing inquiries. Searching in all directions, we shouted Jatinda's name with the urgency of fright. But he had faded into the dark unknown surrounding the little station.

I was completely unnerved, shocked to a peculiar numbness. That God would countenance this depressing episode! The romantic occasion of my first carefully-planned flight after Him was cruelly marred.

"Amar, we must return home." I was weeping like a child. "Jatinda's callous departure is an ill omen. This trip is doomed to failure."

"Is this your love for the Lord? Can't you stand the little test of a treacherous companion?"

Through Amar's suggestion of a divine test, my heart steadied itself. In a few hours, we entrained for Hardwar, via Bareilly. Changing trains at Moghul Serai, we discussed a vital matter as we waited on the platform.

"Amar, we may soon be closely questioned by railroad officials. I am not underrating my brother's ingenuity! No matter what the outcome, I will not speak untruth."

"All I ask of you, Mukunda, is to keep still. Don't laugh or grin while I am talking."

At this moment, a European station agent accosted me. He waved a telegram whose import I immediately grasped.

"Are you running away from home in anger?"

"No!" I was glad his choice of words permitted me to make emphatic reply. Not anger but "divinest melancholy" was responsible, I knew, for my unconventional behavior.

The official then turned to Amar. The duel of wits that followed hardly permitted me to maintain the counseled stoic gravity.

"Where is the third boy?" The man injected a full ring of authority into his voice. "Come on; speak the truth!"

"Sir, I notice you are wearing eyeglasses. Can't you see that we are only two?" Amar smiled impudently. "I am not a magician; I can't conjure up a third companion."

The official, noticeably disconcerted by this impertinence, sought a new field of attack.

"What is your name?"

"I am called Thomas. I am the son of an English mother and a converted Christian Indian father."

"What is your friend's name?"

"I call him Thompson."

By this time my inward mirth had reached a zenith; I unceremoniously made for the train, whistling for departure. Amar followed with the official, who was credulous and obliging enough to put us into a European compartment. After his polite exit, we wore an expression of blithe satisfaction at having outwitted a veteran European official.

The train bore us triumphantly into a dawn arrival at Hardwar. The majestic mountains loomed invitingly in the distance. We dashed through the station and entered the freedom of city crowds.

Deeming it advisable to leave Hardwar at once, we bought tickets to proceed north to Rishikesh. I had already boarded the train, while Amar lagged on the platform. He was brought to an abrupt halt by a shout from a policeman. Our unwelcome guardian escorted us to a station bungalow and took charge of our money. He explained courteously that it was his duty to hold us until my elder brother arrived.

Learning that the truants' destination had been the Himalayas, the officer related a strange story.

"I see you are crazy about saints! You will never meet a greater man of God than the one I saw only yesterday. My brother officer and I first encountered him five days ago. We were patrolling by the Ganges, on a sharp lookout for a certain murderer. Our instructions were to capture him, alive or dead. He was known to be masquerading as a SADHU in order to rob pilgrims. A short way before us, we spied a figure which resembled the description of the criminal. He ignored our command to stop; we ran to overpower him. Approaching his back, I wielded my ax with tremendous force; the man's right arm was severed almost completely from his body.

"Without outcry or any glance at the ghastly wound, the stranger astonishingly continued his swift pace. As we jumped in front of him, he spoke quietly.

"'I am not the murderer you are seeking.'

"I was deeply mortified to see I had injured the person of a divine--looking sage. Prostrating myself at his feet, I implored his pardon, and offered my turban-cloth to staunch the heavy spurts of blood.

"'Son, that was just an understandable mistake on your part.' The saint regarded me kindly. 'Run along, and don't reproach yourself. The Beloved Mother is taking care of me.' He pushed his dangling arm into its stump and lo! it adhered; the blood inexplicably ceased to flow.

"'Come to me under yonder tree in three days and you will find me fully healed. Thus you will feel no remorse.'

"Yesterday my brother officer and I went eagerly to the designated spot. The SADHU was there and allowed us to examine his arm. It bore no scar or trace of hurt!

"'I am going via Rishikesh to the Himalayan solitudes.' He blessed us as he departed quickly. I feel that my life has been uplifted through his sanctity."

We thanked the officer for relieving our tedium with his marvelous story. He was probably intimating that he was more fortunate than we: he had met an illumined saint without effort; our earnest search had ended, not at the feet of a master, but in a coarse police station!

So near the Himalayas and yet, in our captivity, so far, I told Amar I felt doubly impelled to seek freedom.

But alas, Ananta and Amar's brother arrived after three days. Amar greeted his relative with affectionate relief. I was unreconciled; Ananta got no more from me than a severe upbraiding.

"I understand how you feel." My brother spoke soothingly. "All I ask of you is to accompany me to Benares to meet a certain saint, and go on to Calcutta to visit your grieving father for a few days. Then you can resume your search here for a master."

Our party entrained for Benares. There I had a singular and instant response to my prayers.

A clever scheme had been prearranged by Ananta. Before seeing me at Hardwar, he had stopped in Benares to ask a certain scriptural authority to interview me later. Both the pundit and his son had promised to undertake my dissuasion from the path of a SANNYASI.

Ananta took me to their home. The son, a young man of ebullient manner, greeted me in the courtyard. He engaged me in a lengthy philosophic discourse. Professing to have a clairvoyant knowledge of my future, he discountenanced my idea of being a monk.

"You will meet continual misfortune, and be unable to find God, if you insist on deserting your ordinary responsibilities! You cannot work out your past karma without worldly experiences."

Krishna's immortal words rose to my lips in reply: "'Even he with the worst of karma who ceaselessly meditates on Me quickly loses the effects of his past bad actions. Becoming a high-souled being, he soon attains perennial peace. Arjuna, know this for certain: the devotee who puts his trust in Me never perishes!'"

But the forceful prognostications of the young man had slightly shaken my confidence. With all the fervor of my heart I prayed silently to God:

"Please solve my bewilderment and answer me, right here and now, if Thou dost desire me to lead the life of a renunciate or a worldly man!"

I noticed a SADHU of noble countenance standing just outside the compound of the pundit's house. Evidently he had overheard the spirited conversation between the self-styled clairvoyant and myself, for the stranger called me to his side. I felt a tremendous power flowing from his calm eyes.

"Son, don't listen to that ignoramus. In response to your prayer, the Lord tells me to assure you that your sole path in this life is that of the renunciate."

With astonishment as well as gratitude, I smiled happily at this decisive message.

I turned away. To Ananta I remarked that I would not engage in further discussion with our hosts. My brother agreed to an immediate departure; we soon entrained for Calcutta.

At home in Calcutta, Father touchingly requested me to curb my roving feet until, at least, the completion of my high school studies. In my absence, he had lovingly hatched a plot by arranging for a saintly pundit, Swami Kebalananda, to come regularly to the house.

"The sage will be your Sanskrit tutor," my parent announced confidently.

Father hoped to satisfy my religious yearnings by instructions from a learned philosopher. But the tables were subtly turned: my new teacher, far from offering intellectual aridities, fanned the embers of my God-aspiration. Unknown to Father, Swami Kebalananda was an exalted disciple of Lahiri Mahasaya.

Kebalananda was a noted authority on the ancient SHASTRAS or sacred books. But my progress in Sanskrit scholarship was unnoteworthy. I sought every opportunity to forsake prosaic grammar and to talk of yoga and Lahiri Mahasaya. And to my Father's great dismay, I never became a Sanskrit scholar; Kebalananda taught me a diviner syntax.

5

A "Perfume Saint" Displays
His Wonders

Two years elapsed between my flight with Amar toward the Himalayas, and the great day of Sri Yukteswar's arrival into my life. During that interim I met a number of sages – the "Perfume Saint," the "Tiger Swami," Nagendra Nath Bhaduri, Master Mahasaya, and the famous Bengali scientist, Jagadis Chandra Bose.

My encounter with the "Perfume Saint" had two preambles, one harmonious and the other humorous.

"God is simple. Everything else is complex. Do not seek absolute values in the relative world of nature."

These philosophical finalities gently entered my ear as I stood silently before a temple image of Kali. Turning, I confronted a tall man whose garb, or lack of it, revealed him a wandering SADHU.

The sage and I were present in Calcutta's Kalighat Temple, whither I had gone to view its famed magnificence. With a sweeping gesture, my chance companion dismissed the ornate dignity.

"Bricks and mortar sing us no audible tune; the heart opens only to the human chant of being."

We strolled to the inviting sunshine at the entrance, where throngs of devotees were passing to and fro.

"You are young." The sage surveyed me thoughtfully. "India too is young. The ancient RISHIS laid down ineradicable patterns of spiritual living. Their hoary dictums suffice for this day and land. Not outmoded, not unsophisticated against the guiles of materialism, the disciplinary precepts mold India still. By millenniums-more than embarrassed scholars care to compute!-the skeptic Time has validated Vedic worth. Take it for your heritage."

As I was reverently bidding farewell to the eloquent SADHU, he revealed a clairvoyant perception:

"After you leave here today, an unusual experience will come your way."

I quitted the temple precincts and wandered along aimlessly. Turning a corner, I ran into an old acquaintance – one of those long-winded fellows whose conversational powers ignore time and embrace eternity.

"I will let you go in a very short while, if you will tell me all that has happened during the six years of our separation."

"What a paradox! I must leave you now."

But he held me by the hand, forcing out tidbits of information. He was like a ravenous wolf, I thought in amusement; the longer I spoke, the more hungrily he sniffed for news. Inwardly I petitioned the Goddess Kali to devise a graceful means of escape.

My companion left me abruptly. I sighed with relief and doubled my pace, dreading any relapse into the garrulous fever. Hearing rapid footsteps behind me, I quickened my speed. I dared not look back. But with a bound, the youth rejoined me, jovially clasping my shoulder.

"I forgot to tell you of Gandha Baba (Perfume Saint), who is gracing yonder house." He pointed to a dwelling a few yards distant. "Do meet him; he is interesting. You may have an unusual experience. Goodby," and he actually left me.

The similarly worded prediction of the SADHU at Kalighat Temple flashed to my mind. Definitely intrigued, I entered the house and was ushered into a commodious parlor. A crowd of people were sitting, Orient-wise, here and there on a thick orange-colored carpet. An awed whisper reached my ear:

"Behold Gandha Baba on the leopard skin. He can give the natural perfume of any flower to a scentless one, or revive a wilted blossom, or make a person's skin exude delightful fragrance."

I looked directly at the saint; his quick gaze rested on mine. He was plump and bearded, with dark skin and large, gleaming eyes.

"Son, I am glad to see you. Say what you want. Would you like some perfume?"

"What for?" I thought his remark rather childish.

"To experience the miraculous way of enjoying perfumes."

"Harnessing God to make odors?"

"What of it? God makes perfume anyway."

"Yes, but He fashions frail bottles of petals for fresh use and discard. Can you materialize flowers?"

"I materialize perfumes, little friend."

"Then scent factories will go out of business."

"I will permit them to keep their trade! My own purpose is to demonstrate the power of God."

"Sir, is it necessary to prove God? Isn't He performing miracles in everything, everywhere?"

"Yes, but we too should manifest some of His infinite creative ariety."

"How long did it take to master your art?"

"Twelve years."

"For manufacturing scents by astral means! It seems, my honored saint, you have been wasting a dozen years for fragrances which you can obtain with a few rupees from a florist's shop."

"Perfumes fade with flowers."

"Perfumes fade with death. Why should I desire that which pleases the body only?"

"Mr. Philosopher, you please my mind. Now, stretch forth your right hand." He made a gesture of blessing.

I was a few feet away from Gandha Baba; no one else was near enough to contact my body. I extended my hand, which the yogi did not touch.

"What perfume do you want?"

"Rose."

"Be it so."

To my great surprise, the charming fragrance of rose was wafted strongly from the center of my palm. I smilingly took a large white scentless flower from a near-by vase.

"Can this odorless blossom be permeated with jasmine?"

"Be it so."

A jasmine fragrance instantly shot from the petals. I thanked the wonder-worker and seated myself by one of his students. He informed me that Gandha Baba, whose proper name was Vishudhananda, had learned many astonishing yoga secrets from a master in Tibet. The Tibetan yogi, I was assured, had attained the age of over a thousand years.

"His disciple Gandha Baba does not always perform his

perfume-feats in the simple verbal manner you have just witnessed." The student spoke with obvious pride in his master. "His procedure differs widely, to accord with diversity in temperaments. He is marvelous! Many members of the Calcutta intelligentsia are among his followers."

I inwardly resolved not to add myself to their number. A guru too literally "marvelous" was not to my liking. With polite thanks to Gandha Baba, I departed. Sauntering home, I reflected on the three varied encounters the day had brought forth.

6

The Tiger Swami

"I have discovered the Tiger Swami's address. Let us visit him tomorrow."

This welcome suggestion came from Chandi, one of my high school friends. I was eager to meet the saint who, in his premonastic life, had caught and fought tigers with his naked hands. A boyish enthusiasm over such remarkable feats was strong within me.

The next day dawned wintry cold, but Chandi and I sallied forth gaily. After much vain hunting in Bhowanipur, outside Calcutta, we arrived at the right house. A servant approached with leisurely gait and invited us into the parlor. Our long wait there caused uncomfortable misgivings. India's unwritten law for the truth seeker is patience; a master may purposely make a test of one's eagerness to meet him.

Finally summoned by the servant, Chandi and I entered a sleeping apartment. The famous Sohong Swami was seated on his bed. On an immense neck, the swami's fierce yet calm face was adorned with flowing locks, beard and moustache.

Finding our voices, my friend and I greeted the monk, expressing our admiration for his prowess in the extraordinary feline arena.

"Will you not tell us, please, how it is possible to subdue

with bare fists the most ferocious of jungle beasts, the royal Bengals?"

"My sons, it is nothing to me to fight tigers. I could do it today if necessary." He gave a childlike laugh. "You look upon tigers as tigers; I know them as pussycats."

"Swamiji, I think I could impress my subconsciousness with the thought that tigers are pussycats, but could I make tigers believe it?"

"Of course strength also is necessary! One cannot expect victory from a baby who imagines a tiger to be a house cat! Powerful hands are my sufficient weapon."

At our entreaty, the impressive swami consented to tell us something of his own life.

"My earliest ambition was to fight tigers. My will was mighty, but my body was feeble. But it was by indomitable persistency in thoughts of health and strength that I overcame my handicap. I have every reason to extol the compelling mental vigor which I found to be the real subduer of royal Bengals."

"Do you think, revered swami, that I could ever fight tigers?" This was the first, and the last, time that the bizarre ambition ever visited my mind!

"Yes." He was smiling. "But there are many kinds of tigers; some roam in jungles of human desires. No spiritual benefit accrues by knocking beasts unconscious. Rather be victor over the inner prowlers."

"May we hear, sir, how you changed from a tamer of wild tigers to a tamer of wild passions?"

The Tiger Swami fell into silence. Remoteness came into his gaze, summoning visions of bygone years. I discerned his slight mental struggle to decide whether to grant my request. Finally he smiled in acquiescence.

"When my fame reached a zenith, it brought the intoxication of pride. I decided not only to fight tigers but to display them in various tricks. My ambition was to force savage beasts to behave like domesticated ones. I began to perform my feats publicly, with gratifying success.

"One evening my father entered my room in pensive mood.

"'Son, I have words of warning. I would save you from coming ills, produced by the grinding wheels of cause and effect.'

"'Are you a fatalist, Father? Should superstition be allowed to discolor the powerful waters or my activities?'

"'I am no fatalist, son. But I believe in the just law of retribution, as taught in the holy scriptures. There is resentment against you in the jungle family; sometime it may act to your cost.'

"'Father, you astonish me! You well know what tigers are – beautiful but merciless! Even immediately after an enormous meal of some hapless creature, a tiger is fired with fresh lust at sight of new prey.

"'Tigers are the most contemptible of the jungle breed! Who knows? my blows may inject some slight sanity of consideration into their thick heads. I am headmaster in a forest finishing school, to teach them gentle manners!

"'Please, Father, think of me as tiger tamer and never as tiger killer. How could my good actions bring ill upon me? I beg you not to impose any command that I change my way of life.'"

Chandi and I were all attention, understanding the past dilemma. In India a child does not lightly disobey his parents' wishes.

"In stoic silence Father listened to my explanation. He followed it with a disclosure which he uttered gravely.

"'Son, you compel me to relate an ominous prediction from the lips of a saint. He approached me yesterday as I sat on the veranda in my daily meditation.

"'"Dear friend, I come with a message for your belligerent son. Let him cease his savage activities. Otherwise, his next tiger-encounter shall result in his severe wounds, followed by six months of deathly sickness. He shall then forsake his former ways and become a monk."'

"This tale did not impress me. I considered that Father had been the credulous victim of a deluded fanatic."

Grimly silent for a long time, the Tiger Swami seemed oblivious of our presence. When he took up the dangling thread of his narrative, it was suddenly, with subdued voice.

"Not long after Father's warning, I visited the capital city of Cooch Behar. The picturesque territory was new to me, and I expected a restful change. As usual everywhere, a curious crowd followed me on the streets. Within a few hours, the whole city was in a state of excitement over my presence.

"I was relaxing quietly in the evening, when I heard the hoofbeats of galloping horses. They stopped in front of my dwelling place. In came a number of tall, turbaned policemen.

"'Honored Sir, we are sent to welcome you on behalf of the Prince of Cooch Behar. He is pleased to invite you to his palace tomorrow morning.' The officers bowed with unwonted courtesy.

"I had no option but agree to go.

"I was bewildered the next day to be obsequiously escorted from my door into a magnificent coach drawn by four horses. A servant held an ornate umbrella to protect me from the scorching sunlight. I enjoyed the pleasant ride through the city and its woodland outskirts. The royal scion himself was at the palace door to welcome me. He proffered his own gold-brocaded seat, smilingly placing himself in a chair of simpler design.

"'All this politeness is certainly going to cost me something!' I thought in mounting astonishment. The prince's motive emerged after a few casual remarks.

"'My city is filled with the rumor that you can fight wild tigers with nothing more than your naked hands. Is it a fact?'

"'It is quite true.'

"'I challenge you to fight my newly-caught tiger, Raja Begum. If you can successfully resist him, bind him with a chain, and leave his cage in a conscious state, you shall have this royal Bengal! Several thousand rupees and many other gifts shall also be bestowed. If you refuse to meet him in combat, I shall blazon your name throughout the state as an impostor!'

"His insolent words struck me like a volley of bullets. I shot an angry acceptance.

"'The match will be set for a week hence. I regret that I cannot give you permission to view the tiger in advance.'

"Whether the prince feared I might seek to hypnotize the beast, or secretly feed him opium, I know not!

"I left the palace, noting with amusement that the royal umbrella and panoplied coach were now missing.

"The following week I methodically prepared my mind and body for the coming ordeal. My servant apprized me that the prince was in his element as manager of the bout between man and beast. He had supervised the erection of a storm-proof pavilion, designed to accommodate thousands. Its center held Raja Begum in an enormous iron cage, surrounded by an outer safety room. The captive emitted a ceaseless series of blood-curdling roars. He was fed sparingly, to kindle a wrathful appetite. Perhaps the prince expected me to be the meal of reward!

"Crowds from the city and suburbs bought tickets eagerly in response to the beat of drums announcing the unique contest. The day of battle saw hundreds turned away for lack of seats. Many men broke through the tent openings, or crowded any space below the galleries."

As the Tiger Swami's story approached a climax, my excitement mounted with it; Chandi also was raptly mute.

"Amidst piercing sound-explosions from Raja Begum, and the hubbub of the somewhat terrified crowd, I quietly made my appearance. Scantily clad around the waist, I was otherwise unprotected by clothing. I opened the bolt on the door of the safety room and calmly locked it behind me. The tiger sensed blood. Leaping with a thunderous crash on his bars, he sent forth a fearsome welcome. The audience was hushed with pitiful fear; I seemed a meek lamb before the raging beast.

"In a trice I was within the cage; but as I slammed the door, Raja Begum was headlong upon me. My right hand was desperately torn. Human blood, the greatest treat a tiger can know, fell in appalling streams. The prophecy of the saint seemed about to be fulfilled.

"I rallied instantly from the shock of the first serious injury I had ever received. Banishing the sight of my gory fingers by thrusting them beneath my waist cloth, I swung my left arm in a bone-cracking blow. The beast reeled back, swirled around the rear of the cage, and sprang forward convulsively. My famous fistic punishment rained on his head.

"But Raja Begum's taste of blood had acted like the

maddening first sip of wine to a dipsomaniac long-deprived. Punctuated by deafening roar, the brute's assaults grew in fury. My inadequate defense of only one hand left me vulnerable before claws and fangs. But I dealt out dazing retribution. Mutually ensanguined, we struggled as to the death.

"'Shoot him!' 'Kill the tiger!' Shrieks arose from the audience. So fast did man and beast move that a guard's bullet went amiss. I mustered all my will force, bellowed fiercely, and landed a final concussive blow. The tiger collapsed and lay quietly.

"Like a pussycat!" I interjected.

The swami laughed in hearty appreciation, then continued the engrossing tale.

"Raja Begum was vanquished at last. His royal pride was further humbled: with my lacerated hands, I audaciously forced open his jaws. For a dramatic moment, I held my head within the yawning deathtrap. I looked around for a chain. Pulling one from a pile on the floor, I bound the tiger by his neck to the cage bars. In triumph I moved toward the door.

"But that fiend incarnate, Raja Begum, had stamina worthy of his supposed demoniac origin. With an incredible lunge, he snapped the chain and leaped on my back. My shoulder fast in his jaws, I fell violently. But in a trice I had him pinned beneath me. Under merciless blows, the treacherous animal sank into semiconsciousness. This time I secured him more carefully. Slowly I left the cage.

"I found myself in a new uproar, this time one of delight. The crowd's cheer broke as though from a single gigantic throat. Disastrously mauled, I had yet fulfilled the three conditions of the fight-stunning the tiger, binding him with a chain, and leaving him without requiring assistance for myself. In addition, I had so drastically injured and frightened the aggressive beast that he had been content to overlook the opportune prize of my head in his mouth!

"After my wounds were treated, I was honored and garlanded; hundreds of gold pieces showered at my feet. The whole city entered a holiday period. Endless discussions were heard on all sides about my victory over one of the largest and most savage tigers ever seen. Raja Begum was presented to me, as promised, but I felt no elation. A spiritual change had entered my heart. It seemed that with my final exit from the cage I had also closed the door on my worldly ambitions. And finally I was initiated into the spiritual path.

7

The Levitating Saint:
Nagendra Nath Bhaduri

"I saw a yogi remain in the air, several feet above the ground, last night at a group meeting." My friend, Upendra Mohun Chowdhury, spoke impressively.

I gave him an enthusiastic smile. "Perhaps I can guess his name. Was it Bhaduri Mahasaya, of Upper Circular Road?"

Upendra nodded, a little crestfallen not to be a news-bearer. My inquisitiveness about saints was well-known among my friends; they delighted in setting me on a fresh track.

"The yogi lives so close to my home that I often visit him." My words brought keen interest to Upendra's face, and I made a further confidence.

"I heard that the saint never leaves his home." Upendra's tone was a trifle incredulous.

"Indeed it is true! He has lived indoors for the past twenty years."

"How does he remain in the air, defying the law of gravitation?"

"A yogi's body loses its grossness after use of certain PRANAYAMAS. Then it will levitate or hop about like a leaping frog. Even saints who do not practice a formal yoga have been known to levitate during a state of intense devotion to God."

"I would like to know more of this sage. Do you attend his evening meetings?" Upendra's eyes were sparkling with curiosity.

"Yes, I go often. I am vastly entertained by the wit in his wisdom."

On my way home from school one afternoon, I passed Bhaduri Mahasaya's cloister and decided on a visit. The yogi was inaccessible to the general public. A lone disciple, occupying the ground floor, guarded his master's privacy. The student was something of a martinet; he now inquired formally if I had an "engagement." His guru put in an appearance just in time to save me from summary ejection.

"Let Mukunda come when he will."

I followed Bhaduri Mahasaya to his austere quarters on the top floor, from which he seldom stirred.

"Maharishi, you are the first yogi I have known who always stays indoors."

"God plants his saints sometimes in unexpected soil, lest we think we may reduce Him to a rule!"

The saint and I entered the meditative state. After an hour, his gentle voice roused me.

"You go often into the silence, but have you developed ANUBHAVA?" He was reminding me to love God more than meditation. "Do not mistake the technique for the Goal."

He offered me some mangoes. With that good-humored wit that I found so delightful in his grave nature, he remarked, "People in general are more fond of JALA YOGA (union with food) than of DHYANA YOGA (union with God)."

His yogic pun affected me uproariously.

"What a laugh you have!" An affectionate gleam came into his gaze. His own face was always serious, yet touched with an ecstatic smile. His large, lotus eyes held a hidden divine laughter.

"Those letters come from far-off America." The sage indicated several thick envelopes on a table. "I correspond with a few societies there whose members are interested in yoga. They are discovering India anew, with a better sense of direction than Columbus! I am glad to help them. The knowledge of yoga is free to all who will receive, like the ungarnishable daylight.

"What RISHIS perceived as essential for human salvation need not be diluted for the West. Alike in soul though diverse in outer experience, neither West nor East will flourish if some form of disciplinary yoga be not practiced."

The saint held me with his tranquil eyes. I did not realize that his speech was a veiled prophetic guidance. It is only now, as I write these words, that I understand the full meaning in the casual intimations he often gave me that someday I would carry India's teachings to America.

Although it throws me ahead of my story by a number of years, I will recount here the last words given to me by Bhaduri Mahasaya. Shortly before I embarked for the West, I sought him out and humbly knelt for his farewell blessing:

"Son, go to America. Take the dignity of hoary India for your shield. Victory is written on your brow; the noble distant people will well receive you."

8

India's Great Scientist: J.C. Bose

"Jagadis Chandra Bose's wireless inventions antedated those of Marconi."

Overhearing this provocative remark, I walked closer to a sidewalk group of professors engaged in scientific discussion

"What do you mean, sir?"

The professor obligingly explained. "Bose was the first one to invent a wireless coherer and an instrument for indicating the refraction of electric waves. But the Indian scientist did not exploit his inventions commercially. He soon turned his attention from the inorganic to the organic world. His revolutionary discoveries as a plant physiologist are outpacing even his radical achievements as a physicist."

I politely thanked my mentor. He added, "The great scientist is one of my brother professors at Presidency College."

I paid a visit the next day to the sage at his home, which was close to mine on Gurpar Road. The grave and retiring botanist greeted me graciously. The precision in his tones revealed the lifelong scientific habit.

"I have recently returned from an expedition to scientific societies of the West. Their members exhibited intense interest in delicate instruments of my invention which demonstrate the indivisible unity of all life. The Bose crescograph has the enormity of ten million magnifications. The microscope enlarges only a few thousand times; yet it brought vital impetus to biological science. The crescograph opens incalculable vistas."

"You have done much, sir, to hasten the embrace of East and West in the impersonal arms of science."

"I was educated at Cambridge. How admirable is the Western method of submitting all theory to scrupulous experimental verification! That empirical procedure has gone hand in hand with the gift for introspection which is my Eastern heritage. Together they have enabled me to sunder the silences of natural realms long uncommunicative. The telltale charts of my crescograph are evidence for the most skeptical that plants have a sensitive nervous system and a varied emotional life. Love, hate, joy, fear, pleasure, pain, excitability, stupor, and countless appropriate responses to stimuli are as universal in plants as in animals."

"The unique throb of life in all creation could seem only poetic imagery before your advent, Professor!"

"The poet is intimate with truth, while the scientist approaches awkwardly. Come someday to my laboratory and see the unequivocable testimony of the crescograph."

Gratefully I accepted the invitation, and took my departure. I heard later that the botanist had left Presidency College, and was planning a research center in Calcutta.

When the Bose Institute was opened, I attended the dedicatory services. Enthusiastic hundreds strolled over the premises. I was charmed with the artistry and spiritual symbolism of the new home of science.

Bose's speech on this great occasion might have issued from the lips of one of the inspired ancient RISHIS.

"I dedicate today this Institute as not merely a laboratory but a temple. In the pursuit of my investigations I was unconsciously led into the border region of physics and physiology. To my amazement, I found boundary lines vanishing, and points of contact emerging, between the realms of the living and the non-living. Inorganic matter was perceived as anything but inert; it was athrill under the action of multitudinous forces.

"A universal reaction seemed to bring metal, plant and animal under a common law. They all exhibited essentially the same phenomena of fatigue and depression, with possibilities of recovery and of exaltation, as well as the permanent irresponsiveness associated with death. Filled with awe at this stupendous generalization, it was with great hope that I announced my results before the Royal Society--results demonstrated by experiments.

"An unconscious theological bias was also present, which confounds ignorance with faith. It is often forgotten that He who surrounded us with this ever-evolving mystery of creation has also implanted in us the desire to question and understand. Through many years of miscomprehension, I came to know that the life of a devotee of science is inevitably filled with unending struggle. It is for him to cast his life as an ardent offering-regarding gain and loss, success and failure, as one.

"In time the leading scientific societies of the world accepted my theories and results, and recognized the importance of the Indian contribution to science. Can anything small or circumscribed ever satisfy the mind of India? By a continuous living tradition, and a vital power of rejuvenescence, this land has readjusted itself through unnumbered transformations. Indians have always arisen who, discarding the immediate and absorbing prize of the hour, have sought for the realization of the highest ideals in life-not through passive renunciation, but through active struggle. The weakling who has refused the conflict, acquiring nothing, has had nothing to renounce. He alone who has striven and won can enrich the world by bestowing the fruits of his victorious experience.

"The work already carried out in the Bose laboratory on the response of matter, and the unexpected revelations in plant life, have opened out very extended regions of inquiry in physics, in physiology, in medicine, in agriculture, and even in psychology. Problems hitherto regarded as insoluble have now been brought within the sphere of experimental investigation.

"But high success is not to be obtained without rigid exactitude. Hence the long battery of super-sensitive instruments and apparatus of my design, which stand before you today in their cases in the entrance hall. They tell you of the protracted efforts to get behind the deceptive seeming into the reality that remains unseen, of the continuous toil and persistence and resourcefulness called forth to overcome human limitations. All creative scientists know that the true laboratory is the mind, where behind illusions they uncover the laws of truth.

"It is my further wish that the facilities of this Institute be available, so far as possible, to workers from all countries. In this I am attempting to carry on the traditions of my country. So far back as twenty-five centuries, India welcomed to its ancient universities, at Nalanda and Taxila, scholars from all parts of the world.

"Although science is neither of the East nor of the West but rather international in its universality, yet India is specially fitted to make great contributions. The burning Indian imagination, which can extort new order out of a mass of apparently contradictory facts, is held in check by the habit of concentration. This restraint confers the power to hold the mind to the pursuit of truth with an infinite patience."

Tears stood in my eyes at the scientist's concluding words. Is "patience" not indeed a synonym of India, confounding Time and the historians alike?

I visited the research center again, soon after the day of opening. The great botanist, mindful of his promise, took me to his quiet laboratory.

"I will attach the crescograph to this fern; the magnification is tremendous. If a snail's crawl were enlarged in the same proportion, the creature would appear to be traveling like an express train!"

My gaze was fixed eagerly on the screen which reflected the magnified fern-shadow. Minute life-movements were now clearly perceptible; the plant was growing very slowly before my fascinated eyes. The scientist touched the tip of the fern with a small metal bar. The developing pantomime came to an abrupt halt, resuming the eloquent rhythms as soon as the rod was withdrawn.

"You saw how any slight outside interference is detrimental to the sensitive tissues," Bose remarked. "Watch; I will now administer chloroform, and then give an antidote."

The effect of the chloroform discontinued all growth; the antidote was revivifying. The evolutionary gestures on the screen held me more raptly than a "movie" plot. My companion (here in the role of villain) thrust a sharp instrument through a part of the fern; pain was indicated by spasmodic flutters. When he passed a razor partially through the stem, the shadow was violently agitated, then stilled itself with the final punctuation of death.

"By first chloroforming a huge tree, I achieved a successful transplantation. Usually, such monarchs of the forest die very quickly after being moved. Graphs of my delicate apparatus have proved that trees possess a circulatory system; their sap movements correspond to the blood pressure of animal bodies. The ascent of sap is not explicable on the mechanical grounds ordinarily advanced, such as capillary attraction. The phenomenon has been solved through the crescograph as the activity of living cells. Peristaltic waves issue from a cylindrical tube which extends down a tree and serves as an actual heart! The more deeply we perceive, the more striking becomes the evidence that a uniform plan links every form in manifold nature."

The great scientist pointed to another Bose instrument.

"I will show you experiments on a piece of tin. The life-force in metals responds adversely or beneficially to stimuli. Ink markings will register the various reactions."

Deeply engrossed, I watched the graph which recorded the characteristic waves of atomic structure. When the professor applied chloroform to the tin, the vibratory writings stopped. They recommenced as the metal slowly regained its normal state. My companion dispensed a poisonous chemical. Simultaneous with the quivering end of the tin, the needle dramatically wrote on the chart a death-notice.

"Bose instruments have demonstrated that metals, such as the steel used in scissors and machinery, are subject to fatigue, and regain efficiency by periodic rest. The life-pulse in metals is seriously harmed or even extinguished through the application of electric currents or heavy pressure."

I looked around the room at the numerous inventions, eloquent testimony of a tireless ingenuity.

"Sir, it is lamentable that mass agricultural development is not speeded by fuller use of your marvelous mechanisms. Would it not be easily possible to employ some of them in quick laboratory experiments to indicate the influence of various types of fertilizers on plant growth?"

"You are right. Countless uses of Bose instruments will be made by future generations. The scientist seldom knows contemporaneous reward; it is enough to possess the joy of creative service."

With expressions of unreserved gratitude to the indefatigable sage, I took my leave. "Can the astonishing fertility of his genius ever be exhausted?" I thought.

No diminution came with the years. Inventing an intricate instrument, the "Resonant Cardiograph," Bose then pursued extensive researches on innumerable Indian plants. An enormous unsuspected pharmacopoeia of useful drugs was revealed. The cardiograph is constructed with an unerring accuracy by which a one-hundredth part of a second is indicated on a graph. Resonant records measure infinitesimal pulsations in plant, animal and human structure. The great botanist predicted that use of his cardiograph will lead to vivisection on plants instead of animals.

"Side by side recordings of the effects of a medicine given simultaneously to a plant and an animal have shown astounding unanimity in result," he pointed out. "Everything in man has been foreshadowed in the plant. Experimentation on vegetation will contribute to lessening of human suffering."

Years later Bose's pioneer plant findings were substantiated by other scientists. Work done in 1938 at Columbia University was reported by THE NEW YORK TIMES as follows:

It has been determined within the past few years that when

the nerves transmit messages between the brain and other parts of the body, tiny electrical impulses are being generated. These impulses have been measured by delicate galvanometers and magnified millions of times by modern amplifying apparatus. Until now no satisfactory method had been found to study the passages of the impulses along the nerve fibers in living animals or man because of the great speed with which these impulses travel.

Dr's. K. S. Cole and H. J. Curtis reported having discovered that the long single cells of the fresh-water plant nitella, used frequently in goldfish bowls, are virtually identical with those of single nerve fibers. Furthermore, they found that nitella fibers, on being excited, propagate electrical waves that are similar in every way, except velocity, to those of the nerve fibers in animals and man. The electrical nerve impulses in the plant were found to be much slower than those in animals. This discovery was therefore seized upon by the Columbia workers as a means for taking slow motion pictures of the passage of the electrical impulses in nerves.

The nitella plant thus may become a sort of Rosetta stone for deciphering the closely guarded secrets close to the very borderland of mind and matter.

9

The Blissful Devotee and His Cosmic Romance: Master Mahasaya

"Little sir, please be seated. I am talking to my Divine Mother."

Silently I had entered the room in great awe. The angelic appearance of Master Mahasaya fairly dazzled me. With silky white beard and large lustrous eyes, he seemed an incarnation of purity. His upraised chin and folded hands apprized me that my first visit had disturbed him in the midst of his devotions.

His simple words of greeting produced the most violent effect my nature had so far experienced. The bitter separation of my mother's death I had thought the measure of all anguish. Now an agony at separation from my Divine Mother was an indescribable torture of the spirit. I fell moaning to the floor.

"Little sir, quiet yourself!" The saint was sympathetically distressed.

Abandoned in some oceanic desolation, I clutched his feet as the sole raft of my rescue.

"Holy sir, thy intercession! Ask Divine Mother if I find any favor in Her sight!"

This promise is one not easily bestowed; the master was constrained to silence.

Beyond reach of doubt, I was convinced that Master Mahasaya was in intimate converse with the Universal Mother. It was deep humiliation to realize that my eyes were blind to Her who even at this moment was perceptible to the faultless gaze of the saint. Shamelessly gripping his feet, deaf to his gentle remonstrances, I besought him again and again for his intervening grace.

"I will make your plea to the Beloved." The master's capitulation came with a slow, compassionate smile.

What power in those few words, that my being should know release from its stormy exile?

"Sir, remember your pledge! I shall return soon for Her message!" Joyful anticipation rang in my voice that only a moment ago had been sobbing in sorrow.

Descending the long stairway, I was overwhelmed by memories. This house at 50 Amherst Street, now the residence of Master Mahasaya, had once been my family home.

My steps were eager as I returned to my Gurpar Road home. Seeking the seclusion of my small attic, I remained in meditation until ten o'clock. The darkness of the warm Indian night was suddenly lit with a wondrous vision.

Haloed in splendor, the Divine Mother stood before me. Her face, tenderly smiling, was beauty itself.

"Always have I loved thee! Ever shall I love thee!"

The celestial tones still ringing in the air, She disappeared.

The sun on the following morning had hardly risen when I paid my second visit to Master Mahasaya. Climbing the staircase in the house of poignant memories, I reached his fourth-floor room. As I stood irresolutely on the landing, the door was opened by the master's welcoming hand. I knelt at his holy feet. In a playful mood, I wore a solemn mask over my face, hiding the divine elation.

"Sir, I have come-very early, I confess! – for your message. Did the Beloved Mother say anything about me?"

"Mischievous little sir!"

"Why so mysterious, so evasive? Do saints never speak plainly?" Perhaps I was a little provoked.

"Must you test me?" His calm eyes were full of understanding. "Could I add a single word this morning to the assurance you received last night at ten o'clock from the Beautiful Mother Herself?"

Master Mahasaya possessed control over the flood-gates of my soul: again I plunged prostrate at his feet. But this time my tears welled from a bliss, and not a pain, past bearing.

"Think you that your devotion did not touch the Infinite Mercy? The Motherhood of God, that you have worshiped in forms both human and divine, could never fail to answer your forsaken cry."

Who was this simple saint, whose least request to the Universal Spirit met with sweet acquiescence? His role in the world was humble, as befitted the greatest man of humility I ever knew. Consumed by an unsophisticated passion for the Divine Mother, the saint no more demanded the outward forms of respect than a child.

"I am not your guru; he shall come a little later," he told me. "Through his guidance, your experiences of the Divine in terms of love and devotion shall be translated into his terms of fathomless wisdom."

One day found me walking alone near the Howrah railway station. I stood for a moment by a temple, silently criticizing a small group of men with drum and cymbals who were violently reciting a chant.

"How undevotionally they use the Lord's divine name in mechanical repetition," I reflected. My gaze was astonished by the rapid approach of Master Mahasaya. "Sir, how come you here?"

The saint, ignoring my question, answered my thought. "Isn't it true, little sir, that the Beloved's name sounds sweet from all lips, ignorant or wise?" He passed his arm around me affectionately; I found myself carried on his magic carpet to the Merciful Presence.

"Would you like to see some bioscopes?" This question one afternoon from Master Mahasaya was mystifying; the term was then used in India to signify motion pictures. I agreed, glad to be in his company in any circumstances. A brisk walk brought us to the garden fronting Calcutta University. Soon we entered a university hall where a lecture was in progress. It proved abysmally dull, though varied occasionally by lantern slide illustrations, equally uninteresting.

"So this is the kind of bioscope the master wanted me to see!" My thought was impatient, yet I would not hurt the saint by revealing boredom in my face. But he leaned toward me confidentially.

"I see, little sir, that you don't like this bioscope. I have mentioned it to Divine Mother; She is in full sympathy with us both. She tells me that the electric lights will now go out, and won't be relit until we have a chance to leave the room."

As his whisper ended, the hall was plunged into darkness. The professor's strident voice was stilled in astonishment, then remarked, "The electrical system of this hall appears to be defective." By this time, Master Mahasaya and I were safely across the threshold. Glancing back from the corridor, I saw that the scene of our martyrdom had again become illuminated.

"Little sir, you were disappointed in that bioscope, but I think you will like a different one." The saint and I were standing on the sidewalk in front of the university building. He gently slapped my chest over the heart.

A transforming silence ensued. Just as the modern "talkies" become inaudible motion pictures when the sound apparatus goes out of order, so the Divine Hand, by some strange miracle, stifled the earthly bustle. The pedestrians as well as the passing trolley cars, automobiles, bullock carts, and iron-wheeled hackney carriages were all in noiseless transit. As though possessing an omnipresent eye, I beheld the scenes which were behind me, and to each side, as easily as those in front. The whole spectacle of activity in that small section of Calcutta passed before me without a sound. Like a glow of fire dimly seen beneath a thin coat of ashes, a mellow luminescence permeated the panoramic view.

My own body seemed nothing more than one of the many shadows, though it was motionless, while the others flitted mutely to and fro. Several boys, friends of mine, approached and passed on; though they had looked directly at me, it was without recognition.

The unique pantomime brought me an inexpressible ecstasy. I drank deep from some blissful fount. Suddenly my chest received another soft blow from Master Mahasaya.

"Little sir, I see you found the second bioscope to your liking." The saint was smiling. I started to drop in gratitude on the ground before him.

10

I Meet My Master, Sri Yukteswar

My promise to Father had been that I would complete my high school studies. I cannot pretend to diligence. The week of final examinations at the Hindu High School was fast approaching. This interrogatory period, like the sepulchral haunts, inspires a well-known terror. My mind was nevertheless at peace.

"Hello, Mukunda! I catch hardly a glimpse of you these days!" A classmate accosted me one afternoon on Gurpar Road.

"Hello, Nantu! My invisibility at school has actually placed me there in a decidedly awkward position." I unburdened myself under his friendly gaze.

Nantu, who was a brilliant student, laughed heartily; my predicament was not without a comic aspect.

"You are utterly unprepared for the finals! I suppose it is up to me to help you!"

The simple words conveyed divine promise to my ears; with alacrity I visited my friend's home. He kindly outlined the solutions to various problems he considered likely to be set by the instructors.

The night was far gone when I departed. Bursting with

unseasoned erudition, I devoutly prayed it would remain for the next few critical days. Nantu had coached me in my various subjects but, under press of time, had forgotten my course in Sanskrit. Fervently I reminded God of the oversight.

I set out on a short walk the next morning. As I took a short cut through the weeds of a corner lot, my eye fell on a few loose printed sheets. A triumphant pounce proved them to be Sanskrit verse. I sought out a pundit for aid in my stumbling interpretation. His rich voice filled the air with the edgeless, honeyed beauty of the ancient tongue.

"These exceptional stanzas cannot possibly be of aid in your Sanskrit test." The scholar dismissed them skeptically.

But familiarity with that particular poem enabled me on the following day to pass the Sanskrit examination. Through the discerning help Nantu had given, I also attained the minimum grade for success in all my other subjects.

Father was pleased that I had kept my word and concluded my secondary school course. In my new dignity, I was now openly planning to leave home. Together with a young friend, Jitendra Mazumdar, I decided to join a Mahamandal hermitage in Benares, and receive its spiritual discipline. I quickly completed my travel preparations.

"I make one last plea." Father was distressed as I stood before him for final blessing. "Do not forsake me and your grieving brothers and sisters."

"Revered Father, how can I tell my love for you! But even greater is my love for the Heavenly Father, who has given me the gift of a perfect father on earth. Let me go, that I someday return with a more divine understanding."

With reluctant parental consent, I set out to join Jitendra, already in Benares at the hermitage. On my arrival the young head swami, Dyananda, greeted me cordially. Tall and thin, of thoughtful mien, he impressed me favorably. His fair face had a Buddha-like composure.

The ashram members, knowing little of meditation practices, thought I should employ my whole time in organizational duties.

"Don't try to catch God so soon!" This ridicule from a fellow resident accompanied one of my early departures toward the attic. I went to Dyananda, busy in his small sanctum overlooking the Ganges.

"Swamiji, I don't understand what is required of me here. I am seeking direct perception of God. Without Him, I cannot be satisfied with affiliation or creed or performance of good works."

The orange-robed ecclesiastic gave me an affectionate pat. Staging a mock rebuke, he admonished a few near-by disciples. "Don't bother Mukunda. He will learn our ways."

Dyananda had further words for me.

"Mukunda, I see your father is regularly sending you money. Please return it to him; you require none here. A second injunction for your discipline concerns food. Even when you feel hunger, don't mention it."

Whether famishment gleamed in my eye, I knew not. That I was hungry, I knew only too well. The invariable hour for the first hermitage meal was twelve noon. I had been accustomed in my own home to a large breakfast at nine o'clock.

The three-hour gap became daily more interminable. Gone were the Calcutta years when I could rebuke the cook for a ten-minute delay. Now I tried to control my appetite; one day I undertook a twenty-four hour fast. With double zest I awaited the following midday.

"Dyanandaji's train is late; we are not going to eat until he arrives." Jitendra brought me this devastating news. As gesture of welcome to the swami, who had been absent for two weeks, many delicacies were in readiness.

"Lord hasten the train!" I prayed. Darkness was descending as our leader entered the door. My greeting was one of unfeigned joy.

"Dyanandaji will bathe and meditate before we can serve food." Jitendra approached me again as a bird of ill omen.

I was in near-collapse. My young stomach, new to deprivation, protested with gnawing vigor. Pictures I had seen of famine victims passed wraithlike before me. The next Benares death from starvation is due at once in this hermitage," I thought.

Intense absorption yet permitted me to observe that Dyananda ate absent-mindedly. He was apparently above my gross pleasures.

"Swamiji, weren't you hungry?" Happily surfeited, I was alone with the leader in his study.

"O yes! I have spent the last four days without food or drink. I never eat on trains. Strictly I observe the SHASTRIC rules for monks of my particular order.

"Certain problems of our organizational work lie on my mind. Tonight at home I neglected my dinner. What's the hurry? Tomorrow I'll make it a point to have a proper meal." He laughed merrily.

I ventured a further remark.

"Swamiji, I am puzzled. Following your instruction, suppose I never asked for food, and nobody gives me any. I should starve to death."

"Die then!" This alarming counsel split the air. "Die if you must Mukunda! Never admit that you live by the power of food and not by the power of God! He who has created every form of nourishment, He who has bestowed appetite, will certainly see that His devotee is sustained! Do not imagine that rice maintains you, or that money or men support you! Could they aid if the Lord withdraws your life-breath? Mukunda! Cut through the chains of agency and perceive the Single Cause!"

I found his incisive words entering some deep marrow. Gone was an age-old delusion by which bodily imperatives outwit the soul. There and then I tasted the Spirit's all-sufficiency. In how many strange cities, in my later life of ceaseless travel, did occasion arise to prove the serviceability of this lesson in a Benares hermitage!

My relationship with Dyananda's followers grew steadily worse. The household was alienated, hurt by my determined aloofness. My strict adherence to meditation on the very Ideal for which I had left home and all worldly ambitions called forth shallow criticism on all sides.

Torn by spiritual anguish, I entered the attic one dawn, resolved to pray until answer was vouchsafed.

"Merciful Mother of the Universe, teach me Thyself through visions, or through a guru sent by Thee!"

The passing hours found my sobbing pleas without response. Suddenly I felt lifted as though bodily to a sphere uncircumscribed.

"Thy Master cometh today!" A divine womanly voice came from everywhere and nowhere.

This supernal experience was pierced by a shout from a definite locale. A young priest nicknamed Habu was calling me from the downstairs kitchen.

"Mukunda, enough of meditation! You are needed for an errand."

Another day I might have replied impatiently; now I wiped my tear-swollen face and meekly obeyed the summons. Together Habu and I set out for a distant market place in the Bengali section of Benares. Passing an inconspicuous lane, I turned my head and surveyed the narrow length.

A Christlike man in the ocher robes of a swami stood motionless at the end of the road. Instantly and anciently familiar he seemed; my gaze fed hungrily for a trice. Then doubt assailed me.

"You are confusing this wandering monk with someone known to you," I thought. "Dreamer, walk on."

Retracing my steps as though wing-shod, I reached the narrow lane. My quick glance revealed the quiet figure, steadily gazing in my direction. A few eager steps and I was at his feet.

"Gurudeva!" The divine face was none other than he of my thousand visions. These halcyon eyes, in leonine head with pointed beard and flowing locks, had oft peered through gloom of my nocturnal reveries, holding a promise I had not fully understood.

"O my own, you have come to me!" My guru uttered the words again and again in Bengali, his voice tremulous with joy. "How many years I have waited for you!"

We entered a oneness of silence; words seemed the rankest superfluities. With an antenna of irrefragable insight I sensed that my guru knew God, and would lead me to Him.

My hand in his, my guru led me to his temporary residence in the Rana Mahal section of the city. As we made our way to the stone balcony of a house overlooking the Ganges, he said affectionately:

"I will give you my hermitages and all I possess."

"Sir, I come for wisdom and God-contact. Those are your treasure-troves I am after!"

The swift Indian twilight had dropped its half-curtain before my master spoke again. His eyes held unfathomable tenderness.

"I give you my unconditional love."

Precious words! A quarter-century elapsed before I had another auricular proof of his love. His lips were strange to ardor; silence became his oceanic heart.

"Will you give me the same unconditional love?" He gazed at me with childlike trust.

"I will love you eternally, Gurudeva!"

"Ordinary love is selfish, darkly rooted in desires and satisfactions. Divine love is without condition, without boundary, without change. The flux of the human heart is gone forever at the transfixing touch of pure love." He added humbly, "If ever you find me falling from a state of God-realization, please promise to put my head on your lap and help to bring me back to the Cosmic Beloved we both worship."

He rose then in the gathering darkness and guided me to an inner room. I was awe-struck at the grandeur of his wisdom, exquisitely blended with an innate humility.

Like a divine mirror, my guru apparently had caught a reflection of my whole life.

"The living reality of your presence, Master, is joy beyond any symbol."

"It is time for a change, inasmuch as you are unhappily situated in the hermitage."

I had made no references to my life; they now seemed

superfluous! By his natural, unemphatic manner, I understood that he wished no astonished ejaculations at his clairvoyance.

"You should go back to Calcutta. Why exclude relatives from your love of humanity?"

"Sir, I am not returning home. But I will follow you anywhere. Please give me your address, and your name."

"Swami Sri Yukteswar Giri. My chief hermitage is in Serampore, on Rai Ghat Lane. I am visiting my mother here for only a few days."

I wondered at God's intricate play with His devotees. Serampore is but twelve miles from Calcutta, yet in those regions I had never caught a glimpse of my guru. We had had to travel for our meeting to the ancient city of Kasi.

"You will come to me in four weeks." For the first time, Sri Yukteswar's voice was stern. "Now I have told my eternal affection, and have shown my happiness at finding you-that is why you disregard my request. The next time we meet, you will have to reawaken my interest: I won't accept you as a disciple easily. There must be complete surrender by obedience to my strict training."

I remained obstinately silent. My guru easily penetrated my difficulty.

"Do you think your relatives will laugh at you?"

"I will not return."

"You will return in thirty days."

"Never." Bowing reverently at his feet, I departed without lightening the controversial tension. As I made my way in the midnight darkness, I wondered why the miraculous meeting had ended on an inharmonious note.

The next morning I noticed increased hostility in the attitude of the hermitage members. My days became spiked with invariable rudeness. In three weeks, Dyananda left the ashram to attend a conference in Bombay; pandemonium broke over my hapless head.

"Mukunda is a parasite, accepting hermitage hospitality without making proper return." Overhearing this remark, I regretted for the first time that I had obeyed the request to send back my money to Father. With heavy heart, I sought out my sole friend, Jitendra.

"I am leaving. Please convey my respectful regrets to Dyanandaji when he returns."

"I will leave also! My attempts to meditate here meet with no more favor than your own." Jitendra spoke with determination.

"I have met a Christlike saint. Let us visit him in Serampore."

And so the "bird" prepared to "swoop" perilously close to Calcutta!

11

Two Penniless Boys in Brindaban

"It would serve you right if Father disinherited you, Mukunda! How foolishly you are throwing away your life!" An elder-brother sermon was assaulting my ears.

Jitendra and I, fresh from the train, had just arrived at the home of Ananta, recently transferred from Calcutta to the ancient city of Agra. Brother was a supervising accountant for the Bengal-Nagpur Railway.

"You well know, Ananta, I seek my inheritance from the Heavenly Father."

"Money first; God can come later! Who knows? Life may be too long."

"God first; money is His slave! Who can tell? Life may be too short."

My retort was summoned by the exigencies of the moment, and held no presentiment. Yet the leaves of time unfolded to early finality for Ananta; a few years later he entered the land where bank notes avail neither first nor last.

"Wisdom from the hermitage, I suppose! But I see you have left Benares." Ananta's eyes gleamed with satisfaction.

"My sojourn in Benares was not in vain! I found there

everything my heart had been longing for! You may be sure it was not your pundit or his son!"

Ananta joined me in reminiscent laughter; he had had to admit that the Benares "clairvoyant" he selected was a shortsighted one.

"What are your plans, my wandering brother?"

"Jitendra persuaded me to Agra. We shall view the beauties of the Taj Mahal here," I explained. "Then we are going to my newly-found guru, who has a hermitage in Serampore."

Ananta hospitably arranged for our comfort. Several times during the evening I noticed his eyes fixed on me reflectively.

"I know that look!" I thought. "A plot is brewing!"

The denouement took place during our early breakfast.

"So you feel quite independent of Father's wealth." Ananta's gaze was innocent as he resumed the barbs of yesterday's conversation.

"I am conscious of my dependence on God."

"Words are cheap! Life has shielded you thus far! What a plight if you were forced to look to the Invisible Hand for your food and shelter! You would soon be begging on the streets!"

"Never! I would not put faith in passers-by rather than God! He can devise for His devotee a thousand resources besides the begging-bowl!"

"More rhetoric! Suppose I suggest that your vaunted philosophy be put to a test in this tangible world?"

"I would agree! Do you confine God to a speculative world?"

"We shall see; today you shall have opportunity either to enlarge or to confirm my own views!" Ananta paused for a dramatic moment; then spoke slowly and seriously.

"I propose that I send you and your fellow disciple Jitendra this morning to the near-by city of Brindaban. You must not take a single rupee; you must not beg, either for food or money; you must not reveal your predicament to anyone; you must not go without your meals; and you must not be stranded in Brindaban. If you return to my bungalow here before twelve o'clock tonight, without having broken any rule of the test, I shall be the most astonished man in Agra!"

"I accept the challenge." No hesitation was in my words or in my heart.

"Your willingness does you credit. I'll escort you to the train at once." Ananta turned to the open-mouthed Jitendra. "You must go along as a witness and, very likely, a fellow victim!"

A half hour later Jitendra and I were in possession of one-way tickets for our impromptu trip. We submitted, in a secluded corner of the station, to a search of our persons.

As faith invaded the serious realms of finance, my friend spoke protestingly. "Ananta, give me one or two rupees as a safeguard. Then I can telegraph you in case of misfortune."

"Jitendra!" My ejaculation was sharply reproachful. "I will not proceed with the test if you take any money as final security."

"There is something reassuring about the clink of coins." Jitendra said no more as I regarded him sternly.

"Mukunda, I am not heartless." A hint of humility had crept into Ananta's voice. It may be that his conscience was smiting him; perhaps for sending two insolvent boys to a strange city; perhaps for his own religious skepticism. "If by any chance or grace you pass successfully through the Brindaban ordeal, I shall ask you to initiate me as your disciple."

But no time remained for my comment; our train was at point of departure.

Jitendra maintained a lugubrious silence as our train covered the miles. Finally he bestirred himself; leaning over, he pinched me painfully at an awkward spot.

"I see no sign that God is going to supply our next meal!"

"Be quiet, doubting Thomas; the Lord is working with us."

"Can you also arrange that He hurry? Already I am famished merely at the prospect before us. I left Benares to view the Taj's mausoleum, not to enter my own!"

"Cheer up, Jitendra! Are we not to have our first glimpse of the sacred wonders of Brindaban? I am in deep joy at thought of treading the ground hallowed by feet of Lord Krishna."

The door of our compartment opened; two men seated themselves. The next train stop would be the last.

"Young lads, do you have friends in Brindaban?" The stranger opposite me was taking a surprising interest.

"None of your business!" Rudely I averted my gaze.

"You are probably flying away from your families under the enchantment of the Stealer of Hearts. I am of devotional temperament myself. I will make it my positive duty to see that you receive food, and shelter from this overpowering heat."

"No, sir, let us alone. You are very kind; but you are mistaken in judging us to be truants from home."

No further conversation ensued; the train came to a halt. As Jitendra and I descended to the platform, our chance companions linked arms with us and summoned a horse cab.

We alit before a stately hermitage, set amidst the evergreen trees of well-kept grounds. Our benefactors were evidently known here; a smiling lad led us without comment to a parlor. We were soon joined by an elderly woman of dignified bearing.

"Gauri Ma, the princes could not come." One of the men

addressed the ashram hostess. "At the last moment their plans went awry; they send deep regrets. But we have brought two other guests. As soon as we met on the train, I felt drawn to them as devotees of Lord Krishna."

"Good-by, young friends." Our two acquaintances walked to the door. "We shall meet again, if God be willing."

"You are welcome here." Gauri Ma smiled in motherly fashion on her two unexpected charges. "You could not have come on a better day. I was expecting two royal patrons of this hermitage. What a shame if my cooking had found none to appreciate it!"

Lunch was announced; Gauri Ma led the way to a dining patio, spicy with savory odors. She vanished into an adjoining kitchen.

I had been premeditating this moment. Selecting the appropriate spot on Jitendra's anatomy, I administered a pinch as resounding as the one he had given me on the train.

"Doubting Thomas, the Lord works-in a hurry, too!"

The hostess reentered with a PUNKHA. She steadily fanned us in the Oriental fashion as we squatted on ornate blanket-seats. Ashram disciples passed to and fro with some thirty courses. Rather than "meal," the description can only be "sumptuous repast." Since arriving on this planet, Jitendra and I had never before tasted such delicacies.

"Dishes fit for princes indeed, Honored Mother! What your royal patrons could have found more urgent than attending this banquet, I cannot imagine! You have given us a memory for a lifetime!"

We departed with her blessing and an attractive invitation to revisit the hermitage.

Once again Jitendra was beset with misgivings.

"A fine mess you have got me into! Our luncheon was only accidental good fortune! How can we see the sights of this city, without a single pice between us? And how on earth are you going to take me back to Ananta's?"

"Be quiet, Jitendra! The same Lord who fed us will show us Brindaban, and return us to Agra."

A slight young man of pleasing countenance approached at rapid pace. Halting under the tree, he bowed before me.

"Dear friend, you and your companion must be strangers here. Permit me to be your host and guide."

It is scarcely possible for an Indian to pale, but Jitendra's face was suddenly sickly. I politely declined the offer.

"You are surely not banishing me?" The stranger's alarm would have been comic in any other circumstances.

"Why not?"

"You are my guru." His eyes sought mine trustfully. "During my midday devotions, the blessed Lord Krishna appeared in a vision. He showed me two forsaken figures under this very tree. One face was yours, my master! Often have I seen it in meditation! What joy if you accept my humble services!"

"I too am glad you have found me. Neither God nor man has forsaken us!" Though I was motionless, smiling at the eager face before me, an inward obeisance cast me at the Divine Feet.

"Dear friends, will you not honor my home for a visit?"

"You are kind; but the plan is unfeasible. Already we are guests of my brother in Agra."

"At least give me memories of touring Brindaban with you."

I gladly consented. The young man, who said his name was Pratap Chatterji, hailed a horse carriage. We visited

Madanamohana Temple and other Krishna shrines. Night descended while we were at our temple devotions.

"Excuse me while I get SANDESH." Pratap entered a shop near the railroad station. Jitendra and I sauntered along the wide street, crowded now in the comparative coolness. Our friend was absent for some time, but finally returned with gifts of many sweetmeats.

"Please allow me to gain this religious merit." Pratap smiled pleadingly as he held out a bundle of rupee notes and two tickets, just purchased, to Agra.

The reverence of my acceptance was for the Invisible Hand. Scoffed at by Ananta, had Its bounty not far exceeded necessity?

We sought out a secluded spot near the station.

"Pratap, I will instruct you in the KRIYA of Lahiri Mahasaya, the greatest yogi of modern times. His technique will be your guru."

The initiation was concluded in a half hour. "KRIYA is your CHINTAMANI," I told the new student. "The technique, which as you see is simple, embodies the art of quickening man's spiritual evolution. Hindu scriptures teach that the incarnating ego requires a million years to obtain liberation from MAYA. This natural period is greatly shortened through KRIYA YOGA. Be faithful in your practice; you will approach the Guru of all gurus."

"I am transported to find this yogic key, long sought!" Pratap spoke thoughtfully. "Its unshackling effect on my sensory bonds will free me for higher spheres. The vision today of Lord Krishna could only mean my highest good."

We sat awhile in silent understanding, then walked slowly to the station. Joy was within me as I boarded the train.

"How shallow my trust! My heart has been stone! Never in future shall I doubt God's protection!"

Midnight was approaching. The two "Cinderellas," sent forth penniless, entered Ananta's bedroom. His face, as he had promised, was a study in astonishment. Silently I showered the table with rupees.

"Jitendra, the truth!" Ananta's tone was jocular. "Has not this youngster been staging a holdup?"

But as the tale was unfolded, my brother turned sober, then solemn.

Late as it was, my brother insisted that he receive DIKSHA into KRIYA YOGA. The "guru" Mukunda had to shoulder the responsibility of two unsought disciples in one day.

Bidding farewell to Ananta, Jitendra and I were shortly traveling south by train toward Bengal and reached Serampore, twelve miles to the north.

A throb of wonderment stole over me as I realized that twenty-eight days had elapsed since the Benares meeting with my guru. "You will come to me in four weeks!" Here I was, heart pounding, standing within his courtyard on quiet Rai Ghat Lane. I entered for the first time the hermitage where I was to spend the best part of the next ten years with India's JYANAVATAR, "incarnation of wisdom."

12

Years in My Master's Hermitage

"You have come." Sri Yukteswar greeted me from a tiger skin on the floor of a balconied sitting room. His voice was cold, his manner unemotional.

"Yes, dear Master, I am here to follow you." Kneeling, I touched his feet.

"How can that be? You ignore my wishes."

"No longer, Guruji! Your wish shall be my law!"

"That is better! Now I can assume responsibility for your life."

"I willingly transfer the burden, Master."

"My first request, then, is that you return home to your family. I want you to enter college in Calcutta. Your education should be continued."

"Very well, sir." I hid my consternation. Would importunate books pursue me down the years? First Father, now Sri Yukteswar!

"Someday you will go to the West. Its people will lend ears more receptive to India's ancient wisdom if the strange Hindu teacher has a university degree."

"You know best, Guruji." My gloom departed. The reference to the West I found puzzling, remote; but my opportunity to please Master by obedience was vitally immediate.

"You will be near in Calcutta; come here whenever you find time."

"Every day if possible, Master! Gratefully I accept your authority in every detail of my life-on one condition."

"Yes?"

"That you promise to reveal God to me!"

"You are of exacting disposition!" Then Master's consent rang out with compassionate finality:

"Let your wish be my wish."

Lifelong shadow lifted from my heart; the vague search, hither and yon, was over. I had found eternal shelter in a true guru.

"Come; I will show you the hermitage." Master rose from his tiger mat. I glanced about me; my gaze fell with astonishment on a wall picture, garlanded with a spray of jasmine.

"Lahiri Mahasaya!"

"Yes, my divine guru." Sri Yukteswar's tone was reverently vibrant. "Greater he was, as man and yogi, than any other teacher whose life came within the range of my investigations."

Silently I bowed before the familiar picture. Soul-homage sped to the peerless master who, blessing my infancy, had guided my steps to this hour.

Led by my guru, I strolled over the house and its grounds. Large, ancient and well-built, the hermitage was surrounded by a massive-pillared courtyard. Master invited me to stay overnight.

"Guruji, please tell me something of your life." I was squatting on a straw mat near his tiger skin.

"My family name was Priya Nath Karar. I was born here in Serampore, where Father was a wealthy businessman.

He left me this ancestral mansion, now my hermitage. My formal schooling was little. In early manhood, I undertook the responsibilities of a householder, and have one daughter, now married. My middle life was blessed with the guidance of Lahiri Mahasaya. After my wife died, I joined the Swami Order and received the new name of Sri Yukteswar Giri."

Master fell into tranquil silence. Around midnight he led me to a narrow cot. Sleep was sound and sweet the first night under my guru's roof.

Sri Yukteswar chose the following morning to grant me his KRIYA YOGA initiation. The technique I had already received from two disciples of Lahiri Mahasaya – Father and my tutor, Swami Kebalananda – but in Master's presence I felt transforming power. A flood of ineffable bliss, overwhelming my heart to an innermost core, continued during the following day. It was late that afternoon before I could bring myself to leave the hermitage.

"You will return in thirty days." As I reached my Calcutta home, the fulfillment of Master's prediction entered with me. None of my relatives made the pointed remarks I had feared."

"Son, I am happy for us both." Father and I sat together in the evening calm. "You have found your guru, as in miraculous fashion I once found my own. Your master has proved no inaccessible Himalayan saint, but one near-by. My prayers have been answered: you have not in your search for God been permanently removed from my sight."

Father was also pleased that my formal studies would be resumed; he made suitable arrangements. I was enrolled the following day at the Scottish Church College in Calcutta.

The impartiality of saints is rooted in wisdom. Masters have escaped MAYA; its alternating faces of intellect and idiocy no longer cast an influential glance. Sri Yukteswar showed no special consideration to those who happened to be powerful or accomplished; neither did he slight others for their poverty or illiteracy. He would listen respectfully to words of truth from a child, and openly ignore a conceited pundit.

Eight o'clock was the supper hour, and sometimes found lingering guests. My guru would not excuse himself to eat alone; none left his ashram hungry or dissatisfied. Sri Yukteswar was never at a loss, never dismayed by unexpected visitors; scanty food would emerge a banquet under his resourceful direction. Yet he was economical; his modest funds went far. "Be comfortable within your purse," he often said. "Extravagance will buy you discomfort."

Quiet evening hours often brought one of my guru's discourses, treasures against time. His every utterance was measured and chiseled by wisdom. The essence of truth, all-pervasive with even a physiological aspect, came from him like a fragrant exudation of the soul. I was conscious always that I was in the presence of a living manifestation of God. The weight of his divinity automatically bowed my head before him.

My early months with Sri Yukteswar culminated in a useful lesson-"How to Outwit a Mosquito." At home my family always used protective curtains at night. I was dismayed to discover that in the Serampore hermitage this prudent custom was honored in the breach. Yet the insects were in full residency; I was bitten from head to foot. My guru took pity on me.

"Buy yourself a curtain, and also one for me." He laughed and added, "If you buy only one, for yourself, all mosquitoes will concentrate on me!"

I was more than thankful to comply.

The instructive mosquitoes served for an early lesson at the ashram. It was the gentle hour of dusk. My guru was matchlessly interpreting the ancient texts. At his feet, I was in perfect peace. A rude mosquito entered the idyl and competed for my attention. As it dug a poisonous hypodermic needle into my thigh, I automatically raised an avenging hand. Reprieve from impending execution! An opportune memory came to me of one of Patanjali's yoga aphorisms-that on AHIMSA (harmlessness).

"Why didn't you finish the job?"

"Master! Do you advocate taking life?"

"No; but the deathblow already had been struck in your mind."

"I don't understand."

"Patanjali's meaning was the removal of DESIRE to kill." Sri Yukteswar had found my mental processes an open book. "This world is inconveniently arranged for a literal practice of AHIMSA. Man may be compelled to exterminate harmful creatures. He is not under similar compulsion to feel anger or animosity. All forms of life have equal right to the air of MAYA. The saint who uncovers the secret of creation will be in harmony with its countless bewildering expressions. All men may approach that understanding who curb the inner passion for destruction."

"Guruji, should one offer himself a sacrifice rather than kill a wild beast?"

"No; man's body is precious. It has the highest evolutionary value because of unique brain and spinal centers. These enable the advanced devotee to fully grasp and express the loftiest aspects of divinity. No lower form is so equipped. It is true that one incurs the debt of a minor sin if he is forced to kill an animal or any living thing. But the VEDAS teach that wanton loss of a human body is a serious transgression against the karmic law."

I sighed in relief; scriptural reinforcement of one's natural instincts is not always forthcoming.

One afternoon during my early months at the ashram, found Sri Yukteswar's eyes fixed on me piercingly.

"You are too thin, Mukunda."

His remark struck a sensitive point.

"Medicines have limitations; the creative life-force has none. Believe that: you shall be well and strong."

Sri Yukteswar's words aroused a conviction of personally-applicable truth which no other healer – and I had tried many! – had been able to summon within me.

Day by day, behold! I waxed. Two weeks after Master's hidden blessing, I had accumulated the invigorating weight which eluded me in the past. My persistent stomach ailments vanished with a lifelong permanency. On later occasions I witnessed my guru's instantaneous divine healings of persons suffering from ominous disease-tuberculosis, diabetes, epilepsy, or paralysis.

"All creation is governed by law," Sri Yukteswar concluded. "The ones which manifest in the outer universe, discoverable by scientists, are called natural laws. But there are subtler laws ruling the realms of consciousness which can be known only through the inner science of yoga. The hidden spiritual planes also have their natural and lawful principles of operation. It is not the physical scientist but the fully self-realized master who comprehends the true nature of matter. Thus Christ was able to restore the servant's ear after it had been severed by one of the disciples."

Sri Yukteswar was a peerless interpreter of the scriptures. Many of my happiest memories are centered in his discourses. But his jeweled thoughts were not cast into ashes of heedlessness or stupidity. One restless movement of my body, or my slight lapse into absent-mindedness, sufficed to put an abrupt period to Master's exposition.

"You are not here." Master interrupted himself one afternoon with this disclosure. As usual, he was keeping track of my attention with a devastating immediacy.

"Guruji!" My tone was a protest. "I have not stirred; my eyelids have not moved; I can repeat each word you have uttered!"

"Nevertheless you were not fully with me. Your objection forces me to remark that in your mental background you were creating three institutions. One was a sylvan retreat on a plain, another on a hilltop, a third by the ocean."

Those vaguely formulated thoughts had indeed been present almost subconsciously. I glanced at him apologetically.

"What can I do with such a master, who penetrates my random musings?"

"You have given me that right. The subtle truths I am expounding cannot be grasped without your complete concentration. Unless necessary I do not invade the seclusion of others' minds. Man has the natural privilege of roaming secretly among his thoughts. The unbidden Lord does not enter there; neither do I venture intrusion."

"You are ever welcome, Master!"

"Your architectural dreams will materialize later. Now is the time for study!"

Thus incidentally my guru revealed in his simple way the coming of three great events in my life. Since early youth I had

had enigmatic glimpses of three buildings, each in a different setting. In the exact sequence Sri Yukteswar had indicated, these visions took ultimate form. First came my founding of a boys' yoga school on a Ranchi plain, then my American headquarters on a Los Angeles hilltop, finally a hermitage in southern California by the vast Pacific.

I always thrilled at the touch of Sri Yukteswar's holy feet. Yogis teach that a disciple is spiritually magnetized by reverent contact with a master; a subtle current is generated. The devotee's undesirable habit-mechanisms in the brain are often cauterized; the groove of his worldly tendencies beneficially disturbed. Momentarily at least he may find the secret veils of MAYA lifting, and glimpse the reality of bliss. My whole body responded with a liberating glow whenever I knelt in the Indian fashion before my guru.

Master always had young CHELAS in his hermitage. Their spiritual and intellectual education was his lifelong interest: even shortly before he passed on, he accepted for training two six-year-old boys and one youth of sixteen. He directed their minds and lives with that careful discipline in which the word "disciple" is etymologically rooted. The ashram residents loved and revered their guru.

Master spoke fluent English, French, Hindi, and Bengali; his Sanskrit was fair. He patiently instructed his young disciples by certain short cuts which he had ingeniously devised for the study of English and Sanskrit.

Sri Yukteswar's health was excellent; I never saw him unwell. He permitted students to consult doctors if it seemed advisable. His purpose was to give respect to the worldly custom: "Physicians must carry on their work of healing through God's laws as applied to matter." But he extolled the superiority of mental therapy, and often repeated: "Wisdom is the greatest cleanser."

"The body is a treacherous friend. Give it its due; no more," he said. "Pain and pleasure are transitory; endure all dualities with calmness, while trying at the same time to remove their hold. Imagination is the door through which disease as well as healing enters. Disbelieve in the reality of sickness even when you are ill; an unrecognized visitor will flee!"

Sri Yukteswar counseled his students to be living liaisons of Western and Eastern virtues. Himself an executive Occidental in outer habits, inwardly he was the spiritual Oriental. He praised the progressive, resourceful and hygienic habits of the West, and the religious ideals which give a centuried halo to the East.

Discipline had not been unknown to me: at home Father was strict, Ananta often severe. But Sri Yukteswar's training cannot be described as other than drastic. A perfectionist, my guru was hypercritical of his disciples, whether in matters of moment or in the subtle nuances of behavior.

Master was apparently satisfied with my spiritual progress, for he seldom referred to it; in other matters my ears were no strangers to reproof. My chief offenses were absentmindedness, intermittent indulgence in sad moods, non-observance of certain rules of etiquette, and occasional unmethodical ways.

My guru could never be bribed, even by love. He showed no leniency to anyone who, like myself, willingly offered to be his disciple. Whether Master and I were surrounded by his students or by strangers, or were alone together, he always spoke plainly and upbraided sharply. No trifling lapse into shallowness or inconsistency escaped his rebuke. This flattening treatment was hard to endure, but my resolve was to allow Sri Yukteswar to iron out each of my psychological kinks. As he labored at this titanic transformation, I shook many times under the weight of his disciplinary hammer.

But divine insight is painful to worldly ears; Master was not popular with superficial students. The wise, always few in number, deeply revered him. I daresay Sri Yukteswar would have been the most soughtafter guru in India had his words not been so candid and so censorious.

"I am hard on those who come for my training," he admitted to me. "That is my way; take it or leave it. I will never compromise. But you will be much kinder to your disciples; that is your way. I try to purify only in the fires of severity, searing beyond the average toleration. The gentle approach of love is also transfiguring. The inflexible and the yielding methods are equally effective if applied with wisdom. You will go to foreign lands, where blunt assaults on the ego are not appreciated. A teacher could not spread India's message in the West without an ample fund of accommodative patience and forbearance." I refuse to state the amount of truth I later came to find in Master's words!

Though Sri Yukteswar's undissembling speech prevented a large following during his years on earth, nevertheless his living spirit manifests today over the world, through sincere students of his KRIYA YOGA and other teachings.

During my early months with Master, I had experienced a sensitive fear of his reprimands. These were reserved, I soon saw, for disciples who had asked for his verbal vivisection. If any writhing student made a protest, Sri Yukteswar would become unoffendedly silent. His words were never wrathful, but impersonal with wisdom.

Master's insight was not for the unprepared ears of

casual visitors; he seldom remarked on their defects, even if conspicuous. But toward students who sought his counsel, Sri Yukteswar felt a serious responsibility. Brave indeed is the guru who undertakes to transform the crude ore of ego-permeated humanity! A saint's courage roots in his compassion for the stumbling eyeless of this world.

When I had abandoned underlying resentment, I found a marked decrease in my chastisement. In a very subtle way, Master melted into comparative clemency. In time I demolished every wall of rationalization and subconscious reservation behind which the human personality generally shields itself. The reward was an effortless harmony with my guru. I discovered him then to be trusting, considerate, and silently loving. Undemonstrative, however, he bestowed no word of affection.

My own temperament is principally devotional. It was disconcerting at first to find that my guru, saturated with JNANA but seemingly dry of BHAKTI, expressed himself only in terms of cold spiritual mathematics. But as I tuned myself to his nature, I discovered no diminution but rather increase in my devotional approach to God. A self-realized master is fully able to guide his various disciples along natural lines of their essential bias.

My relationship with Sri Yukteswar, somewhat inarticulate, nonetheless possessed all eloquence. Often I found his silent signature on my thoughts, rendering speech inutile. Quietly sitting beside him, I felt his bounty pouring peacefully over my being.

Sri Yukteswar's impartial justice was notably demonstrated during the summer vacation of my first college year. I welcomed the opportunity to spend uninterrupted months at Serampore with my guru.

"You may be in charge of the hermitage." Master was pleased over my enthusiastic arrival. "Your duties will be the reception of guests, and supervision of the work of the other disciples."

Kumar, a young villager from east Bengal, was accepted a fortnight later for hermitage training. Remarkably intelligent, he quickly won Sri Yukteswar's affection. For some unfathomable reason, Master was very lenient to the new resident.

"Mukunda, let Kumar assume your duties. Employ your own time in sweeping and cooking." Master issued these instructions after the new boy had been with us for a month.

Exalted to leadership, Kumar exercised a petty household tyranny.

In silent mutiny, the other disciples continued to seek me out for daily counsel.

"Mukunda is impossible! You made me supervisor, yet the others go to him and obey him." Three weeks later Kumar was complaining to our guru. I overheard him from an adjoining room.

"That's why I assigned him to the kitchen and you to the parlor." Sri Yukteswar's withering tones were new to Kumar. "In this way you have come to realize that a worthy leader has the desire to serve, and not to dominate. You wanted Mukunda's position, but could not maintain it by merit. Return now to your earlier work as cook's assistant."

After this humbling incident, Master resumed toward Kumar a former attitude of unwonted indulgence. Who can solve the mystery of attraction? In Kumar our guru discovered a charming fount which did not spurt for the fellow disciples. Though the new boy was obviously Sri Yukteswar's favorite,

I felt no dismay. Personal idiosyncrasies, possessed even by masters, lend a rich complexity to the pattern of life. My nature is seldom commandeered by a detail; I was seeking from Sri Yukteswar a more inaccessible benefit than an outward praise.

Kumar spoke venomously to me one day without reason; I was deeply hurt.

"Your head is swelling to the bursting point!" I added a warning whose truth I felt intuitively: "Unless you mend your ways, someday you will be asked to leave this ashram."

Laughing sarcastically, Kumar repeated my remark to our guru, who had just entered the room. Fully expecting to be scolded, I retired meekly to a corner.

"Maybe Mukunda is right." Master's reply to the boy came with unusual coldness. I escaped without castigation.

A year later, Kumar set out for a visit to his childhood home. He ignored the quiet disapproval of Sri Yukteswar, who never authoritatively controlled his disciples' movements. On the boy's return to Serampore in a few months, a change was unpleasantly apparent. Gone was the stately Kumar with serenely glowing face. Only an undistinguished peasant stood before us, one who had lately acquired a number of evil habits.

Master summoned me and brokenheartedly discussed the fact that the boy was now unsuited to the monastic hermitage life.

"Mukunda, I will leave it to you to instruct Kumar to leave the ashram tomorrow; I can't do it!" Tears stood in Sri Yukteswar's eyes, but he controlled himself quickly. "The boy would never have fallen to these depths had he listened to me and not gone away to mix with undesirable companions. He has rejected my protection; the callous world must be his guru still."

My guru mixed freely with men and women disciples, treating all as his children. Perceiving their soul equality, he showed no distinction or partiality.

"In sleep, you do not know whether you are a man or a woman," he said. "Just as a man, impersonating a woman, does not become one, so the soul, impersonating both man and woman, has no sex. The soul is the pure, changeless image of God."

Sri Yukteswar never avoided or blamed women as objects of seduction. Men, he said, were also a temptation to women. I once inquired of my guru why a great ancient saint had called women "the door to hell."

"A girl must have proved very troublesome to his peace of mind in his early life," my guru answered caustically. "Otherwise he would have denounced, not woman, but some imperfection in his own self-control."

If a visitor dared to relate a suggestive story in the hermitage, Master would maintain an unresponsive silence. "Do not allow yourself to be thrashed by the provoking whip of a beautiful face," he told the disciples. "How can sense slaves enjoy the world? Its subtle flavors escape them while they grovel in primal mud. All nice discriminations are lost to the man of elemental lusts." Students seeking to escape from the dualistic MAYA delusion received from Sri Yukteswar patient and understanding counsel.

"Just as the purpose of eating is to satisfy hunger, not greed, so the sex instinct is designed for the propagation of the species according to natural law, never for the kindling of insatiable longings," he said. "Destroy wrong desires now; otherwise they will follow you after the astral body is torn from its physical casing. Even when the flesh is weak, the mind should be constantly resistant. If temptation assails you with cruel force, overcome it by impersonal analysis and indomitable will. Every natural passion can be mastered.

"Conserve your powers. Be like the capacious ocean, absorbing within all the tributary rivers of the senses. Small yearnings are openings in the reservoir of your inner peace, permitting healing waters to be wasted in the desert soil of materialism. The forceful activating impulse of wrong desire is the greatest enemy to the happiness of man. Roam in the world as a lion of self-control; see that the frogs of weakness don't kick you around."

The devotee is finally freed from all instinctive compulsions. He transforms his need for human affection into aspiration for God alone, a love solitary because omnipresent.

The monastic regulations do not allow a swami to retain connection with worldly ties after their formal severance. He cannot perform the ceremonial family rites which are obligatory on the householder. Yet Shankara, the ancient founder of the Swami Order, disregarded the injunctions. At the death of his beloved mother, he cremated her body with heavenly fire which he caused to spurt from his upraised hand.

Sri Yukteswar also ignored the restrictions, in a fashion less spectacular. When his mother passed on, he arranged the crematory services by the holy Ganges in Benares, and fed many Brahmins in conformance with age-old custom.

My guru's ready wit and rollicking laugh enlivened every discussion. Often grave, Master was never gloomy. "To seek the Lord, one need not disfigure his face," he would remark. "Remember that finding God will mean the funeral of all sorrows."

Among the philosophers, professors, lawyers and scientists

who came to the hermitage, a number arrived for their first visit with the expectation of meeting an orthodox religionist. A supercilious smile or a glance of amused tolerance occasionally betrayed that the newcomers anticipated nothing more than a few pious platitudes. Yet their reluctant departure would bring an expressed conviction that Sri Yukteswar had shown precise insight into their specialized fields.

My guru ordinarily was gentle and affable to guests; his welcome was given with charming cordiality. Yet inveterate egotists sometimes suffered an invigorating shock. They confronted in Master either a frigid indifference or a formidable opposition: ice or iron!

Master stressed on other occasions the futility of mere book learning.

"Do not confuse understanding with a larger vocabulary," he remarked. "Sacred writings are beneficial in stimulating desire for inward realization, if one stanza at a time is slowly assimilated. Continual intellectual study results in vanity and the false satisfaction of an undigested knowledge."

Sri Yukteswar related one of his own experiences in scriptural edification. The scene was a forest hermitage in eastern Bengal, where he observed the procedure of a renowned teacher, Dabru Ballav. His method, at once simple and difficult, was common in ancient India.

Dabru Ballav had gathered his disciples around him in the sylvan solitudes. The holy BHAGAVAD GITA was open before them. Steadfastly they looked at one passage for half an hour, then closed their eyes. Another half hour slipped away. The master gave a brief comment. Motionless, they meditated again for an hour. Finally the guru spoke.

"Have you understood?"

"Yes, sir." One in the group ventured this assertion.

"No; not fully. Seek the spiritual vitality that has given these words the power to rejuvenate India century after century." Another hour disappeared in silence. The master dismissed the students, and turned to Sri Yukteswar.

"Do you know the BHAGAVAD GITA?"

"No, sir, not really; though my eyes and mind have run through its pages many times."

"Thousands have replied to me differently!" The great sage smiled at Master in blessing. "If one busies himself with an outer display of scriptural wealth, what time is left for silent inward diving after the priceless pearls?"

Sri Yukteswar directed the study of his own disciples by the same intensive method of one-pointedness. "Wisdom is not assimilated with the eyes, but with the atoms," he said. "When your conviction of a truth is not merely in your brain but in your being, you may diffidently vouch for its meaning." He discouraged any tendency a student might have to construe book-knowledge as a necessary step to spiritual realization.

"The RISHIS wrote in one sentence profundities that commentating scholars busy themselves over for generations," he remarked. "Endless literary controversy is for sluggard minds. What more liberating thought than 'God is'-nay, 'God'?"

But man does not easily return to simplicity. It is seldom "God" for him, but rather learned pomposities. His ego is pleased, that he can grasp such erudition.

Men who were pridefully conscious of high worldly position were likely, in Master's presence, to add humility to their other possessions. A local magistrate once arrived for an interview at the seaside hermitage in Puri. The man, who held a reputation for ruthlessness, had it well within his power to oust us from the ashram. I cautioned my guru about the despotic possibilities. But he seated himself with an uncompromising air, and did not rise to greet the visitor. Slightly nervous, I squatted near the door. The man had to content himself with a wooden box; my guru did not request me to fetch a chair. There was no fulfillment of the magistrate's obvious expectation that his importance would be ceremoniously acknowledged.

A metaphysical discussion ensued. The guest blundered through misinterpretations of the scriptures. As his accuracy sank, his ire rose.

"Do you know that I stood first in the M. A. examination?" Reason had forsaken him, but he could still shout.

"Mr. Magistrate, you forget that this is not your courtroom," Master replied evenly. "From your childish remarks I would have surmised that your college career was unremarkable. A university degree, in any case, is not remotely related to Vedic realization. Saints are not produced in batches every semester like accountants."

After a stunned silence, the visitor laughed heartily.

"This is my first encounter with a heavenly magistrate," he said. Later he made a formal request, couched in the legal terms which were evidently part and parcel of his being, to be accepted as a "probationary" disciple.

My guru personally attended to the details connected with the management of his property. Unscrupulous persons on various occasions attempted to secure possession of Master's ancestral land. With determination and even by instigating lawsuits, Sri Yukteswar outwitted every opponent. He underwent these painful experiences from a desire never to be a begging guru, or a burden on his disciples.

His financial independence was one reason why my alarmingly outspoken Master was innocent of the cunnings of diplomacy. Unlike those teachers who have to flatter their supporters, my guru was impervious to the influences, open or subtle, of others' wealth. Never did I hear him ask or even hint for money for any purpose. His hermitage training was given free and freely to all disciples.

An insolent court deputy arrived one day at the Serampore ashram to serve Sri Yukteswar with a legal summons. A disciple named Kanai and myself were also present. The officer's attitude toward Master was offensive.

"It will do you good to leave the shadows of your hermitage and breathe the honest air of a courtroom." The deputy grinned contemptuously. I could not contain myself.

"Another word of your impudence and you will be on the floor!" I advanced threateningly.

"You wretch!" Kanai's shout was simultaneous with my own. "Dare you bring your blasphemies into this sacred ashram?"

But Master stood protectingly in front of his abuser. "Don't get excited over nothing. This man is only doing his rightful duty."

The officer, dazed at his varying reception, respectfully offered a word of apology and sped away.

I often reflected that my majestic Master could easily have been an emperor or world-shaking warrior had his mind been centered on fame or worldly achievement. He had chosen instead to storm those inner citadels of wrath and egotism whose fall is the height of a man.

13

The Sleepless Saint

"Please permit me to go to the Himalayas. I hope in unbroken solitude to achieve continuous divine communion."

I actually once addressed these ungrateful words to my Master. Seized by one of the unpredictable delusions which occasionally assail the devotee, I felt a growing impatience with hermitage duties and college studies. A feebly extenuating circumstance is that my proposal was made when I had been only six months with Sri Yukteswar. Not yet had I fully surveyed his towering stature.

"Many hillmen live in the Himalayas, yet possess no God-perception." My guru's answer came slowly and simply. "Wisdom is better sought from a man of realization than from an inert mountain."

Ignoring Master's plain hint that he, and not a hill, was my teacher, I repeated my plea. Sri Yukteswar vouchsafed no reply. I took his silence for consent, a precarious interpretation readily accepted at one's convenience.

In my Calcutta home that evening, I busied myself with travel preparations. The following morning I sought out Behari Pundit, my Sanskrit professor at Scottish Church College.

"Sir, you have told me of your friendship with a great disciple of Lahiri Mahasaya. Please give me his address."

"You mean Ram Gopal Muzumdar. I call him the 'sleepless saint.' He is always awake in an ecstatic consciousness. His home is at Ranbajpur, near Tarakeswar."

I thanked the pundit, and entrained immediately for Tarakeswar. I hoped to silence my misgivings by wringing a sanction from the "sleepless saint" to engage myself in lonely Himalayan meditation. Behari's friend, I heard, had received illumination after many years of KRIYA YOGA practice in isolated caves.

At Tarakeswar I approached a famous shrine. Hindus regard it with the same veneration that Catholics give to the Lourdes sanctuary in France. I entered the sacred Tarakeswar shrine; the altar contains nothing but a round stone. Its circumference, beginningless and endless, makes it aptly significant of the Infinite. Cosmic abstractions are not alien even to the humblest Indian peasant; he has been accused by Westerners, in fact, of living on abstractions!

My own mood at the moment was so austere that I felt disinclined to bow before the stone symbol. God should be sought, I reflected, only within the soul.

I left the temple without genuflection and walked briskly toward the outlying village of Ranbajpur. I wended my way alongside the banks of a canal. Darkness fell; the outskirts of the jungle village were alive with winking fireflies and the howls of near-by jackals. The moonlight was too faint to supply any reassurance; I stumbled on for two hours.

Welcome clang of a cowbell! My repeated shouts eventually brought a peasant to my side.

"I am looking for Ram Gopal Babu."

"No such person lives in our village." The man's tone was surly. "You are probably a lying detective."

Hoping to allay suspicion in his politically troubled mind, I touchingly explained my predicament. He took me to his home and offered a hospitable welcome. After a relishable meal of coarse rice, lentil-DHAL, and curry of potatoes with raw bananas, I retired to a small hut adjoining the courtyard. Sleep was inconsiderable that night; I prayed deeply to be directed to the secret yogi, Ram Gopal.

As the first streaks of dawn penetrated the fissures of my dark room, I set out for Ranbajpur. At midafternoon my world was still an endless paddy field. Heat pouring from the avoidless sky was bringing me to near-collapse. As a man approached at leisurely pace, I hardly dared utter my usual question.

The stranger halted beside me. Short and slight, he was physically unimpressive save for an extraordinary pair of piercing dark eyes.

"I was planning to leave Ranbajpur, but your purpose was good, so I awaited you." He shook his finger in my astounded face. "Aren't you clever to think that, unannounced, you could pounce on me? That professor Behari had no right to give you my address."

Considering that introduction of myself would be mere verbosity in the presence of this master, I stood speechless, somewhat hurt at my reception. His next remark was abruptly put.

"Tell me; where do you think God is?"

"Why, He is within me and everywhere." I doubtless looked as bewildered as I felt.

"All-pervading, eh?" The saint chuckled. "Then why, young sir, did you fail to bow before the Infinite in the stone symbol at the Tarakeswar temple yesterday? Your pride caused you the punishment of being misdirected by the passer-by who was not bothered by fine distinctions of left and right. Today, too, you have had a fairly uncomfortable time of it!"

I agreed wholeheartedly, wonder-struck that an omniscient eye hid within the unremarkable body before me. Healing strength emanated from the yogi; I was instantly refreshed in the scorching field.

"The devotee inclines to think his path to God is the only way," he said. "Yoga, through which divinity is found within, is doubtless the highest road: so Lahiri Mahasaya has told us. But discovering the Lord within, we soon perceive Him without. Holy shrines at Tarakeswar and elsewhere are rightly venerated as nuclear centers of spiritual power." The saint's censorious attitude vanished; his eyes became compassionately soft. He patted my shoulder.

"Young yogi, I see you are running away from your master. He has everything you need; you must return to him. Mountains cannot be your guru." Ram Gopal was repeating the same thought which Sri Yukteswar had expressed at our last meeting.

"Masters are under no cosmic compulsion to limit their residence." My companion glanced at me quizzically. "The Himalayas in India and Tibet have no monopoly on saints. What one does not trouble to find within will not be discovered by transporting the body hither and yon. As soon as the devotee is WILLING to go even to the ends of the earth for spiritual enlightenment, his guru appears near-by."

I silently agreed, recalling my prayer in the Benares hermitage, followed by the meeting with Sri Yukteswar in a crowded lane.

"Are you able to have a little room where you can close the door and be alone?"

"Yes." I reflected that this saint descended from the general to the particular with disconcerting speed.

"That is your cave." The yogi bestowed on me a gaze of illumination which I have never forgotten. "That is your sacred mountain. That is where you will find the kingdom of God."

His simple words instantaneously banished my lifelong obsession for the Himalayas. In a burning paddy field I awoke from the monticolous dreams of eternal snows.

"Young sir, your divine thirst is laudable. I feel great love for you." Ram Gopal took my hand and led me to a quaint hamlet. The adobe houses were covered with coconut leaves and adorned with rustic entrances.

The saint seated me on the umbrageous bamboo platform of his small cottage. After giving me sweetened lime juice and a piece of rock candy, he entered his patio and assumed the lotus posture. In about four hours I opened my meditative eyes and saw that the moonlit figure of the yogi was still motionless. As I was sternly reminding my stomach that man does not live by bread alone, Ram Gopal approached me.

"I see you are famished; food will be ready soon."

A fire was kindled under a clay oven on the patio; rice and DHAL were quickly served on large banana leaves. My host courteously refused my aid in all cooking chores. "The guest is God," a Hindu proverb, has commanded devout observance from time immemorial.

Ram Gopal arranged some torn blankets on the floor for my bed, and seated himself on a straw mat. Overwhelmed by his spiritual magnetism, I ventured a request.

"Sir, why don't you grant me a SAMADHI?"

"Dear one, I would be glad to convey the divine contact, but it is not my place to do so." The saint looked at me with half-closed eyes. "Your master will bestow that experience shortly. Your body is not tuned just yet. As a small lamp cannot withstand excessive electrical voltage, so your nerves are unready for the cosmic current. If I gave you the infinite ecstasy right now, you would burn as if every cell were on fire.

"You are asking illumination from me," the yogi continued musingly, "while I am wondering-inconsiderable as I am, and with the little meditation I have done-if I have succeeded in pleasing God, and what worth I may find in His eyes at the final reckoning."

"Sir, have you not been singleheartedly seeking God for a long time?"

"I have not done much. Behari must have told you something of my life. For twenty years I occupied a secret grotto, meditating eighteen hours a day. Then I moved to a more inaccessible cave and remained there for twenty-five years, entering the yoga union for twenty hours daily. I did not need sleep, for I was ever with God. My body was more rested in the complete calmness of the superconsciousness than it could be by the partial peace of the ordinary subconscious state.

"The muscles relax during sleep, but the heart, lungs, and circulatory system are constantly at work; they get no rest. In superconsciousness, the internal organs remain in a state of suspended animation, electrified by the cosmic energy. By such means I have found it unnecessary to sleep for years. The time will come when you too will dispense with sleep."

"My goodness, you have meditated for so long and yet are unsure of the Lord's favor!" I gazed at him in astonishment. "Then what about us poor mortals?"

"Well, don't you see, my dear boy, that God is Eternity

Itself? To assume that one can fully know Him by forty-five years of meditation is rather a preposterous expectation. Babaji assures us, however, that even a little meditation saves one from the dire fear of death and after-death states. Do not fix your spiritual ideal on a small mountain, but hitch it to the star of unqualified divine attainment. If you work hard, you will get there."

Enthralled by the prospect, I asked him for further enlightening words. He related a wondrous story of his first meeting with Lahiri Mahasaya's guru, Babaji. {FN13-3} Around midnight Ram Gopal fell into silence, and I lay down on my blankets. Closing my eyes, I saw flashes of lightning; the vast space within me was a chamber of molten light. I opened my eyes and observed the same dazzling radiance. The room became a part of that infinite vault which I beheld with interior vision.

"Why don't you go to sleep?"

"Sir, how can I sleep in the presence of lightning, blazing whether my eyes are shut or open?"

"You are blessed to have this experience; the spiritual radiations are not easily seen." The saint added a few words of affection.

At dawn Ram Gopal gave me rock candies and said I must depart. I felt such reluctance to bid him farewell that tears coursed down my cheeks.

"I will not let you go empty-handed," the yogi spoke tenderly. "I will do something for you."

He smiled and looked at me steadfastly. I stood rooted to the ground, peace rushing like a mighty flood through the gates of my eyes. I was instantaneously healed of a pain in my back, which had troubled me intermittently for years. After touching the saint's feet, I sauntered into the jungle, making my way through its tropical tangle until I reached Tarakeswar.

I entrained happily an hour later for Calcutta. My travels ended, not in the lofty mountains, but in the Himalayan presence of my Master.

14

An Experience in
Cosmic Consciousness

"I am here, Guruji." My shamefacedness spoke more
eloquently for me.

"Let us go to the kitchen and find something to eat." Sri
Yukteswar's manner was as natural as if hours and not days
had separated us.

"Master, I must have disappointed you by my abrupt
departure from my duties here; I thought you might be angry
with me."

"No, of course not! Wrath springs only from thwarted
desires. I do not expect anything from others, so their actions
cannot be in opposition to wishes of mine. I would not use
you for my own ends; I am happy only in your own true
happiness."

"Sir, one hears of divine love in a vague way, but for the
first time I am having a concrete example in your angelic self!
In the world, even a father does not easily forgive his son if he
leaves his parent's business without warning. But you show
not the slightest vexation, though you must have been put
to great inconvenience by the many unfinished tasks I left
behind."

We looked into each other's eyes, where tears were shining. A blissful wave engulfed me; I was conscious that the Lord, in the form of my guru, was expanding the small ardors of my heart into the incompressible reaches of cosmic love.

A few mornings later I made my way to Master's empty sitting room. I planned to meditate, but my laudable purpose was unshared by disobedient thoughts. They scattered like birds before the hunter.

"Mukunda!" Sri Yukteswar's voice sounded from a distant inner balcony.

I felt as rebellious as my thoughts. "Master always urges me to meditate," I muttered to myself. "He should not disturb me when he knows why I came to his room."

He summoned me again; I remained obstinately silent. The third time his tone held rebuke.

"Sir, I am meditating," I shouted protestingly.

"I know how you are meditating," my guru called out, "with your mind distributed like leaves in a storm! Come here to me."

Snubbed and exposed, I made my way sadly to his side.

"Poor boy, the mountains couldn't give what you wanted." Master spoke caressively, comfortingly. His calm gaze was unfathomable. "Your heart's desire shall be fulfilled."

Sri Yukteswar seldom indulged in riddles; I was bewildered. He struck gently on my chest above the heart.

My body became immovably rooted; breath was drawn out of my lungs as if by some huge magnet. Soul and mind instantly lost their physical bondage, and streamed out like a fluid piercing light from my every pore. My sense of identity was no longer narrowly confined to a body, but embraced the circumambient atoms. All objects within my panoramic gaze trembled and vibrated like quick motion pictures. My body, Master's, the pillared courtyard, the furniture and floor, the trees and sunshine, occasionally became violently agitated, until all melted into a luminescent sea; even as sugar crystals, thrown into a glass of water, dissolve after being shaken. The unifying light alternated with materializations of form, the metamorphoses revealing the law of cause and effect in creation.

An oceanic joy broke upon calm endless shores of my soul. The Spirit of God, I realized, is exhaustless Bliss; His body is countless tissues of light.

I cognized the center of the empyrean as a point of intuitive perception in my heart. Irradiating splendor issued from my nucleus to every part of the universal structure. Blissful AMRITA, the nectar of immortality, pulsed through me with a quicksilverlike fluidity. The creative voice of God I heard resounding as AUM, the vibration of the Cosmic Motor.

Suddenly the breath returned to my lungs. With a disappointment almost unbearable, I realized that my infinite immensity was lost. Once more I was limited to the humiliating cage of a body, not easily accommodative to the Spirit. Like a prodigal child, I had run away from my macrocosmic home and imprisoned myself in a narrow microcosm.

My guru was standing motionless before me; I started to drop at his holy feet in gratitude for the experience in cosmic consciousness which I had long passionately sought. He held me upright, and spoke calmly, unpretentiously.

"You must not get overdrunk with ecstasy. Much work yet remains for you in the world. Come; let us sweep the balcony floor; then we shall walk by the Ganges."

I fetched a broom; Master, I knew, was teaching me the

secret of balanced living. The soul must stretch over the cosmogonic abysses, while the body performs its daily duties.

The cosmic vision left many permanent lessons. By daily stilling my thoughts, I could win release from the delusive conviction that my body was a mass of flesh and bones, traversing the hard soil of matter. The breath and the restless mind, I saw, were like storms which lashed the ocean of light into waves of material forms-earth, sky, human beings, animals, birds, trees. No perception of the Infinite as One Light could be had except by calming those storms. As often as I silenced the two natural tumults, I beheld the multitudinous waves of creation melt into one lucent sea, even as the waves of the ocean, their tempests subsiding, serenely dissolve into unity.

A master bestows the divine experience of cosmic consciousness when his disciple, by meditation, has strengthened his mind to a degree where the vast vistas would not overwhelm him. The experience can never be given through one's mere intellectual willingness or open-mindedness. Only adequate enlargement by yoga practice and devotional BHAKTI can prepare the mind to absorb the liberating shock of omnipresence.

Sri Yukteswar taught me how to summon the blessed experience at will, and also how to transmit it to others if their intuitive channels were developed. For months I entered the ecstatic union, comprehending why the UPANISHADS say God is RASA, "the most relishable." One day, however, I took a problem to Master.

"I want to know, sir-when shall I find God?"

"You have found Him."

"O no, sir, I don't think so!"

My guru was smiling. "I am sure you aren't expecting a venerable Personage, adorning a throne in some antiseptic corner of the cosmos! I see, however, that you are imagining that the possession of miraculous powers is knowledge of God. One might have the whole universe, and find the Lord elusive still! Spiritual advancement is not measured by one's outward powers, but only by the depth of his bliss in meditation.

"EVER-NEW JOY IS GOD. He is inexhaustible; as you continue your meditations during the years, He will beguile you with an infinite ingenuity.

"How quickly we weary of earthly pleasures! Desire for material things is endless; man is never satisfied completely, and pursues one goal after another. The 'something else' he seeks is the Lord, who alone can grant lasting joy.

"Outward longings drive us from the Eden within; they offer false pleasures which only impersonate soul-happiness. The lost paradise is quickly regained through divine meditation. As God is unanticipatory Ever-Newness, we never tire of Him. Can we be surfeited with bliss, delightfully varied throughout eternity?"

"I understand now, sir, why saints call the Lord unfathomable. Even everlasting life could not suffice to appraise Him."

"That is true; but He is also near and dear. After the mind has been cleared by KRIYA YOGA of sensory obstacles, meditation furnishes a twofold proof of God. Ever-new joy is evidence of His existence, convincing to our very atoms. Also, in meditation one finds His instant guidance, His adequate response to every difficulty."

"I see, Guruji; you have solved my problem." I smiled gratefully. "I do realize now that I have found God."

15

The Cauliflower Robbery

"Master, a gift for you! These six huge cauliflowers were planted with my hands; I have watched over their growth with the tender care of a mother nursing her child." I presented the basket of vegetables with a ceremonial flourish.

"Thank you!" Sri Yukteswar's smile was warm with appreciation. "Please keep them in your room; I shall need them tomorrow for a special dinner."

I had just arrived in Puri to spend my college summer vacation with my guru at his seaside hermitage.

I awoke early the following morning, refreshed by the salty sea breezes and the charm of my surroundings. Sri Yukteswar's melodious voice was calling; I took a look at my cherished cauliflowers and stowed them neatly under my bed.

"Come, let us go to the beach." Master led the way; several young disciples and myself followed in a scattered group. Our guru surveyed us in mild criticism.

"Halt!" My guru's eyes sought mine. "Did you remember to lock the back door of the hermitage?"

"I think so, sir."

Sri Yukteswar was silent for a few minutes, a half-suppressed smile on his lips. "No, you forgot," he said finally. "Divine contemplation must not be made an excuse for material carelessness. You have neglected your duty in safeguarding the ashram; you must be punished."

I thought he was obscurely joking when he added: "Your six cauliflowers will soon be only five."

We turned around at Master's orders and marched back until we were close to the hermitage.

"Rest awhile. Mukunda, look across the compound on our left; observe the road beyond. A certain man will arrive there presently; he will be the means of your chastisement."

I concealed my vexation at these incomprehensible remarks. A peasant soon appeared on the road; he was dancing grotesquely and flinging his arms about with meaningless gestures. Almost paralyzed with curiosity, I glued my eyes on the hilarious spectacle. As the man reached a point in the road where he would vanish from our view, Sri Yukteswar said, "Now, he will return."

The peasant at once changed his direction and made for the rear of the ashram. Crossing a sandy tract, he entered the building by the back door. I had left it unlocked, even as my guru had said. The man emerged shortly, holding one of my prized cauliflowers. He now strode along respectably, invested with the dignity of possession.

The unfolding farce, in which my role appeared to be that of bewildered victim, was not so disconcerting that I failed in indignant pursuit. I was halfway to the road when Master recalled me. He was shaking from head to foot with laughter.

"That poor crazy man has been longing for a cauliflower," he explained between outbursts of mirth. "I thought it would be a good idea if he got one of yours, so ill-guarded!"

I dashed to my room, where I found that the thief, evidently one with a vegetable fixation, had left untouched my gold rings, watch, and money, all lying openly on the blanket. He had crawled instead under the bed where, completely hidden from casual sight, one of my cauliflowers had aroused his singlehearted desire.

I asked Sri Yukteswar that evening to explain the incident which had, I thought, a few baffling features.

My guru shook his head slowly. "You will understand it someday. Science will soon discover a few of these hidden laws."

When the wonders of radio burst some years later on an astounded world, I remembered Master's prediction. Age-old concepts of time and space were annihilated; no peasant's home so narrow that London or Calcutta could not enter! The dullest intelligence enlarged before indisputable proof of one aspect of man's omnipresence.

The "plot" of the cauliflower comedy can be best understood by a radio analogy. Sri Yukteswar was a perfect human radio. Thoughts are no more than very gentle vibrations moving in the ether. Just as a sensitized radio picks up a desired musical number out of thousands of other programs from every direction, so my guru had been able to catch the thought of the half-witted man who hankered for a cauliflower, out of the countless thoughts of broadcasting human wills in the world. By his powerful will, Master was also a human broadcasting station, and had successfully directed the peasant to reverse his steps and go to a certain room for a single cauliflower.

Intuition is soul guidance, appearing naturally in man during those instants when his mind is calm. Nearly everyone has had the experience of an inexplicably correct "hunch," or has transferred his thoughts effectively to another person.

The human mind, free from the static of restlessness, can

perform through its antenna of intuition all the functions of complicated radio mechanisms – sending and receiving thoughts, and tuning out undesirable ones. As the power of a radio depends on the amount of electrical current it can utilize, so the human radio is energized according to the power of will possessed by each individual.

All thoughts vibrate eternally in the cosmos. By deep concentration, a Master is able to detect the thoughts of any mind, living or dead. Thoughts are universally and not individually rooted; a truth cannot be created, but only perceived. The erroneous thoughts of man result from imperfections in his discernment. The goal of yoga science is to calm the mind, that without distortion it may mirror the divine vision in the universe.

Radio and television have brought the instantaneous sound and sight of remote persons to the firesides of millions: the first faint scientific intimations that man is an all-pervading spirit. Not a body confined to a point in space, but the vast soul, which the ego in most barbaric modes conspires in vain to cramp.

"Very strange, very wonderful, seemingly very improbable phenomena may yet appear which, when once established, will not astonish us more than we are now astonished at all that science has taught us during the last century," Charles Robert Richet, Nobel Prizeman in physiology, has declared. "It is assumed that the phenomena, which we now accept without surprise, do not excite our astonishment because they are understood. But this is not the case. If they do not surprise us it is not because they are understood, it is because they are familiar; for if that which is not understood ought to surprise us, we should be surprised at everything – the fall of a stone thrown into the air, the acorn which becomes an oak, mercury which expands when it is heated, iron attracted by a magnet, phosphorus which burns when it is rubbed. . . . The science of today is a light matter; the revolutions and evolutions which it will experience in a hundred thousand years will far exceed the most daring anticipations."

A humorous occurrence took place a few days after I had been so implausibly robbed of a cauliflower. A certain kerosene lamp could not be found. Having so lately witnessed my guru's omniscient insight, I thought he would demonstrate that it was child's play to locate the lamp.

Master perceived my expectation. With exaggerated gravity he questioned all ashram residents. A young disciple confessed that he had used the lamp to go to the well in the back yard.

Sri Yukteswar gave the solemn counsel: "Seek the lamp near the well."

I rushed there; no lamp! Crestfallen, I returned to my guru. He was now laughing heartily, without compunction for my disillusionment.

"Too bad I couldn't direct you to the vanished lamp; I am not a fortune teller!" With twinkling eyes, he added, "I am not even a satisfactory Sherlock Holmes!"

I realized that Master would never display his powers when challenged, or for a triviality.

Delightful weeks sped by. Sri Yukteswar was planning a religious procession. He asked me to lead the disciples over the town and beach of Puri. The festive day dawned as one of the hottest of the summer.

"Guruji, how can I take the barefooted students over the fiery sands?" I spoke despairingly.

"I will tell you a secret," Master responded. "The Lord will send an umbrella of clouds; you all shall walk in comfort."

I happily organized the procession; our group started from the ashram with a SAT-SANGA banner. Designed by Sri Yukteswar, it bore the symbol of the single eye, the telescopic gaze of intuition.

No sooner had we left the hermitage than the part of the sky which was overhead became filled with clouds as though by magic. To the accompaniment of astonished ejaculations from all sides, a very light shower fell, cooling the city streets and the burning seashore. The soothing drops descended during the two hours of the parade. The exact instant at which our group returned to the ashram, the clouds and rain passed away tracelessly.

"You see how God feels for us," Master replied after I had expressed my gratitude. "The Lord responds to all and works for all. Just as He sent rain at my plea, so He fulfills any sincere desire of the devotee. Seldom do men realize how often God heeds their prayers. He is not partial to a few, but listens to everyone who approaches Him trustingly. His children should ever have implicit faith in the loving-kindness of their Omnipresent Father."

The festivities started in the morning with a barefoot procession along the streets. A SANKIRTAN (group chanting), accompanied by the harmonium and hand-played Indian drums, was in progress on the second floor. Sri Yukteswar listened appreciatively; his musical sense was acutely perfect.

"They are off key!" Master left the cooks and joined the artists. The melody was heard again, this time correctly rendered.

In India, music as well as painting and the drama is considered a divine art. Brahma, Vishnu, and Shiva – the Eternal

Trinity – were the first musicians. The Divine Dancer Shiva is scripturally represented as having worked out the infinite modes of rhythm in His cosmic dance of universal creation, preservation, and dissolution, while Brahma accentuated the time-beat with the clanging cymbals, and Vishnu sounded the holy MRIDANGA or drum. Krishna, an incarnation of Vishnu, is always shown in Hindu art with a flute, on which he plays the enrapturing song that recalls to their true home the human souls wandering in MAYA-delusion. Saraswati, goddess of wisdom, is symbolized as performing on the VINA, mother of all stringed instruments. The SAMA VEDA of India contains the world's earliest writings on musical science.

The foundation stone of Hindu music is the RAGAS or fixed melodic scales. The six basic RAGAS branch out into 126 derivative RAGINIS (wives) and PUTRAS (sons). Each RAGA has a minimum of five notes: a leading note (VADI or king), a secondary note (SAMAVADI or prime minister), helping notes (ANUVADI, attendants), and a dissonant note (VIVADI, the enemy).

Each one of the six basic RAGAS has a natural correspondence with a certain hour of the day, season of the year, and a presiding deity who bestows a particular potency. Thus, (1) the HINDOLE RAGA is heard only at dawn in the spring, to evoke the mood of universal love; (2) DEEPAKA RAGA is played during the evening in summer, to arouse compassion; (3) MEGHA RAGA is a melody for midday in the rainy season, to summon courage; (4) BHAIRAVA RAGA is played in the mornings of August, September, October, to achieve tranquillity; (5) SRI RAGA is reserved for autumn twilights, to attain pure love; (6) MALKOUNSA RAGA is heard at midnights in winter, for valor.

The ancient rishis discovered these laws of sound alliance between nature and man. Because nature is an objectification of AUM, the Primal Sound or Vibratory Word, man can obtain control over all natural manifestations through the use of certain MANTRAS or chants. Historical documents tell of the remarkable powers possessed by Miyan Tan Sen, sixteenth century court musician for Akbar the Great. Commanded by the Emperor to sing a night RAGA while the sun was overhead, Tan Sen intoned a MANTRA which instantly caused the whole palace precincts to become enveloped in darkness.

Indian music divides the octave into 22 SRUTIS or demi-semitones. These microtonal intervals permit fine shades of musical expression unattainable by the Western chromatic scale of 12 semitones. Each one of the seven basic notes of the octave is associated in Hindu mythology with a color, and the natural cry of a bird or beast-DO with green, and the peacock; RE with red, and the skylark; MI with golden, and the goat; FA with yellowish white, and the heron; SOL with black, and the nightingale; LA with yellow, and the horse; SI with a combination of all colors, and the elephant.

Three scales-major, harmonic minor, melodic minor-are the only ones which Occidental music employs, but Indian music outlines 72 THATAS or scales. Ancient Sanskrit literature describes 120 TALAS or time-measures. The traditional founder of Hindu music, Bharata, is said to have isolated 32 kinds of TALA in the song of a lark. The origin of TALA or rhythm is rooted in human movements – the double time of walking, and the triple time of respiration in sleep, when inhalation is twice the length of exhalation. India has always recognized the human voice as the most perfect instrument of sound.

The deeper aim of the early rishi-musicians was to blend the singer with the Cosmic Song which can be heard through awakening of man's occult spinal centers. Indian music is a subjective, spiritual, and individualistic art, aiming not at symphonic brilliance but at personal harmony with the Oversoul. The Sanskrit word for musician is BHAGAVATHAR, "he who sings the praises of God." The SANKIRTANS or musical gatherings are an effective form of yoga or spiritual discipline, necessitating deep concentration, intense absorption in the seed thought and sound. The SANKIRTAN on the day of the festival was inspiring to the cooks amidst the steaming pots. My brother disciples and I joyously sang the refrains, beating time with our hands.

By sunset we had served our hundreds of visitors with KHICHURI (rice and lentils), vegetable curry, and rice pudding. We laid cotton blankets over the courtyard; soon the assemblage was squatting under the starry vault, quietly attentive to the wisdom pouring from Sri Yukteswar's lips. His public speeches emphasized the value of KRIYA YOGA, and a life of self-respect, calmness, determination, simple diet, and regular exercise.

A group of very young disciples then chanted a few sacred hymns; the meeting concluded with SANKIRTAN. From ten o'clock until midnight, the ashram residents washed pots and pans, and cleared the courtyard. My guru called me to his side.

"I am pleased over your cheerful labors today and during the past week of preparations. I want you with me; you may sleep in my bed tonight."

This was a privilege I had never thought would fall to my lot. We sat awhile in a state of intense divine tranquillity.

16

Outwitting the Stars

"Mukunda, why don't you get an astrological armlet?"

"Should I, Master? I don't believe in astrology."

"It is never a question of BELIEF; the only scientific attitude one can take on any subject is whether it is TRUE. The law of gravitation worked as efficiently before Newton as after him. The cosmos would be fairly chaotic if its laws could not operate without the sanction of human belief.

"Charlatans have brought the stellar science to its present state of disrepute. Astrology is too vast, both mathematically and philosophically, to be rightly grasped except by men of profound understanding. If ignoramuses misread the heavens, and see there a scrawl instead of a script, that is to be expected in this imperfect world. One should not dismiss the wisdom with the 'wise.'

"All parts of creation are linked together and interchange their influences. The balanced rhythm of the universe is rooted in reciprocity," my guru continued. "Man, in his human aspect, has to combat two sets of forces – first, the tumults within his being, caused by the admixture of earth, water, fire, air, and ethereal elements; second, the outer disintegrating powers of nature. So long as man struggles with his mortality, he is affected by the myriad mutations of heaven and earth.

"Astrology is the study of man's response to planetary stimuli. The stars have no conscious benevolence or animosity; they merely send forth positive and negative radiations. Of themselves, these do not help or harm humanity, but offer a lawful channel for the outward operation of cause-effect equilibriums which each man has set into motion in the past.

"A child is born on that day and at that hour when the celestial rays are in mathematical harmony with his individual karma. His horoscope is a challenging portrait, revealing his unalterable past and its probable future results. But the natal chart can be rightly interpreted only by men of intuitive wisdom: these are few.

"The message boldly blazoned across the heavens at the moment of birth is not meant to emphasize fate – the result of past good and evil – but to arouse man's will to escape from his universal thralldom. What he has done, he can undo. None other than himself was the instigator of the causes of whatever effects are now prevalent in his life. He can overcome any limitation, because he created it by his own actions in the first place, and because he has spiritual resources which are not subject to planetary pressure.

"Superstitious awe of astrology makes one an automaton, slavishly dependent on mechanical guidance. The wise man defeats his planets – which is to say, his past – by transferring his allegiance from the creation to the Creator. The more he realizes his unity with Spirit, the less he can be dominated by matter. The soul is ever-free; it is deathless because birthless. It cannot be regimented by stars.

"Man IS a soul, and HAS a body. When he properly places his sense of identity, he leaves behind all compulsive patterns. So long as he remains confused in his ordinary state of spiritual amnesia, he will know the subtle fetters of environmental law.

"God is harmony; the devotee who attunes himself will never perform any action amiss. His activities will be correctly and naturally timed to accord with astrological law. After deep prayer and meditation he is in touch with his divine consciousness; there is no greater power than that inward protection."

"Then, dear Master, why do you want me to wear an astrological bangle?" I ventured this question after a long silence, during which I had tried to assimilate Sri Yukteswar's noble exposition.

"It is only when a traveler has reached his goal that he is justified in discarding his maps. During the journey, he takes advantage of any convenient short-cut. The ancient rishis discovered many ways to curtail the period of man's exile in delusion. There are certain mechanical features in the law of karma which can be skillfully adjusted by the fingers of wisdom.

"All human ills arise from some transgression of universal law. The scriptures point out that man must satisfy the laws of nature, while not discrediting the divine omnipotence. He should say: 'Lord, I trust in Thee, and know Thou canst help me, but I too will do my best to undo any wrong I have done.' By a number of means – by prayer, by will power, by yoga meditation, by consultation with saints, by use of astrological bangles – the adverse effects of past wrongs can be minimized or nullified.

"Just as a house can be fitted with a copper rod to absorb the shock of lightning, so the bodily temple can be benefited by various protective measures. Ages ago our yogis discovered that pure metals emit an astral light which is powerfully counteractive to negative pulls of the planets. Subtle electrical and magnetic radiations are constantly circulating in the universe; when a man's body is being aided, he does not know it; when it is being disintegrated, he is still in ignorance. Can he do anything about it?

"This problem received attention from our rishis; they found helpful not only a combination of metals, but also of plants and-most effective of all-faultless jewels of not less than two carats. The preventive uses of astrology have seldom been seriously studied outside of India. One little-known fact is that the proper jewels, metals, or plant preparations are valueless unless the required weight is secured, and unless these remedial agents are worn next to the skin."

"Sir, of course I shall take your advice and get a bangle. I am intrigued at the thought of outwitting a planet!"

"For general purposes I counsel the use of an armlet made of gold, silver, and copper. But for a specific purpose I want you to get one of silver and lead." Sri Yukteswar added careful directions.

"Guruji, what 'specific purpose' do you mean?"

"The stars are about to take an unfriendly interest in you, Mukunda. Fear not; you shall be protected. In about a month your liver will cause you much trouble. The illness is scheduled to last for six months, but your use of an astrological armlet will shorten the period to twenty-four days."

I sought out a jeweler the next day, and was soon wearing the bangle. My health was excellent; Master's prediction slipped from my mind. He left Serampore to visit Benares. Thirty days after our conversation, I felt a sudden pain in the region of my liver. The following weeks were a nightmare of excruciating pain. Reluctant to disturb my guru, I thought I would bravely endure my trial alone.

But twenty-three days of torture weakened my resolution; I entrained for Benares. There Sri Yukteswar greeted me with unusual warmth, but gave me no opportunity to tell him my woes in private. Many devotees visited Master that day, just for a DARSHAN. Ill and neglected, I sat in a corner. It was not until after the evening meal that all guests had departed. My guru summoned me to the octagonal balcony of the house.

"You must have come about your liver disorder." Sri Yukteswar's gaze was averted; he walked to and fro, occasionally intercepting the moonlight. "Let me see; you have been ailing for twenty-four days, haven't you?"

"Yes, sir."

"Please do the stomach exercise I have taught you."

"If you knew the extent of my suffering, Master, you would not ask me to exercise." Nevertheless I made a feeble attempt to obey him.

"You say you have pain; I say you have none. How can such contradictions exist?" My guru looked at me inquiringly.

I was dazed and then overcome with joyful relief. No longer could I feel the continuous torment that had kept me nearly sleepless for weeks; at Sri Yukteswar's words the agony vanished as though it had never been.

I started to kneel at his feet in gratitude, but he quickly prevented me.

"Don't be childish. Get up and enjoy the beauty of the moon over the Ganges." But Master's eyes were twinkling happily as I stood in silence beside him. I understood by his attitude that he wanted me to feel that not he, but God, had been the Healer.

Sri Yukteswar discovered the mathematical application of a 24,000-year equinoctial cycle to our present age. The cycle is divided into an Ascending Arc and a Descending Arc, each of 12,000 years. Within each Arc fall four YUGAS or Ages, called KALI, DWAPARA, TRETA, and SATYA, corresponding to the Greek ideas of Iron, Bronze, Silver, and Golden Ages.

My guru determined by various calculations that the last KALI YUGA or Iron Age, of the Ascending Arc, started about A.D. 500. The Iron Age, 1200 years in duration, is a span of materialism; it ended about A.D. 1700. That year ushered in DWAPARA YUGA, a 2400-year period of electrical and atomic-energy developments, the age of telegraph, radio, airplanes, and other space-annihilators.

The 3600-year period of TRETA YUGA will start in A.D. 4100; its age will be marked by common knowledge of telepathic communications and other time-annihilators. During the 4800 years of SATYA YUGA, final age in an ascending arc, the intelligence of a man will be completely developed; he will work in harmony with the divine plan.

A descending arc of 12,000 years, starting with a descending Golden Age of 4800 years, then begins for the world; man gradually sinks into ignorance. These cycles are the eternal rounds of MAYA, the contrasts and relativities of the phenomenal universe. Man, one by one, escapes from creation's prison of duality as he awakens to consciousness of his inseverable divine unity with the Creator.

Master enlarged my understanding not only of astrology but of the world's scriptures. Master expounded the Christian Bible with a beautiful clarity. It was from my Hindu guru, unknown to the roll call of Christian membership, that I learned to perceive the deathless essence of the Bible, and to understand the truth in Christ's assertion-surely the most thrillingly intransigent ever uttered: "Heaven and earth shall pass away, but my words shall not pass away."

"The Adam and Eve story is incomprehensible to me!" I observed with considerable heat one day in my early struggles with the allegory. "Why did God punish not only the guilty pair, but also the innocent unborn generations?"

Master was more amused by my vehemence than my ignorance. "GENESIS is deeply symbolic, and cannot be grasped by a literal interpretation," he explained. "Its 'tree of life' is the human body. The spinal cord is like an upturned tree, with man's hair as its roots, and afferent and efferent nerves as branches. The tree of the nervous system bears many enjoyable fruits, or sensations of sight, sound, smell, taste, and touch. In these, man may rightfully indulge; but he was forbidden the experience of sex, the 'apple' at the center of the bodily garden.

"The 'serpent' represents the coiled-up spinal energy which stimulates the sex nerves. 'Adam' is reason, and 'Eve' is feeling. When the emotion or Eve-consciousness in any human being is overpowered by the sex impulse, his reason or Adam also succumbs."

As Sri Yukteswar ended his discourse, I glanced with new respect at the pages of GENESIS.

"Dear Master," I said, "for the first time I feel a proper filial obligation toward Adam and Eve!"

17

Sasi and the Three Sapphires

"Because you and my son think so highly of Swami Sri Yukteswar, I will take a look at him." The tone of voice used by Dr. Narayan Chunder Roy implied that he was humoring the whim of half-wits. I concealed my indignation, in the best traditions of the proselyter.

My companion, a veterinary surgeon, was a confirmed agnostic. His young son Santosh had implored me to take an interest in his father. So far my invaluable aid had been a bit on the invisible side.

Dr. Roy accompanied me the following day to the Serampore hermitage. After Master had granted him a brief interview, marked for the most part by stoic silence on both sides, the visitor brusquely departed.

"Why bring a dead man to the ashram?" Sri Yukteswar looked at me inquiringly as soon as the door had closed on the Calcutta skeptic.

"Sir! The doctor is very much alive!"

"But in a short time he will be dead."

I was shocked. "Sir, this will be a terrible blow to his son. Santosh yet hopes for time to change his father's materialistic views. I beseech you, Master, to help the man."

"Very well; for your sake." My guru's face was impassive. "The proud horse doctor is far gone in diabetes, although he does not know it. In fifteen days he will take to his bed. The physicians will give him up for lost; his natural time to leave this earth is six weeks from today. Due to your intercession, however, on that date he will recover. But there is one condition. You must get him to wear an astrological bangle; he will doubtless object as violently as one of his horses before an operation!" Master chuckled.

After a silence, during which I wondered how Santosh and I could best employ the arts of cajolery on the recalcitrant doctor, Sri Yukteswar made further disclosures.

"As soon as the man gets well, advise him not to eat meat. He will not heed this counsel, however, and in six months, just as he is feeling at his best, he will drop dead. Even that six-month extension of life is granted him only because of your plea."

The following day I suggested to Santosh that he order an armlet at the jeweler's. It was ready in a week, but Dr. Roy refused to put it on.

"I am in the best of health. You will never impress me with these astrological superstitions." The doctor glanced at me belligerently.

I recalled with amusement that Master had justifiably compared the man to a balky horse. Another seven days passed; the doctor, suddenly ill, meekly consented to wear the bangle. Two weeks later the physician in attendance told me that his patient's case was hopeless. He supplied harrowing details of the ravages inflicted by diabetes.

I shook my head. "My guru has said that, after a sickness lasting one month, Dr. Roy will be well."

The physician stared at me incredulously. But he sought me out a fortnight later, with an apologetic air.

"Dr. Roy has made a complete recovery!" he exclaimed. "It is the most amazing case in my experience. Never before have I seen a dying man show such an inexplicable comeback. Your guru must indeed be a healing prophet!"

After one interview with Dr. Roy, during which I repeated Sri Yukteswar's advice about a meatless diet, I did not see the man again for six months. He stopped for a chat one evening as I sat on the piazza of my family home on Gurpar Road.

"Tell your teacher that by eating meat frequently, I have wholly regained my strength. His unscientific ideas on diet have not influenced me." It was true that Dr. Roy looked a picture of health.

But the next day Santosh came running to me from his home on the next block. "This morning Father dropped dead!"

This case was one of my strangest experiences with Master. Sri Yukteswar was boundless in his kindness when confronted by the urgent prayer of a devotee.

It was my proudest privilege to bring college friends to meet my guru. Many of them would lay aside – at least in the ashram! – their fashionable academic cloak of religious skepticism.

One of my friends, Sasi, spent a number of happy week ends in Serampore. Master became immensely fond of the boy, and lamented that his private life was wild and disorderly.

"Sasi, unless you reform, one year hence you will be dangerously ill." Sri Yukteswar gazed at my friend with affectionate exasperation. "Mukunda is the witness: don't say later that I didn't warn you."

Sasi laughed. "Master, I will leave it to you to interest

a sweet charity of cosmos in my own sad case! My spirit is willing but my will is weak. You are my only savior on earth; I believe in nothing else."

"At least you should wear a two-carat blue sapphire. It will help you."

"I can't afford one. Anyhow, dear guruji, if trouble comes, I fully believe you will protect me."

"In a year you will bring three sapphires," Sri Yukteswar replied cryptically. "They will be of no use then."

Variations on this conversation took place regularly. "I can't reform!" Sasi would say in comical despair. "And my trust in you, Master, is more precious to me than any stone!"

A year later I was visiting my guru at the Calcutta home of his disciple, Naren Babu. About ten o'clock in the morning, as Sri Yukteswar and I were sitting quietly in the second-floor parlor, I heard the front door open. Master straightened stiffly.

"It is that Sasi," he remarked gravely. "The year is now up; both his lungs are gone. He has ignored my counsel; tell him I don't want to see him."

Half stunned by Sri Yukteswar's sternness, I raced down the stairway. Sasi was ascending.

"O Mukunda! I do hope Master is here; I had a hunch he might be."

"Yes, but he doesn't wish to be disturbed."

Sasi burst into tears and brushed past me. He threw himself at Sri Yukteswar's feet, placing there three beautiful sapphires.

"Omniscient guru, the doctors say I have galloping tuberculosis! They give me no longer than three more months! I humbly implore your aid; I know you can heal me!"

"Isn't it a bit late now to be worrying over your life? Depart with your jewels; their time of usefulness is past." Master then sat sphinxlike in an unrelenting silence, punctuated by the boy's sobs for mercy.

An intuitive conviction came to me that Sri Yukteswar was merely testing the depth of Sasi's faith in the divine healing power. I was not surprised a tense hour later when Master turned a sympathetic gaze on my prostrate friend.

"Get up, Sasi; what a commotion you make in other people's houses! Return your sapphires to the jeweler's; they are an unnecessary expense now. But get an astrological bangle and wear it. Fear not; in a few weeks you shall be well."

Sasi's smile illumined his tear-marred face like sudden sun over a sodden landscape. "Beloved guru, shall I take the medicines prescribed by the doctors?"

Sri Yukteswar's glance was longanimous. "Just as you wish – drink them or discard them; it does not matter. It is more possible for the sun and moon to interchange their positions than for you to die of tuberculosis." He added abruptly, "Go now, before I change my mind!"

With an agitated bow, my friend hastily departed. I visited him several times during the next few weeks, and was aghast to find his condition increasingly worse.

"Sasi cannot last through the night." These words from his physician, and the spectacle of my friend, now reduced almost to a skeleton, sent me posthaste to Serampore. My guru listened coldly to my tearful report.

"Why do you come here to bother me? You have already heard me assure Sasi of his recovery."

I bowed before him in great awe, and retreated to the door. Sri Yukteswar said no parting word, but sank into silence, his unwinking eyes half-open, their vision fled to another world.

I returned at once to Sasi's home in Calcutta. With astonishment I found my friend sitting up, drinking milk.

"O Mukunda! What a miracle! Four hours ago I felt Master's presence in the room; my terrible symptoms immediately disappeared. I feel that through his grace I am entirely well."

In a few weeks Sasi was stouter and in better health than ever before. But his singular reaction to his healing had an ungrateful tinge: he seldom visited Sri Yukteswar again! My friend told me one day that he so deeply regretted his previous mode of life that he was ashamed to face Master.

I could only conclude that Sasi's illness had had the contrasting effect of stiffening his will and impairing his manners.

The first two years of my course at Scottish Church College were drawing to a close. On his return from Puri, Sri Yukteswar gave me a pleasant surprise. "Your Calcutta studies are now over. I will see that you pursue your last two years of university work right here in Serampore."

I was puzzled. "Sir, there is no Bachelor of Arts course in this town." Serampore College, the sole institution of higher learning, offered only a two-year course in Intermediate Arts.

Master smiled mischievously. "I am too old to go about collecting donations to establish an A.B. college for you. I guess I shall have to arrange the matter through someone else."

Two months later Professor Howells, president of Serampore College, publicly announced that he had succeeded in raising sufficient funds to offer a four-year course. Serampore College became a branch affiliation of the University of Calcutta. I was one of the first students to enroll in Serampore as an A.B. candidate.

18

A Mohammedan Wonder-Worker

"Years ago, right in this very room you now occupy, a Mohammedan wonder-worker performed four miracles before me!"

Sri Yukteswar made this surprising statement during his first visit to my new quarters. Immediately after entering Serampore College, I had taken a room in a nearby boardinghouse, called PANTHI.

"Master, what a coincidence! Are these newly decorated walls really ancient with memories?"

"It is a long story." My guru smiled reminiscently. "The name of the FAKIR was Afzal Khan. He had acquired his extraordinary powers through a chance encounter with a Hindu yogi.

"'Son, I am thirsty; fetch me some water.' A dust-covered SANNYASI made this request of Afzal one day during his early boyhood in a small village of eastern Bengal.

"'Master, I am a Mohammedan. How could you, a Hindu, accept a drink from my hands?'

"'Your truthfulness pleases me, my child. I do not observe the ostracizing rules of ungodly sectarianism. Go; bring me water quickly.'

"Afzal's reverent obedience was rewarded by a loving glance from the yogi.

"'You possess good karma from former lives,' he observed solemnly. 'I am going to teach you a certain yoga method which will give you command over one of the invisible realms. The great powers that will be yours should be exercised for worthy ends; never employ them selfishly! I perceive, alas! that you have brought over from the past some seeds of destructive tendencies. Do not allow them to sprout by watering them with fresh evil actions. The complexity of your previous karma is such that you must use this life to reconcile your yogic accomplishments with the highest humanitarian goals.'

"After instructing the amazed boy in a complicated technique, the master vanished.

"Afzal faithfully followed his yoga exercise for twenty years. His miraculous feats began to attract widespread attention. It seems that he was always accompanied by a disembodied spirit whom he called 'Hazrat.' This invisible entity was able to fulfill the FAKIR's slightest wish.

"Ignoring his master's warning, Afzal began to misuse his powers. Whatever object he touched and then replaced would soon disappear without a trace. This disconcerting eventuality usually made the Mohammedan an objectionable guest!

"He visited large jewelry stores in Calcutta from time to time, representing himself as a possible purchaser. Any jewel he handled would vanish shortly after he had left the shop.

"Afzal was often surrounded by several hundred students, attracted by the hope of learning his secrets. The FAKIR occasionally invited them to travel with him. At the railway station he would manage to touch a roll of tickets. These he would return to the clerk, remarking: 'I have changed my mind, and won't buy them now.' But when he boarded the train with his retinue, Afzal would be in possession of the required tickets.

"These exploits created an indignant uproar; Bengali jewelers and ticket-sellers were succumbing to nervous breakdowns! The police who sought to arrest Afzal found themselves helpless; the FAKIR could remove incriminating evidence merely by saying: 'Hazrat, take this away.'"

Sri Yukteswar rose from his seat and walked to the balcony of my room which overlooked the Ganges. I followed him, eager to hear more of the baffling Mohammedan Raffles.

"This PANTHI house formerly belonged to a friend of mine. He became acquainted with Afzal and asked him here. My friend also invited about twenty neighbors, including myself. I was only a youth then, and felt a lively curiosity about the notorious FAKIR." Master laughed. "I took the precaution of not wearing anything valuable! Afzal looked me over inquisitively, then remarked:

"'You have powerful hands. Go downstairs to the garden; get a smooth stone and write your name on it with chalk; then throw the stone as far as possible into the Ganges.'

"I obeyed. As soon as the stone had vanished under distant waves, the Mohammedan addressed me again:

"'Fill a pot with Ganges water near the front of this house.'

"After I had returned with a vessel of water, the FAKIR cried, 'Hazrat, put the stone in the pot!'

"The stone appeared at once. I pulled it from the vessel and found my signature as legible as when I had written it.

"Babu, one of my friends in the room, was wearing a heavy antique gold watch and chain. The FAKIR examined them with ominous admiration. Soon they were missing!

"'Afzal, please return my prized heirloom!' Babu was nearly in tears.

"The Mohammedan was stoically silent for awhile, then

said, 'You have five hundred rupees in an iron safe. Bring them to me, and I will tell you where to locate your timepiece.'

"The distraught Babu left immediately for his home. He came back shortly and handed Afzal the required sum.

"'Go to the little bridge near your house,' the FAKIR instructed Babu. 'Call on Hazrat to give you the watch and chain.'

"Babu rushed away. On his return, he was wearing a smile of relief and no jewelry whatever.

"'When I commanded Hazrat as directed,' he announced, 'my watch came tumbling down from the air into my right hand! You may be sure I locked the heirloom in my safe before rejoining the group here!'

"Babu's friends, witnesses of the comicotragedy of the ransom for a watch, were staring with resentment at Afzal. He now spoke placatingly.

"'Please name any drink you want; Hazrat will produce it.'

"A number asked for milk, others for fruit juices. I was not too much shocked when the unnerved Babu requested whisky! The Mohammedan gave an order; the obliging Hazrat sent sealed containers sailing down the air and thudding to the floor. Each man found his desired beverage.

"The promise of the fourth spectacular feat of the day was doubtless gratifying to our host: Afzal offered to supply an instantaneous lunch!

"'Let us order the most expensive dishes,' Babu suggested gloomily. 'I want an elaborate meal for my five hundred rupees! Everything should be served on gold plates!'

"As soon as each man had expressed his preferences, the FAKIR addressed himself to the inexhaustible Hazrat. A great rattle ensued; gold platters filled with intricately-prepared curries, hot LUCHIS, and many out-of-season fruits, landed from nowhere at our feet. All the food was delicious. After feasting for an hour, we started to leave the room. A tremendous noise, as though dishes were being piled up, caused us to turn around. Lo! there was no sign of the glittering plates or the remnants of the meal."

"Guruji," I interrupted, "if Afzal could easily secure such things as gold dishes, why did he covet the property of others?"

"The FAKIR was not highly developed spiritually," Sri Yukteswar explained. "His mastery of a certain yoga technique gave him access to an astral plane where any desire is immediately materialized. Through the agency of an astral being, Hazrat, the Mohammedan could summon the atoms of any object from etheric energy by an act of powerful will. But such astrally-produced objects are structurally evanescent; they cannot be long retained. Afzal still yearned for worldly wealth which, though more hardly earned, has a more dependable durability."

I laughed. "It too sometimes vanishes most unaccountably!"

"Afzal was not a man of God-realization," Master went on. "Miracles of a permanent and beneficial nature are performed by true saints because they have attuned themselves to the omnipotent Creator. Afzal was merely an ordinary man with an extraordinary power of penetrating a subtle realm not usually entered by mortals until death."

"I understand now, Guruji. The after-world appears to have some charming features."

Master agreed. "I never saw Afzal after that day, but a few years later Babu came to my home to show me a newspaper account of the Mohammedan's public confession. From it I learned the facts I have just told you about Afzal's early initiation from a Hindu guru."

The gist of the latter part of the published document, as recalled by Sri Yukteswar, was as follows: "I, Afzal Khan, am writing these words as an act of penance and as a warning to those who seek the possession of miraculous powers. For years I have been misusing the wondrous abilities imparted to me through the grace of God and my master. I became drunk with egotism, feeling that I was beyond the ordinary laws of morality. My day of reckoning finally arrived.

"Recently I met an old man on a road outside Calcutta. He limped along painfully, carrying a shining object which looked like gold. I addressed him with greed in my heart.

"'I am Afzal Khan, the great FAKIR. What have you there?'

"'This ball of gold is my sole material wealth; it can be of no interest to a FAKIR. I implore you, sir, to heal my limp.'

"I touched the ball and walked away without reply. The old man hobbled after me. He soon raised an outcry: 'My gold is gone!'

"As I paid no attention, he suddenly spoke in a stentorian voice that issued oddly from his frail body:

"'Do you not recognize me?'

"I stood speechless, aghast at the belated discovery that this unimpressive old cripple was none other than the great saint who, long, long ago, had initiated me into yoga. He straightened himself; his body instantly became strong and youthful.

"'So!' My guru's glance was fiery. 'I see with my own eyes that you use your powers, not to help suffering humanity, but to prey on it like a common thief! I withdraw your occult gifts; Hazrat is now freed from you. No longer shall you be a terror in Bengal!'

"I called on Hazrat in anguished tones; for the first time, he did not appear to my inner sight. But some dark veil suddenly lifted within me; I saw clearly the blasphemy of my life.

"'My guru, I thank you for coming to banish my long delusion.' I was sobbing at his feet. 'I promise to forsake my worldly ambitions. I will retire to the mountains for lonely meditation on God, hoping to atone for my evil past.'

"My master regarded me with silent compassion. 'I feel your sincerity,' he said finally. 'Because of your earlier years of strict obedience, and because of your present repentance, I will rant you one boon. Your other powers are now gone, but whenever food and clothing are needed, you may still call successfully on Hazrat to supply them. Devote yourself wholeheartedly to divine understanding in the mountain solitudes.'

"My guru then vanished; I was left to my tears and reflections. I go to seek the forgiveness of the Cosmic Beloved."

19

My Master, in Calcutta, Appears in Serampore

"I am often beset by atheistic doubts. Yet a torturing surmise sometimes haunts me: may not untapped soul possibilities exist? Is am not missing his real destiny if he fails to explore them?"

These remarks of Dijen Babu, my roommate at the PANTHI boardinghouse, were called forth by my invitation that he meet my guru.

"Sri Yukteswarji will initiate you into KRIYA YOGA," I replied. It calms the dualistic turmoil by a divine inner certainty."

That evening Dijen accompanied me to the hermitage. In Master's presence my friend received such spiritual peace that he was soon constant visitor. The trivial preoccupations of daily life are not enough for man; wisdom too is a native hunger. In Sri Yukteswar's words Dijen found an incentive to those attempts – first painful, then effortlessly liberating – to locate a real self within his bosom than the humiliating ego of a temporary birth, seldom ample enough for the Spirit.

As Dijen and I were both pursuing the A.B. course at Serampore College, we got into the habit of walking together to the ashram as soon as classes were over. We would often see Sri Yukteswar standing on his second-floor balcony, welcoming our approach with smile.

One afternoon Kanai, a young hermitage resident, met Dijen at the door with disappointing news.

"Master is not here; he was summoned to Calcutta by an urgent note."

The following day I received a post card from my guru. "I shall leave Calcutta Wednesday morning," he had written. "You and Dijen meet the nine o'clock train at Serampore station."

About eight-thirty on Wednesday morning, a telepathic message from Sri Yukteswar flashed insistently to my mind: "I am delayed; don't meet the nine o'clock train."

I conveyed the latest instructions to Dijen, who was already dressed for departure.

"You and your intuition!" My friend's voice was edged in scorn. "I refer to trust Master's written word."

I shrugged my shoulders and seated myself with quiet finality. Uttering angrily, Dijen made for the door and closed it noisily behind him.

As the room was rather dark, I moved nearer to the window overlooking the street. The scant sunlight suddenly increased to an intense brilliancy in which the iron-barred window completely vanished. Against this dazzling background appeared the clearly materialized figure of Sri Yukteswar!

Bewildered to the point of shock, I rose from my chair and knelt before him. With my customary gesture of respectful greeting at my guru's feet, I touched his shoes. His ocher swami cloth rushed against me; I distinctly felt not only the texture of his robe, but also the gritty surface of the shoes, and the pressure of his toes within them. Too much astounded to utter a word, I stood up and gazed at him questioningly.

"I was pleased that you got my telepathic message." Master's voice as calm, entirely normal. "I have now finished my business in Calcutta, and shall arrive in Serampore by the ten o'clock train."

As I still stared mutely, Sri Yukteswar went on, "This is not an apparition, but my flesh and blood form. I have been divinely commanded to give you this experience, rare to achieve on earth. Meet me at the station; you and Dijen will see me coming toward you, dressed as I am now. I shall be preceded by a fellow passenger – a little boy carrying a silver jug."

My guru placed both hands on my head, with a murmured blessing. His body began to melt gradually within the piercing light. First his feet and legs vanished, then his torso and head, like a scroll being rolled up.

I remained in a half-stupor of confusion, questioning whether I had not been the victim of a hallucination. A crestfallen Dijen soon entered the room.

"Master was not on the nine o'clock train, nor even the nine-thirty." My friend made his announcement with a slightly apologetic air.

"Come then; I know he will arrive at ten o'clock." I took Dijen's hand and rushed him forcibly along with me, heedless of his protests. In about ten minutes we entered the station, where the train was already puffing to a halt.

"Let us wait here." I told my friend details of the way in which our guru would approach us. As I finished my description, Sri Yukteswar came into view, wearing the same clothes I had seen a short time earlier. He walked slowly in the wake of a small lad bearing a silver jug.

Soon Sri Yukteswar, a modern Yogi-Christ, reached the spot where Dijen and I were speechlessly rooted. Master smiled at us and immediately we rushed to the hermitage.

20

We Do Not Visit Kashmir

"Father, I want to invite Master and four friends to accompany me to the Himalayan foothills during my summer vacation. May I have six train passes to Kashmir and enough money to cover our travel expenses?"

As I had expected, Father laughed heartily. "This is the third time you have given me the same cock-and-bull story. Didn't you make a similar request last summer, and the year before that? At the last moment, Sri Yukteswarji refuses to go."

"It is true, Father; I don't know why my guru will not give me his definite word about Kashmir. But if I tell him that I have already secured the passes from you, somehow I think that this time he will consent to make the journey."

Father was unconvinced at the moment, but the following day, after some good-humored gibes, he handed me six passes and a roll of ten-rupee bills.

"I hardly think your theoretical trip needs such practical props," he remarked, "but here they are."

That afternoon I exhibited my booty to Sri Yukteswar. Though he smiled at my enthusiasm, his words were noncommittal: "I would like to go; we shall see." He made no comment when I asked his little hermitage disciple, Kanai, to accompany us. I also invited three other friends--Rajendra Nath Mitra, Jotin Auddy, and one other boy. Our date of departure was set for the following Monday.

I arrived in Serampore with my luggage early Monday morning. Rajendra met me at the hermitage door.

"Master is out, walking. He has refused to go."

I was equally grieved and obdurate. "I will not give Father a third chance to ridicule my chimerical plans for Kashmir. Come; the rest of us will go anyhow."

Rajendra agreed; I left the ashram to find a servant. As I walked along briskly, I met my guru in front of the Christian church near Serampore Courthouse.

"Where are you going?" Sri Yukteswar's face was unsmiling.

"Sir, I hear that you and Kanai will not take the trip we have been planning. I am seeking Behari. You will recall that last year he was so anxious to see Kashmir that he even offered to serve without pay."

"I remember. Nevertheless, I don't think Behari will be willing to go."

I was exasperated. "He is just eagerly waiting for this opportunity!"

My guru silently resumed his walk; I soon reached the schoolmaster's house. Behari, in the courtyard, greeted me with a friendly warmth that abruptly vanished as soon as I mentioned Kashmir. With a murmured word of apology, the servant left me and entered his employer's house. I waited half an hour, nervously assuring myself that Behari's delay was being caused by preparations for his trip. Finally I knocked at the front door.

"Behari left by the back stairs about thirty minutes ago," a man informed me. A slight smile hovered about his lips.

I departed sadly, wondering whether my invitation had been too coercive or whether Master's unseen influences were at work. Passing the Christian church, again I saw my guru walking slowly toward me. Without waiting to hear my report, he exclaimed:

"So Behari would not go! Now, what are your plans?"

I felt like a recalcitrant child who is determined to defy his masterful father. "Sir, I am going to ask my uncle to lend me his servant, Lal Dhari."

"See your uncle if you want to," Sri Yukteswar replied with a chuckle. "But I hardly think you will enjoy the visit."

Apprehensive but rebellious, I left my guru and entered Serampore Courthouse. My paternal uncle, Sarada Ghosh, a government attorney, welcomed me affectionately.

"I am leaving today with some friends for Kashmir," I told him. "For years I have been looking forward to this Himalayan trip."

"I am happy for you, Mukunda. Is there anything I can do to make your journey more comfortable?"

These kind words gave me a lift of encouragement. "Dear uncle," I said, "could you possibly spare me your servant, Lal Dhari?"

My simple request had the effect of an earthquake. Uncle jumped so violently that his chair overturned, the papers on the desk flew in every direction, and his pipe, a long, coconut-stemmed hubble-bubble, fell to the floor with a great clatter.

"You selfish young man," he shouted, quivering with wrath, "what a preposterous idea! Who will look after me, if you take my servant on one of your pleasure jaunts?"

I concealed my surprise, reflecting that my amiable uncle's sudden change of front was only one more enigma in a day fully devoted to incomprehensibility. My retreat from the courthouse office was more alacritous than dignified.

I returned to the hermitage, where my friends were expectantly gathered. Conviction was growing on me that some sufficient if exceedingly recondite motive was behind Master's attitude. Remorse seized me that I had been trying to thwart my guru's will.

"Mukunda, wouldn't you like to stay awhile longer with me?" Sri Yukteswar inquired. "Rajendra and the others can go ahead now, and wait for you at Calcutta. There will be plenty of time to catch the last evening train leaving Calcutta for Kashmir."

"Sir, I don't care to go without you," I said mournfully.

My friends paid not the slightest attention to my remark. They summoned a hackney carriage and departed with all the luggage. Kanai and I sat quietly at our guru's feet. After a half hour of complete silence, Master rose and walked toward the second-floor dining patio.

"Kanai, please serve Mukunda's food. His train leaves soon."

Getting up from my blanket seat, I staggered suddenly with nausea and a ghastly churning sensation in my stomach. The stabbing pain was so intense that I felt I had been abruptly hurled into some violent hell. Groping blindly toward my guru, I collapsed before him, attacked by all symptoms of the dread Asiatic cholera. Sri Yukteswar and Kanai carried me to the sitting room.

Racked with agony, I cried, "Master, I surrender my life to you;" for I believed it was indeed fast ebbing from the shores of my body.

Sri Yukteswar put my head on his lap, stroking my forehead with angelic tenderness.

"You see now what would have happened if you were at the station with your friends," he said. "I had to look after you in this strange way, because you chose to doubt my judgment about taking the trip at this particular time."

I understood at last. Inasmuch as great masters seldom see fit to display their powers openly, a casual observer of the day's events would have imagined that their sequence was quite natural. My guru's intervention had been too subtle to be suspected. He had worked his will through Behari and my Uncle Sarada and Rajendra and the others in such an inconspicuous manner that probably everyone but myself thought the situations had been logically normal.

As Sri Yukteswar never failed to observe his social obligations, he instructed Kanai to go for a specialist, and to notify my uncle.

"Master," I protested, "only you can heal me. I am too far gone for any doctor."

"Child, you are protected by the Divine Mercy. Don't worry about the doctor; he will not find you in this state. You are already healed."

With my guru's words, the excruciating suffering left me. I sat up feebly. A doctor soon arrived and examined me carefully.

"You appear to have passed through the worst," he said. "I will take some specimens with me for laboratory tests."

The following morning the physician arrived hurriedly. I was sitting up, in good spirits.

"Well, well, here you are, smiling and chatting as though you had had no close call with death." He patted my hand gently. "I hardly expected to find you alive, after I had discovered from the specimens that your disease was Asiatic cholera. You are fortunate, young man, to have a guru with divine healing powers! I am convinced of it!"

I agreed wholeheartedly.

Master entered the room. I permitted myself a convalescent's liberty, and captured his hand lovingly.

"Guruji," I said, "from my twelfth year on, I have made many unsuccessful attempts to reach the Himalayas. I am finally convinced that without your blessings the Goddess Parvati will not receive me!"

21

We Visit Kashmir

"You are strong enough now to travel. I will accompany you to Kashmir," Sri Yukteswar informed me two days after my miraculous recovery from Asiatic cholera.

That evening our party of six entrained for the north. Our first leisurely stop was at Simla, a queenly city resting on the throne of Himalayan hills. We strolled over the steep streets, admiring the magnificent views.

"English strawberries for sale," cried an old woman, squatting in a picturesque open market place.

Master was curious about the strange little red fruits. He bought a basketful and offered it to Kanai and myself, who were near-by. I tasted one berry but spat it hastily on the ground.

"Sir, what a sour fruit! I could never like strawberries!"

My guru laughed. "Oh, you will like them-in America. At a dinner there, your hostess will serve them with sugar and cream. After she has mashed the berries with a fork, you will taste them and say: 'What delicious strawberries!' Then you will remember this day in Simla."

Sri Yukteswar's forecast vanished from my mind, but reappeared there many years later, shortly after my arrival in America. I was a dinner guest at the home of Mrs. Alice T.

Hasey (Sister Yogmata) in West Somerville, Massachusetts. When a dessert of strawberries was put on the table, my hostess picked up her fork and mashed my berries, adding cream and sugar. "The fruit is rather tart; I think you will like it fixed this way," she remarked.

I took a mouthful. "What delicious strawberries!" I exclaimed. At once my guru's prediction in Simla emerged from the fathomless cave of memory.

Our party soon left Simla and entrained for Rawalpindi and then to a seven-day trip to Srinagar, capital city of Kashmir.

We continued on the labyrinthine way, adorned by views of rivers, valleys, precipitous crags, and multitudinous mountain tiers. Joyous anticipations filled our hearts as we neared central Kashmir, paradise land of lotus lakes, floating gardens, gaily canopied houseboats, the many-bridged Jhelum River, and flower-strewn pastures, all ringed round by the Himalayan majesty. Our approach to Srinagar was through an avenue of tall, welcoming trees. We engaged rooms at a double-storied inn overlooking the noble hills.

We made a pilgrimage to the ancient Srinagar temple of Swami Shankara. As I gazed upon the mountain-peak hermitage, standing bold against the sky, I fell into an ecstatic trance. A vision appeared of a hilltop mansion in a distant land. The lofty Shankara ashram before me was transformed into the structure where, years later, I established the Self-Realization Fellowship headquarters in America. When I first visited Los Angeles, and saw the large building on the crest of Mount Washington, I recognized it at once from my long-past visions in Kashmir and elsewhere.

A few days at Srinagar; then on to Gulmarg ("mountain paths of flowers"), elevated by six thousand feet. Our next excursions were to the famous royal "pleasure gardens" of the Emperor Jehangir, at Shalimar and Nishat Bagh. The ancient palace at Nishat Bagh is built directly over a natural waterfall. Rushing down from the mountains, the torrent has been regulated through ingenious contrivances to flow over colorful terraces and to gush into fountains amidst the dazzling flower-beds.

We took several trips in the SHIKARAS or houseboats, shaded by red-embroidered canopies, coursing along the intricate channels of Dal Lake, a network of canals like a watery spider web.

In this storied vale one finds an epitome of all the earth's beauties. The Lady of Kashmir is mountain-crowned, lake-garlanded, and flower-shod. In later years, after I had toured many distant lands, I understood why Kashmir is often called the world's most scenic spot. It possesses some of the charms of the Swiss Alps, and of Loch Lomond in Scotland, and of the exquisite English lakes. An American traveler in Kashmir finds much to remind him of the rugged grandeur of Alaska and of Pikes Peak near Denver.

Most of the Hindus of Kashmir, world-famed for their beauty, are as white as Europeans and have similar features and bone structure; many have blue eyes and blonde hair. Dressed in Western clothes, they look like Americans. The cold Himalayas protect the Kashmiris from the sultry sun and preserve their light complexions. As one travels to the southern and tropical latitudes of India, he finds progressively that the people become darker and darker.

After spending happy weeks in Kashmir, I was forced to return to Bengal for the fall term of Serampore College. Sri Yukteswar remained in Srinagar, with Kanai and Auddy.

Before I departed, Master hinted that his body would be subject to suffering in Kashmir.

"Sir, you look a picture of health," I protested.

"There is a chance that I may even leave this earth."

"Guruji!" I fell at his feet with an imploring gesture. "Please promise that you won't leave your body now. I am utterly unprepared to carry on without you."

Sri Yukteswar was silent, but smiled at me so compassionately that I felt reassured. Reluctantly I left him.

"Master dangerously ill." This telegram from Auddy reached me shortly after my return to Serampore.

"Sir," I wired my guru frantically, "I asked for your promise not to leave me. Please keep your body; otherwise, I also shall die."

"Be it as you wish." This was Sri Yukteswar's reply from Kashmir.

A letter from Auddy arrived in a few days, informing me that Master had recovered. On his return to Serampore during the next fortnight, I was grieved to find my guru's body reduced to half its usual weight.

Fortunately for his disciples, Sri Yukteswar burned many of their sins in the fire of his severe fever in Kashmir. The metaphysical method of physical transfer of disease is known to highly advanced yogis. By a secret method, the yogi unites his mind and astral vehicle with those of a suffering individual; the disease is conveyed, wholly or in part, to the saint's body. Having harvested God on the physical field, a master no longer cares what happens to that material form. Though he may allow it to register a certain disease in order to relieve others, his mind is never affected; he considers himself fortunate in being able to render such aid.

The spiritual law does not require a master to become ill whenever he heals another person. Healings ordinarily take place through the saint's knowledge of various methods of instantaneous cure in which no hurt to the spiritual healer is involved. On rare occasions, however, a master who wishes to greatly quicken his disciples' evolution may then voluntarily work out on his own body a large measure of their undesirable karma.

Jesus signified himself as a ransom for the sins of many. With his divine powers, his body could never have been subjected to death by crucifixion if he had not willingly cooperated with the subtle cosmic law of cause and effect. He thus took on himself the consequences of others' karma, especially that of his disciples. In this manner they were highly purified and made fit to receive the omnipresent consciousness which later descended on them.

Only great gurus are able to assume the karma of disciples. Sri Yukteswar would not have suffered in Kashmir unless he had received permission from the Spirit within him to help his disciples in that strange way.

22

The Heart of a Stone Image

"As a loyal Hindu wife, I do not wish to complain of my husband. But I yearn to see him turn from his materialistic views. He delights in ridiculing the pictures of saints in my meditation room. Dear brother, I have deep faith that you can help him. Will you?"

My eldest sister Roma gazed beseechingly at me. I was paying a short visit at her Calcutta home on Girish Vidyaratna Lane. Her plea touched me, for she had exercised a profound spiritual influence over my early life, and had lovingly tried to fill the void left in the family circle by Mother's death.

"Beloved sister, of course I will do anything I can." I smiled, eager to lift the gloom plainly visible on her face, in contrast to her usual calm and cheerful expression.

Roma and I sat awhile in silent prayer for guidance. A year earlier, my sister had asked me to initiate her into KRIYA YOGA, in which she was making notable progress.

An inspiration seized me. "Tomorrow," I said, "I am going to the Dakshineswar temple. Please come with me, and persuade your husband to accompany us. I feel that in the vibrations of that holy place, Divine Mother will touch his heart. But don't disclose our object in wanting him to go."

Sister agreed hopefully. Very early the next morning I was

pleased to find that Roma and her husband were in readiness for the trip. As our hackney carriage rattled along Upper Circular Road toward Dakshineswar, my brother-in-law, Satish Chandra Bose, amused himself by deriding spiritual gurus of the past, present, and future. I noticed that Roma was quietly weeping.

"Sister, cheer up!" I whispered. "Don't give your husband the satisfaction of believing that we take his mockery seriously."

"Mukunda, how can you admire worthless humbugs?" Satish was saying. "A SADHU'S very appearance is repulsive. He is either as thin as a skeleton, or as unholily fat as an elephant!"

I shouted with laughter. My good-natured reaction was annoying to Satish; he retired into sullen silence. As our cab entered the Dakshineswar grounds, he grinned sarcastically.

"This excursion, I suppose, is a scheme to reform me?"

As I turned away without reply, he caught my arm. "Young Mr. Monk," he said, "don't forget to make proper arrangements with the temple authorities to provide for our noon meal."

"I am going to meditate now. Do not worry about your lunch," I replied sharply. "Divine Mother will look after it."

"I don't trust Divine Mother to do a single thing for me. But I do hold you responsible for my food." Satish's tones were threatening.

I proceeded alone to the colonnaded hall which fronts the large temple of Kali, or Mother Nature. Selecting a shady spot near one of the pillars, I arranged my body in the lotus posture. The world receded as I became devotionally entranced. My mind was concentrated on Goddess Kali.

"Silent Mother with stony heart," I prayed, "Thou

becamest filled with life at the request of Thy beloved devotee Ramakrishna; why dost Thou not also heed the wails of this yearning son of Thine?"

My aspiring zeal increased boundlessly, accompanied by a divine peace. Yet, when five hours had passed, and the Goddess whom I was inwardly visualizing had made no response, I felt slightly disheartened. Sometimes it is a test by God to delay the fulfillment of prayers. But He eventually appears to the persistent devotee in whatever form he holds dear.

Reluctantly I opened my eyes, and saw that the temple doors were being locked by a priest, in conformance with a noon-hour custom. I rose from my secluded seat under the open, roofed hall, and stepped into the courtyard. Its stone floor was scorching under the midday sun; my bare feet were painfully burned.

"Divine Mother," I silently remonstrated, "Thou didst not come to me in vision, and now Thou art hidden in the temple behind closed doors. I wanted to offer a special prayer to Thee today on behalf of my brother-in-law."

My inward petition was instantly acknowledged. First, a delightful cold wave descended over my back and under my feet, banishing all discomfort. Then, to my amazement, the temple became greatly magnified. Its large door slowly opened, revealing the stone figure of Goddess Kali. Gradually it changed into a living form, smilingly nodding in greeting, thrilling me with joy indescribable. As if by a mystic syringe, the breath was withdrawn from my lungs; my body became very still, though not inert.

Though I was breathless and my body in a strangely quiet state, yet I was able to move my hands and feet freely. For several minutes I experimented in closing and opening my eyes; in either state I saw distinctly the whole Dakshineswar panorama.

In my sacred experience at Dakshineswar, the only extraordinarily-enlarged objects were the temple and the form of the Goddess. Everything else appeared in its normal dimensions, although each was enclosed in a halo of mellow light-white, blue, and pastel rainbow hues.

Behind the temple walls I suddenly glimpsed my brother-in-law as he sat under the thorny branches of a sacred BEL tree. I could effortlessly discern the course of his thoughts. Somewhat uplifted under the holy influence of Dakshineswar, his mind yet held unkind reflections about me. I turned directly to the gracious form of the Goddess.

"Divine Mother," I prayed, "wilt Thou not spiritually change my sister's husband?"

The beautiful figure, hitherto silent, spoke at last: "Thy wish is granted!"

I looked happily at Satish. As though instinctively aware that some spiritual power was at work, he rose resentfully from his seat on the ground. I saw him running behind the temple; he approached me, shaking his fist.

"You little fool," my brother-in-law blurted out, "you have been sitting there cross-legged and cross-eyed for six hours. I have gone back and forth watching you. Where is my food? Now the temple is closed; you failed to notify the authorities; we are left without lunch!"

The exaltation I had felt at the Goddess' presence was still vibrant within my heart. I was emboldened to exclaim, "Divine Mother will feed us!"

Satish was beside himself with rage. "Once and for all," he shouted, "I would like to see your Divine Mother giving us food here without prior arrangements!"

His words were hardly uttered when a temple priest crossed the courtyard and joined us.

"Son," he addressed me, "I have been observing your face serenely glowing during hours of meditation. I saw the arrival of your party this morning, and felt a desire to put aside ample food for your lunch. It is against the temple rules to feed those who do not make a request beforehand, but I have made an exception for you."

I thanked him, and gazed straight into Satish's eyes. He flushed with emotion, lowering his gaze in silent repentance. When we were served a lavish meal, including out-of-season mangoes, I noticed that my brother-in-law's appetite was meager. He was bewildered, diving deep into the ocean of thought. On the return journey to Calcutta, Satish, with softened expression, occasionally glanced at me pleadingly. But he did not speak a single word after the moment the priest had appeared to invite us to lunch, as though in direct answer to Satish's challenge.

The following afternoon I visited my sister at her home. She greeted me affectionately.

"Dear brother," she cried, "what a miracle! Last evening my husband wept openly before me.

"'Beloved DEVI,' he said, 'I am happy beyond expression that this reforming scheme of your brother's has wrought a transformation. I am going to undo every wrong I have done you. From tonight we will use our large bedroom only as a place of worship; your small meditation room shall be changed into our sleeping quarters. I am sincerely sorry that I have ridiculed your brother. For the shameful way I have been acting, I will punish myself by not talking to Mukunda until I have progressed in the spiritual path. Deeply I will seek the Divine Mother from now on; someday I must surely find Her!'"

Years later, I visited my brother-in-law in Delhi. I was overjoyed to perceive that he had developed highly in self-realization, and had been blessed by the vision of Divine Mother. During my stay with him, I noticed that Satish secretly spent the greater part of every night in divine meditation, though he was suffering from a serious ailment, and was engaged during the day at his office.

The thought came to me that my brother-in-law's life span would not be a long one. Roma must have read my mind.

"Dear brother," she said, "I am well, and my husband is sick. Nevertheless, I want you to know that, as a devoted Hindu wife, I am going to be the first one to die. It won't be long now before I pass on."

Taken aback at her ominous words, I yet realized their sting of truth. I was in America when my sister died, about a year after her prediction.

23

I Receive My University Degree

"You ignore your textbook assignments in philosophy. No doubt you are depending on an unlaborious 'intuition' to get you through the examinations. But unless you apply yourself in a more scholarly manner, I shall see to it that you don't pass this course."

Professor D. C. Ghoshal of Serampore College was addressing me sternly. If I failed to pass his final written classroom test, I would be ineligible to take the conclusive examinations.

I took an ingenious step to nullify Professor Ghoshal's threat to me of failure in philosophy. When the results of the final tests were about to be publicly announced, I asked a classmate to accompany me to the professor's study.

"Come along; I want a witness," I told my companion. "I shall be very much disappointed if I have not succeeded in outwitting the instructor."

Professor Ghoshal shook his head after I had inquired what rating he had given my paper.

"You are not among those who have passed," he said in triumph. He hunted through a large pile on his desk. "Your paper isn't here at all; you have failed, in any case, through non-appearance at the examination."

I chuckled. "Sir, I was there. May I look through the stack myself?"

The professor, nonplused, gave his permission; I quickly found my paper, where I had carefully omitted any identification mark except my roll call number. Unwarned by the "red flag" of my name, the instructor had given a high rating to my answers even though they were unembellished by textbook quotations.

Seeing through my trick, he now thundered, "Sheer brazen luck!" He added hopefully, "You are sure to fail in the A.B. finals."

Now, after four years of college, I was eligible to sit for the A.B. examinations.

One night about eleven o'clock, as I was putting on my shoes in preparation for the ride to the boardinghouse, Master questioned me gravely.

"When do your A.B. examinations start?"

"Five days hence, sir."

"I hope you are in readiness for them."

Transfixed with alarm, I held one shoe in the air. "Sir," I protested, "you know how my days have been passed with you rather than with the professors. How can I enact a farce by appearing for those difficult finals?"

Sri Yukteswar's eyes were turned piercingly on mine. "You must appear." His tone was coldly peremptory. "We should not give cause for your father and other relatives to criticize your preference for ashram life. Just promise me that you will be present for the examinations; answer them the best way you can."

"I will appear if you wish it," I said amidst sobs. "But no time remains for proper preparation." Under my breath

I muttered, "I will fill up the sheets with your teachings in answer to the questions!"

When I entered the hermitage the following day at my usual hour, I presented my bouquet with a certain mournful solemnity. Sri Yukteswar laughed at my woebegone air.

"Mukunda, has the Lord ever failed you, at an examination or elsewhere?"

"No, sir," I responded warmly. Grateful memories came in a revivifying flood.

"Not laziness but burning zeal for God has prevented you from seeking college honors," my guru said kindly. After a silence, he quoted, "'Seek ye first the kingdom of God, and His righteousness; and all these things shall be added unto you.'"

For the thousandth time, I felt my burdens lifted in Master's presence. When we had finished our early lunch, he suggested that I return to the PANTHI.

"Does your friend, Romesh Chandra Dutt, still live in your boardinghouse?"

"Yes, sir."

"Get in touch with him; the Lord will inspire him to help you with the examinations."

"Very well, sir." Saying this I bicycled back to the PANTHI. The first person I met in the boardinghouse compound was the scholarly Romesh. As though his days were quite free, he obligingly agreed to my diffident request.

"Of course; I am at your service." He spent several hours of that afternoon and of succeeding days in coaching me in my various subjects.

When I sat for the examination in English literature the following day, my first glance at the questions caused tears of gratitude to pour forth, wetting my paper. The classroom monitor came to my desk and made a sympathetic inquiry.

"My guru foretold that Romesh would help me," I explained. "Look; the very questions dictated to me by Romesh are here on the examination sheet! Fortunately for me, there are very few questions this year on English authors, whose lives are wrapped in deep mystery so far as I am concerned!"

Thinking over the examination in English literature, I realized one morning that I had made a serious error. One section of the questions had been divided into two parts of A or B, and C or D. Instead of answering one question from each part, I had carelessly answered both questions in Group I, and had failed to consider anything in Group II. The best mark I could score in that paper would be 33, three less than the passing mark of 36. I rushed to Master and poured out my troubles.

"Sir, I have made an unpardonable blunder. I don't deserve the divine blessings through Romesh; I am quite unworthy."

"Cheer up, Mukunda." Sri Yukteswar's tones were light and unconcerned. He pointed to the blue vault of the heavens. "It is more possible for the sun and moon to interchange their positions in space than it is for you to fail in getting your degree!"

I left the hermitage in a more tranquil mood, though it seemed mathematically inconceivable that I could pass. I looked once or twice apprehensively into the sky; the Lord of Day appeared to be securely anchored in his customary orbit!

As I reached the PANTHI, I overheard a classmate's remark: "I have just learned that this year, for the first time, the required passing mark in English literature has been lowered."

I entered the boy's room with such speed that he looked up in alarm. I questioned him eagerly.

"Long-haired monk," he said laughingly, "why this sudden interest in scholastic matters? Why cry in the eleventh hour? But it is true that the passing mark has just been lowered to 33 points."

A few joyous leaps took me into my own room, where I sank to my knees and praised the mathematical perfections of my Divine Father.

Every day I thrilled with the consciousness of a spiritual presence that I clearly felt to be guiding me through Romesh. A significant incident occurred in connection with the examination in Bengali. Romesh, who had touched little on that subject, called me back one morning as I was leaving the boardinghouse on my way to the examination hall.

"There is Romesh shouting for you," a classmate said to me impatiently. "Don't return; we shall be late at the hall."

Ignoring the advice, I ran back to the house.

"The Bengali examination is usually easily passed by our Bengali boys," Romesh told me. "But I have just had a hunch that this year the professors have planned to massacre the students by asking questions from our ancient literature." My friend then briefly outlined two stories from the life of Vidyasagar, a renowned philanthropist.

I thanked Romesh and quickly bicycled to the college hall. The examination sheet in Bengali proved to contain two parts. The first instruction was: "Write two instances of the charities of Vidyasagar." As I transferred to the paper the lore that I had so recently acquired, I whispered a few words of thanksgiving that I had heeded Romesh's last-minute summons.

The second instruction on the sheet read: "Write an essay in Bengali on the life of the man who has most inspired you." Gentle reader, I need not inform you what man I chose for my theme. As I covered page after page with praise of my guru, I smiled to realize that my muttered prediction was coming true: "I will fill up the sheets with your teachings!"

I had not felt inclined to question Romesh about my course in philosophy. Trusting my long training under Sri Yukteswar, I safely disregarded the textbook explanations. The highest mark given to any of my papers was the one in philosophy. My score in all other subjects was just barely within the passing mark.

It is a pleasure to record that my unselfish friend Romesh received his own degree CUM LAUDE.

Father was wreathed in smiles at my graduation. On the day I received my degree from Calcutta University, I knelt at my guru's feet and thanked him for all the blessings flowing from his life into mine.

24

I Become a Monk of the Swami Order

"Master, my father has been anxious for me to accept an executive position with the Bengal-Nagpur Railway. But I have definitely refused it." I added hopefully, "Sir, will you not make me a monk of the Swami Order?" I looked pleadingly at my guru. During preceding years, in order to test the depth of my determination, he had refused this same request. Today, however, he smiled graciously.

"Very well; tomorrow I will initiate you into swamiship." He went on quietly, "I am happy that you have persisted in your desire to be a monk. Lahiri Mahasaya often said: 'If you don't invite God to be your summer Guest, He won't come in the winter of your life.'"

The following day was one of the most memorable days in my life. It was a sunny Thursday, I remember, in July, 1914, a few weeks after my graduation from college. On the inner balcony of his Serampore hermitage, Master dipped a new piece of white silk into a dye of ocher, the traditional color of the Swami Order. After the cloth had dried, my guru draped it around me as a renunciate's robe.

"Someday you will go to the West, where silk is preferred,"

he said "As a symbol, I have chosen for you this silk material instead of the customary cotton."

In India, where monks embrace the ideal of poverty, a silk-clad swami is an unusual sight. Many yogis, however, wear garments of silk, which preserves certain subtle bodily currents better than cotton.

"I am averse to ceremonies," Sri Yukteswar remarked. "I will make you a swami in the BIDWAT (non-ceremonious) manner."

The BIBIDISA or elaborate initiation into swamiship includes a fire ceremony, during which symbolical funeral rites are performed. The physical body of the disciple is represented as dead, cremated in the flame of wisdom. The newly-made swami is then given a chant, such as: "This ATMA is Brahma" or "Thou art That" or "I am He." Sri Yukteswar, however, with his love of simplicity, dispensed with all formal rites and merely asked me to select a new name.

"I will give you the privilege of choosing it yourself," he said, smiling.

"Yogananda," I replied, after a moment's thought. The name literally means "Bliss (ANANDA) through divine union (YOGA)."

"Be it so. Forsaking your family name of Mukunda Lal Ghosh, henceforth you shall be called Yogananda of the Giri branch of the Swami Order."

As I knelt before Sri Yukteswar, and for the first time heard him pronounce my new name, my heart overflowed with gratitude. How lovingly and tirelessly had he labored, that the boy Mukunda be someday transformed into the monk Yogananda!

In addition to his new name, usually ending in ANANDA,

the swami takes a title which indicates his formal connection with one of the ten subdivisions of the Swami Order. These DASANAMIS or ten agnomens include the GIRI (mountain), to which Sri Yukteswar, and hence myself, belong. Among the other branches are the SAGAR (sea), BHARATI (land), ARANYA (forest), PURI (tract), TIRTHA (place of pilgrimage), and SARASWATI (wisdom of nature).

The ideal of selfless service to all mankind, and of renunciation of personal ties and ambitions, leads the majority of swamis to engage actively in humanitarian and educational work in India, or occasionally in foreign lands. Ignoring all prejudices of caste, creed, class, color, sex, or race, a swami follows the precepts of human brotherhood. His goal is absolute unity with Spirit.

Sri Yukteswar was both a swami and a yogi. A swami, formally a monk by virtue of his connection with the ancient order, is not always a yogi. Anyone who practices a scientific technique of God-contact is a yogi; he may be either married or unmarried, either a worldly man or one of formal religious ties. A swami may conceivably follow only the path of dry reasoning, of cold renunciation; but a yogi engages himself in a definite, step-by-step procedure by which the body and mind are disciplined, and the soul liberated.

Like any other science, yoga is applicable to people of every clime and time. Yoga is a method for restraining the natural turbulence of thoughts, which otherwise impartially prevent all men, of all lands, from glimpsing their true nature of Spirit. Yoga cannot know a barrier of East and West any more than does the healing and equitable light of the sun. So long as man possesses a mind with its restless thoughts, so long will there be a universal need for yoga or control.

The ancient rishi Patanjali defines "yoga" as "control of the fluctuations of the mind-stuff." His very short and masterly expositions, the YOGA SUTRAS, form one of the six systems of Hindu philosophy. In contradistinction to Western philosophies, all six Hindu systems embody not only theoretical but practical teachings. In addition to every conceivable ontological inquiry, the six systems formulate six definite disciplines aimed at the permanent removal of suffering and the attainment of timeless bliss.

The YOGA system as outlined by Patanjali is known as the Eight-fold Path. The first steps, (1) YAMA and (2) NIYAMA, require observance of ten negative and positive moralities – avoidance of injury to others, of untruthfulness, of stealing, of incontinence, of gift-receiving (which brings obligations); and purity of body and mind, contentment, self-discipline, study, and devotion to God.

The next steps are (3) ASANA (right posture); the spinal column must be held straight, and the body firm in a comfortable position for meditation; (4) PRANAYAMA (control of PRANA, subtle life currents); and (5) PRATYAHARA (withdrawal of the senses from external objects).

The last steps are forms of yoga proper: (6) DHARANA (concentration); holding the mind to one thought; (7) DHYANA (meditation), and (8) SAMADHI (superconscious perception). This is the Eightfold Path of Yoga which leads one to the final goal of KAIVALYA (Absoluteness), a term which might be more comprehensibly put as "realization of the Truth beyond all intellectual apprehension."

"Which is greater," one may ask, "a swami or a yogi?" If and when final oneness with God is achieved, the distinctions of the various paths disappear. There are a number of great souls, living in American or European or other non-Hindu bodies today who, though they may never have heard the words YOGI and SWAMI, are yet true exemplars of those terms. Through their disinterested service to mankind, or through their mastery over passions and thoughts, or through their single hearted love of God, or through their great powers of concentration, they are, in a sense, yogis; they have set themselves the goal of yoga-self-control. These men could rise to even greater heights if they were taught the definite science of yoga, which makes possible more conscious direction of one's mind and life.

25

Brother Ananta and Sister Nalini

"Ananta cannot live; the sands of his karma for this life have run out."

These inexorable words reached my inner consciousness as I sat one morning in deep meditation. Shortly after I had entered the Swami Order, I paid a visit to my birthplace, Gorakhpur, as a guest of my elder brother Ananta. A sudden illness confined him to his bed; I nursed him lovingly.

The solemn inward pronouncement filled me with grief. I felt that I could not bear to remain longer in Gorakhpur, only to see my brother removed before my helpless gaze. Amidst uncomprehending criticism from my relatives, I left India on the first available boat. It cruised along Burm and the China Sea to Japan. I disembarked at Kobe, where I spent only a few days. My heart was too heavy for sightseeing.

On the return trip to India, the boat touched at Shanghai. There Dr. Misra, the ship's physician, guided me to several curio shops, where I selected various presents for Sri Yukteswar and my family and friends. For Ananta I purchased a large carved bamboo piece. No sooner had the Chinese salesman handed me the bamboo souvenir than I dropped it on the floor, crying out, "I have bought this for my dear dead brother!"

A clear realization had swept over me that his soul was

just being freed in the Infinite. The souvenir was sharply and symbolically cracked by its fall; amidst sobs, I wrote on the bamboo surface: "For my beloved Ananta, now gone."

My companion, the doctor, was observing these proceedings with a sardonic smile.

"Save your tears," he remarked. "Why shed them until you are sure he is dead?"

When our boat reached Calcutta, Dr. Misra again accompanied me. My youngest brother Bishnu was waiting to greet me at the dock.

"I know Ananta has departed this life," I said to Bishnu, before he had had time to speak. "Please tell me, and the doctor here, when Ananta died."

Bishnu named the date, which was the very day that I had bought the souvenirs in Shanghai.

Father embraced me warmly as I entered our Gurpar Road home. "You have come," he said tenderly. Two large tears dropped from his eyes. Ordinarily undemonstrative, he had never before shown me these signs of affection. Outwardly the grave father, inwardly he possessed the melting heart of a mother. In all his dealings with the family, his dual parental role was distinctly manifest.

Soon after Ananta's passing, my younger sister Nalini was brought back from death's door by a divine healing. Before relating the story, I will refer to a few phases of her earlier life.

The childhood relationship between Nalini and myself had not been of the happiest nature. I was very thin; she was thinner still. Time passed; Nalini was betrothed to a young Calcutta physician, Panchanon Bose. He received a generous dowry from Father, presumably (as I remarked to Sister) to compensate the bridegroom-to-be for his fate in allying himself with a human bean-pole.

Elaborate marriage rites were celebrated in due time. On the wedding night, I sheltered myself behind the pillow of my new brother-in-law and grinned at him in friendly fashion. He had never seen Nalini until the day of the nuptial ceremony, when he finally learned what he was getting in the matrimonial lottery.

Feeling my sympathy, Dr. Bose pointed unobtrusively to Nalini, and whispered in my ear, "Say, what's this?"

"Why, Doctor," I replied, "it is a skeleton for your observation!"

Convulsed with mirth, my brother-in-law and I were hard put to it to maintain the proper decorum before our assembled relatives.

As the years went on, Dr. Bose and I became fast friends, often joking together, usually with Nalini as our target.

"It is a medical curiosity," my brother-in-law remarked to me one day. "I have tried everything on your lean sister – cod liver oil, butter, malt, honey, fish, meat, eggs, tonics. Still she fails to bulge even one-hundredth of an inch."

A few days later I visited the Bose home. My errand there took only a few minutes; I was leaving, unnoticed, I thought, by Nalini. As I reached the front door, I heard her voice, cordial but commanding.

"Brother, come here. You are not going to give me the slip this time. I want to talk to you."

I mounted the stairs to her room. To my surprise, she was in tears.

"Dear brother," she said, "let us bury the old hatchet. I see that your feet are now firmly set on the spiritual path. Also, you are now robust in appearance. Can you help me? My husband does not come near me, and I love him so dearly! But still more I want to progress in God-realization, even if I must remain thin and unattractive."

My heart was deeply touched at her plea. Our new friendship steadily progressed; one day she asked to become my disciple.

As a test of her faith, I asked her to omit from her diet all fish, meat, and eggs.

After several months, during which Nalini had strictly followed the various rules I had outlined, and had adhered to her vegetarian diet in spite of numerous difficulties, I paid her a visit.

"Sis, you have been conscientiously observing the spiritual injunctions; your reward is near." I smiled mischievously. "How plump do you want to be-as fat as our aunt who hasn't seen her feet in years?"

"No! But I long to be as stout as you are."

I replied solemnly. "By the grace of God, your body shall verily change from today; in one month it shall have the same weight as mine."

And in thirty days, Nalini's weight equalled mine. The new roundness gave her beauty; her husband fell deeply in love. Their marriage, begun so inauspiciously, turned out to be ideally happy.

On my return from Japan, I learned that during my absence Nalini had been stricken with typhoid fever. I rushed to her home, and was aghast to find her reduced to a mere skeleton. She was in a coma.

"Before her mind became confused by illness," my brother-in-law told me, "she often said: 'If brother Mukunda were here, I would not be faring thus.'" He added despairingly, "The other doctors and myself see no hope. Blood dysentery has set in, after her long bout with typhoid."

I began to move heaven and earth with my prayers. Engaging an Anglo-Indian nurse, who gave me full cooperation, I applied to my sister various yoga techniques of healing. The blood dysentery disappeared.

But Dr. Bose shook his head mournfully. "She simply has no more blood left to shed."

"She will recover," I replied stoutly. "In seven days her fever will be gone."

A week later I was thrilled to see Nalini open her eyes and gaze at me with loving recognition. From that day her recovery was swift. Although she regained her usual weight, she bore one sad scar of her nearly fatal illness: her legs were paralyzed. Indian and English specialists pronounced her a hopeless cripple.

The incessant war for her life which I had waged by prayer had exhausted me. I went to Serampore to ask Sri Yukteswar's help. His eyes expressed deep sympathy as I told him of Nalini's plight.

"Your sister's legs will be normal at the end of one month." He added, "Let her wear, next to her skin, a band with an unperforated two-carat pearl, held on by a clasp."

I prostrated myself at his feet with joyful relief.

"Sir, you are a master; your word of her recovery is enough. But if you insist I shall immediately get her a pearl."

My guru nodded. "Yes, do that." He went on to correctly describe the physical and mental characteristics of Nalini, whom he had never seen.

"Sir," I inquired, "is this an astrological analysis? You do not know her birth day or hour."

Sri Yukteswar smiled. "There is a deeper astrology, not dependent on the testimony of calendars and clocks. Each man is a part of the Creator, or Cosmic Man; he has a heavenly body as well as one of earth. The human eye sees the physical form, but the inward eye penetrates more profoundly, even to the universal pattern of which each man is an integral and individual part."

I returned to Calcutta and purchased a pearl for Nalini. A month later, her paralyzed legs were completely healed.

Sister asked me to convey her heartfelt gratitude to my guru. He listened to her message in silence. But as I was taking my leave, he made a pregnant comment.

"Your sister has been told by many doctors that she can never bear children. Assure her that in a few years she will give birth to two daughters."

Some years later, to Nalini's joy, she bore a girl, followed in a few years by another daughter.

"Your master has blessed our home, our entire family," my sister said. "The presence of such a man is a sanctification on the whole of India. Dear brother, please tell Sri Yukteswarji that, through you, I humbly count myself as one of his KRIYA YOGA disciples."

Nagendra Nath Bhaduri
"The Levitating Saint"

Swami Kebalananda
Yoganandaji's beloved Sanskrit tutor

Master Mahasaya
"The Blissful Devotee"

Swami Pranabananda
The Banaras "Saint with Two Bodies"

My mother, Gyana Prabha Ghosh,
a disciple of Lahiri Mahasaya

My father, Bhagabati Charan Ghosh,
a disciple of Lahiri Mahasaya

Yoganandaji at the age of six

Yoganandaji at the age of sixteen

Yoganandaji (*standing*) as a
high-school youth,
with his elder brother Ananta

Yogananda in Ranchi,
India, 1919 at the age of 26

My master, Sri Sri Swami Yukteswar Giri, a disciple of Sri Sri Lahiri Mahasaya

Swami Sri Sri
Yukteswar Giri
in lotus posture

Administration
building of Yogoda
Satsanga Society of
India Branch Math
and Ashram, Ranchi

Jagadis Chandra Bose, India's great physicist, botanist, and inventor of the Crescograph

Ram Gopal Muzumdar
"The Sleepless Saint"

Kashi, Student at Ranchi School

Rabindranath Tagore, inspired poet of Bengal, and Nobel Prize winner for literature.

SRI SRI MAHAVATAR BABAJI
Guru of Sri Sri Lahiri Mahasaya

Lahiri Mahasaya,
disciple of Babaji and
Guru of Swami Sri Sri
Yukteswar

Babaji's Cave in the Himalayas.
It was in this cave near Ranikhet that
Lahiri Mahasaya met the secluded master,
who initiated him in the science of
Kriya Yoga. A grandson of Lahiri
Mahasaya, Ananda Mohan Lahiri
(*in white*), and three other devotees are
visiting the sacred spot.

Paramahansa Yoganandaji with a few of the delegates to the International Congress of Religious Liberals, October 1920, Boston, USA, at which Yoganandaji gave his maiden speech in America.

Paramahansa Yoganandaji giving a lecture in Washington, D.C.

Luther Burbank and Yoganandaji, Santa Rosa, California, 1924

Yoganandaji with the Neumann brothers

Sri Sri Paramahansa Yogananda and Mr. John Balfour at the White House, Washington, D.C. in 1927, where Sri Yoganandaji was received by President Coolidge.

Therese Neumann, the famous Catholic Stigmatist who inspired my 1935 pilgrimage to Konnersreuth, Bavaria

Swami Sri Sri Yukteshwar and Paramahansa Yogananda in a religious procession, Calcutta, 1935

Last Solstice Festival celebrated by Swami Sri Sri Yukteswar, December 1935. Yoganandaji is seated next to his great guru (*centre*) at the table in the large courtyard of the ashram in Serampore.

Dining patio of Swami Sri Sri Yukteswar's Serampore hermitage. I am seated (*centre*) at my guru's feet.

Swami Keshabananda, Yogananandji and
C. Richard Wright at Keshabanandaji's
Ashram, Vrindaban, 1936

Panchanon Bhattacharya, disciple of
Sri Sri Lahiri Mahasaya

Yoganandaji with Giri Bala,
non-eating Saint

Shankari Mai Jiew,
the only living disciple
of Trailanga Swami,
at the *Kumbha Mela*
in Haridwar, 1938.
The yogini was then
112 years old.

Yoganandaji and Swami Dayananda, Mahamandal hermitage, Banaras, 1936.

Ramana Maharshi and Yoganandaji at Sri Ramana's Arunachala ashram.

Yoganandaji with Mahatma Gandhi in his ashram in Wardha.

Swami Krishnanda, at the 1936 *Kumbha Mela* in Allahabad, with his tame vgetarian lioness that utters *Aum* in a deep, attractive growl.

Yoganandaji with Sri Sri Ananda Moyi Ma and her husband Bholanath, Calcutta, 1935.

26

The Science of Kriya Yoga

The science of KRIYA YOGA became widely known in modern India through the instrumentality of Lahiri Mahasaya, my guru's guru. The Sanskrit root of KRIYA is KRI, to do, to act and react; the same root is found in the word KARMA, the natural principle of cause and effect. KRIYA YOGA is thus "union (yoga) with the Infinite through a certain action or rite." A yogi who faithfully follows its technique is gradually freed from karma or the universal chain of causation.

Because of certain ancient yogic injunctions, I cannot give a full explanation of KRIYA YOGA in the pages of a book intended for the general public. The actual technique must be learned from a KRIYABAN or KRIYA YOGI; here a broad reference must suffice.

KRIYA YOGA is a simple, psychophysiological method by which the human blood is decarbonized and recharged with oxygen. The atoms of this extra oxygen are transmuted into life current to rejuvenate the brain and spinal centers. By stopping the accumulation of venous blood, the yogi is able to lessen or prevent the decay of tissues; the advanced yogi transmutes his cells into pure energy. Elijah, Jesus, Kabir and other prophets were past masters in the use of KRIYA or a similar technique, by which they caused their bodies to dematerialize at will.

KRIYA is an ancient science. Lahiri Mahasaya received it from his guru, Babaji, who rediscovered and clarified the technique after it had been lost in the Dark Ages.

"The KRIYA YOGA which I am giving to the world through you in this nineteenth century," Babaji told Lahiri Mahasaya, "is a revival of the same science which Krishna gave, millenniums ago, to Arjuna, and which was later known to Patanjali, and to Christ, St. John, St. Paul, and other disciples."

Krishna also relates that it was he, in a former incarnation, who communicated the indestructible yoga to an ancient illuminato, Vivasvat, who gave it to Manu, the great legislator. He, in turn, instructed Ikshwaku, the father of India's solar warrior dynasty. Passing thus from one to another, the royal yoga was guarded by the rishis until the coming of the materialistic ages. Then, due to priestly secrecy and man's indifference, the sacred knowledge gradually became inaccessible.

KRIYA YOGA is mentioned twice by the ancient sage Patanjali, foremost exponent of yoga, who wrote: "KRIYA YOGA consists of body discipline, mental control, and meditating on AUM." Patanjali speaks of God as the actual Cosmic Sound of AUM heard in meditation. AUM is the Creative Word, the sound of the Vibratory Motor. Even the yoga-beginner soon inwardly hears the wondrous sound of AUM. Receiving this blissful spiritual encouragement, the devotee becomes assured that he is in actual touch with divine realms.

Patanjali refers a second time to the life-control or KRIYA technique thus: "Liberation can be accomplished by that PRANAYAMA which is attained by disjoining the course of inspiration and expiration."

St. Paul knew KRIYA YOGA, or a technique very similar to it, by which he could switch life currents to and from the senses.

"KRIYA YOGA is an instrument through which human evolution can be quickened," Sri Yukteswar explained to his students. "The ancient yogis discovered that the secret of cosmic consciousness is intimately linked with breath mastery. This is India's unique and deathless contribution to the world's treasury of knowledge. The life force, which is ordinarily absorbed in maintaining the heart-pump, must be freed for higher activities by a method of calming and stilling the ceaseless demands of the breath."

The KRIYA YOGI mentally directs his life energy to revolve, upward and downward, around the six spinal centers (medullary, cervical, dorsal, lumbar, sacral, and coccygeal plexuses) which correspond to the twelve astral signs of the zodiac, the symbolic Cosmic Man. One-half minute of revolution of energy around the sensitive spinal cord of man effects subtle progress in his evolution; that half-minute of KRIYA equals one year of natural spiritual unfoldment.

The astral system of a human being, with six (twelve by polarity) inner constellations revolving around the sun of the omniscient spiritual eye, is interrelated with the physical sun and the twelve zodiacal signs. All men are thus affected by an inner and an outer universe.

KRIYA YOGA has nothing in common with the unscientific breathing exercises taught by a number of misguided zealots. Their attempts to forcibly hold breath in the lungs is not only unnatural but decidedly unpleasant. KRIYA, on the other hand, is accompanied from the very beginning by an accession of peace, and by soothing sensations of regenerative effect in the spine.

The ancient yogic technique converts the breath into mind. By spiritual advancement, one is able to cognize the breath as an act of mind-a dream-breath.

Many illustrations could be given of the mathematical relationship between man's respiratory rate and the variations in his states of consciousness. A person whose attention is wholly engrossed, as in following some closely knit intellectual argument, or in attempting some delicate or difficult physical feat, automatically breathes very slowly. Fixity of attention depends on slow breathing; quick or uneven breaths are an inevitable accompaniment of harmful emotional states: fear, lust, anger. The restless monkey breathes at the rate of 32 times a minute, in contrast to man's average of 18 times. The elephant, tortoise, snake and other animals noted for heir longevity have a respiratory rate which is less than man's. The tortoise, for instance, who may attain the age of 300 years, breathes only 4 times per minute.

The rejuvenating effects of sleep are due to man's temporary unawareness of body and breathing. The sleeping man becomes a yogi; each night he unconsciously performs the yogic rite of releasing himself from bodily identification, and of merging the life force with healing currents in the main brain region and the six sub-dynamos of his spinal centers. The sleeper thus dips unknowingly into the reservoir of cosmic energy which sustains all life.

The voluntary yogi performs a simple, natural process consciously, not unconsciously like the slow-paced sleeper. The KRIYA YOGI uses his technique to saturate and feed all his physical cells with undecaying light and keep them in a magnetized state. He scientifically makes breath unnecessary, without producing the states of subconscious sleep or unconsciousness.

By KRIYA, the outgoing life force is not wasted and abused in the senses, but constrained to reunite with subtler spinal energies. By such reinforcement of life, the yogi's body and brain cells are electrified with the spiritual elixir. Thus he removes himself from studied observance of natural laws, which can only take him-by circuitous means as given by proper food, sunlight, and harmonious thoughts-to a million-year Goal. It needs twelve years of normal healthful living to effect even slight perceptible change in brain structure, and a million solar returns are exacted to sufficiently refine the cerebral tenement for manifestation of cosmic consciousness.

Untying the cord of breath which binds the soul to the body, KRIYA serves to prolong life and enlarge the consciousness to infinity. The yoga method overcomes the tug of war between the mind and the matter-bound senses, and frees the devotee to reinherit his eternal kingdom. He knows his real nature is bound neither by physical encasement nor by breath, symbol of the mortal enslavement to air, to nature's elemental compulsions.

KRIYA, controlling the mind DIRECTLY through the life force, is the easiest, most effective, and most scientific avenue of approach to the Infinite. In contrast to the slow, uncertain "bullock cart" theological path to God, KRIYA may justly be called the "airplane" route.

The yogic science is based on an empirical consideration of all forms of concentration and meditation exercises. Yoga enables the devotee to switch off or on, at will, life current from the five sense telephones of sight, sound, smell, taste, and touch. Attaining this power of sense-disconnection, the yogi finds it simple to unite his mind at will with divine realms or with the world of matter. No longer is he unwillingly brought back by the life force to the mundane sphere of rowdy sensations and restless thoughts. Master of his body and mind, the KRIYA YOGI ultimately achieves victory over the "last enemy," death.

So shalt thou feed on Death, that feeds on men: And Death once dead, there's no more dying then.

The life of an advanced KRIYA YOGI is influenced, not by effects of past actions, but solely by directions from the soul. The devotee thus avoids the slow, evolutionary monitors of egoistic actions, good and bad, of common life, cumbrous and snail-like to the eagle hearts.

Referring to yoga's sure and methodical efficacy, Lord Krishna praises the technological yogi in the following words: "The yogi is greater than body-disciplining ascetics, greater even than the followers of the path of wisdom (JNANA YOGA), or of the path of action (KARMA YOGA); be thou, O disciple Arjuna, a yogi!"

27

Founding a Yoga School at Ranchi

The ideal of an all-sided education for youth had always been close to my heart. I saw clearly the arid results of ordinary instruction, aimed only at the development of body and intellect. Moral and spiritual values, without whose appreciation no man can approach happiness, were yet lacking in the formal curriculum. I determined to found a school where young boys could develop to the full stature of manhood. My first step in that direction was made with seven children at Dihika, a small country site in Bengal.

A year later, in 1918, through the generosity of Sir Manindra Chandra Nundy, the Maharaja of Kasimbazar, I was able to transfer my fast-growing group to Ranchi. The Kasimbazar Palace at Ranchi was transformed into the headquarters for the new school, which I called BRAHMACHARYA VIDYALAYA in accordance with the educational ideals of the rishis.

At Ranchi I organized an educational program for both grammar and high school grades. It included agricultural, industrial, commercial, and academic subjects. The students were also taught yoga concentration and meditation, and a unique system of physical development, "Yogoda," whose principles I had discovered in 1916.

The boys responded wonderfully to this training,

developing extraordinary ability to shift the life energy from one part of the body to another part, and to sit in perfect poise in difficult body postures. My youngest brother, Bishnu Charan Ghosh, joined the Ranchi school; he later became a leading physical culturist in Bengal. At the end of the first year at Ranchi, applications for admission reached two thousand.

With a large fruit orchard and twenty-five fertile acres at our disposal, the students, teachers, and myself enjoyed many happy hours of outdoor labor in these ideal surroundings. We had many pets, including a young deer who was fairly idolized by the children. I too loved the fawn so much that I allowed it to sleep in my room.

One day I fed the pet earlier than usual, as I had to attend to some business in the town of Ranchi. Although I cautioned the boys not to feed the fawn until my return, one of them was disobedient, and gave the baby deer a large quantity of milk. When I came back in the evening, sad news greeted me: "The little fawn is nearly dead, through over feeding."

In tears, I placed the apparently lifeless pet on my lap. I prayed piteously to God to spare its life. Hours later, the small creature opened its eyes, stood up, and walked feebly. The whole school shouted for joy.

But a deep lesson came to me that night, one I can never forget. I stayed up with the fawn until two o'clock, when I fell asleep. The deer appeared in a dream, and spoke to me:

"You are holding me back. Please let me go; let me go!"

"All right," I answered in the dream.

I awoke immediately, and ran to the corner of the room where I had placed the pet. It made a last effort to rise, stumbled toward me, then dropped at my feet, dead.

According to the mass karma which guides and regulates the destinies of animals, the deer's life was over, and it was ready to progress to a higher form. But by my deep attachment, which I later realized was selfish, and by my fervent prayers, I had been able to hold it in the limitations of the animal form from which the soul was struggling for release. All sorrow left me; I realized anew that God wants His children to love everything as a part of Him, and not to feel delusively that death ends all.

The Ranchi school grew from small and simple beginnings to an institution now well-known in India. Under the general name of YOGODA SAT-SANGA, flourishing branch schools have been established at Midnapore, Lakshmanpur, and Puri.

The school, now in its twenty-eighth year and the center of many activities, has been honored by visits of eminent men from the East and the West. One of the earliest great figures to inspect the VIDYALAYA in its first year was Swami Pranabananda, the Benares "saint with two bodies."

Sometime after Swami Pranabananda had visited Ranchi, I accompanied my father to the Calcutta house where the yogi was temporarily staying. Pranabananda's prediction, made to me so many years before, came rushing to my mind: "I shall see you, with your father, later on."

As Father entered the swami's room, the great yogi rose from his seat and embraced my parent with loving respect.

"Bhagabati," he said, "what are you doing about yourself? Don't you see your son racing to the Infinite?" I blushed to hear his praise before my father. The swami went on, "You recall how often our blessed guru used to say: 'BANAT, BANAT, BAN JAI.' {FN26-6} So keep up KRIYA YOGA ceaselessly, and reach the divine portals quickly."

Noticing that Pranabananda's room contained many plants and packages of seed, I asked their purpose.

"I have left Benares permanently," he said, "and am now on my way to the Himalayas. There I shall open an ashram for my disciples. These seeds will produce spinach and a few other vegetables. My dear ones will live simply, spending their time in blissful God-union. Nothing else is necessary."

Father asked his brother disciple when he would return to Calcutta.

"Never again," the saint replied. "This year is the one in which Lahiri Mahasaya told me I would leave my beloved Benares forever and go to the Himalayas, there to throw off my mortal frame."

Months later I met an old friend, Sanandan, who was one of Pranabananda's close disciples.

"My adorable guru is gone," he told me, amidst sobs.

I inquired where Pranabananda was to be reborn.

"That's a sacred trust I cannot divulge to anyone," Sanandan replied. "Perhaps you may find out some other way."

Years later I discovered from Swami Keshabananda that Pranabananda, a few years after his birth in a new body, had gone to Badrinarayan in the Himalayas, and there joined the group of saints around the great Babaji.

28

Kashi, Reborn and Rediscovered

"Please do not go into the water. Let us bathe by dipping our buckets."

I was addressing the young Ranchi students who were accompanying me on an eight-mile hike to a neighboring hill. The pond before us was inviting, but a distaste for it had arisen in my mind. The group around me followed my example of dipping buckets, but a few lads yielded to the temptation of the cool waters. No sooner had they dived than large water snakes wiggled around them. The boys came out of the pond with comical alacrity.

We enjoyed a picnic lunch after we reached our destination. I sat under a tree, surrounded by a group of students. Finding me in an inspirational mood, they plied me with questions.

After answering many questions, I was addressed by a lad named Kashi. He was about twelve years old, a brilliant student, and beloved by all.

"Sir," he said, "what will be my fate?"

"You shall soon be dead." The reply came from my lips with an irresistible force.

This unexpected disclosure shocked and grieved me as well as everyone present. Silently rebuking myself as an ENFANT TERRIBLE, I refused to answer further questions.

On our return to the school, Kashi came to my room.

"If I die, will you find me when I am reborn, and bring me again to the spiritual path?" He sobbed.

"Yes," I promised. "If the Heavenly Father lends His aid, I will try to find you."

During the summer vacation, I started on a short trip. Regretting that I could not take Kashi with me, I called him to my room before leaving, and carefully instructed him to remain, against all persuasion, in the spiritual vibrations of the school. Somehow I felt that if he did not go home, he might avoid the impending calamity.

No sooner had I left than Kashi's father arrived in Ranchi. For fifteen days he tried to break the will of his son, explaining that if Kashi would go to Calcutta for only four days to see his mother, he could then return. Kashi persistently refused. The father finally said he would take the boy away with the help of the police. The threat disturbed Kashi, who was unwilling to be the cause of any unfavorable publicity to the school. He saw no choice but to go.

I returned to Ranchi a few days later. When I heard how Kashi had been removed, I entrained at once for Calcutta. There I engaged a horse cab. Very strangely, as the vehicle passed beyond the Howrah Bridge over the Ganges, I beheld Kashi's father and other relatives in mourning clothes. Shouting to my driver to stop, I rushed out and glared at the unfortunate father.

"Mr. Murderer," I cried somewhat unreasonably, "you have killed my boy!"

The father had already realized the wrong he had done in forcibly bringing Kashi to Calcutta. During the few days the boy had been there, he had eaten contaminated food, contracted cholera, and passed on.

My love for Kashi, and the pledge to find him after death, night and day haunted me. No matter where I went, his face loomed up before me. I began a memorable search for him, even as long ago I had searched for my lost mother.

I felt that inasmuch as God had given me the faculty of reason, I must utilize it and tax my powers to the utmost in order to discover the subtle laws by which I could know the boy's astral whereabouts. He was a soul vibrating with unfulfilled desires, I realized-a mass of light floating somewhere amidst millions of luminous souls in the astral regions. How was I to tune in with him, among so many vibrating lights of other souls?

Using a secret yoga technique, I broadcasted my love to Kashi's soul through the microphone of the spiritual eye, the inner point between the eyebrows. With the antenna of upraised hands and fingers, I often turned myself round and round, trying to locate the direction in which he had been reborn as an embryo. I hoped to receive response from him in the concentration-tuned radio of my heart.

I intuitively felt that Kashi would soon return to the earth, and that if I kept unceasingly broadcasting my call to him, his soul would reply. I knew that the slightest impulse sent by Kashi would be felt in my fingers, hands, arms, spine, and nerves.

With undiminished zeal, I practiced the yoga method steadily for about six months after Kashi's death. Walking with a few friends one morning in the crowded Bowbazar section of Calcutta, I lifted my hands in the usual manner. For the first time, there was response. I thrilled to detect electrical impulses trickling down my fingers and palms. These currents translated themselves into one overpowering thought from a deep recess of my consciousness: "I am Kashi; I am Kashi; come to me!"

The thought became almost audible as I concentrated on my heart radio. In the characteristic, slightly hoarse whisper of Kashi, I heard his summons again and again.

I began to turn round and round, to the undisguised amusement of my friends and the passing throng. The electrical impulses tingled through my fingers only when I faced toward a near-by path, aptly named "Serpentine Lane." The astral currents disappeared when I turned in other directions.

"Ah," I exclaimed, "Kashi's soul must be living in the womb of some mother whose home is in this lane."

My companions and I approached closer to Serpentine Lane; the vibrations in my upraised hands grew stronger, more pronounced. As if by a magnet, I was pulled toward the right side of the road. Reaching the entrance of a certain house, I was astounded to find myself transfixed. I knocked at the door in a state of intense excitement, holding my very breath. I felt that the successful end had come for my long, arduous, and certainly unusual quest!

The door was opened by a servant, who told me her master was at home. He descended the stairway from the second floor and smiled at me inquiringly. I hardly knew how to frame my question, at once pertinent and impertinent.

"Please tell me, sir, if you and your wife have been expecting a child for about six months?"

"Yes, it is so." Seeing that I was a swami, a renunciate attired in the traditional orange cloth, he added politely, "Pray inform me how you know my affairs."

When he heard about Kashi and the promise I had given, the astonished man believed my story.

"A male child of fair complexion will be born to you," I told him. "He will have a broad face, with a cowlick atop his forehead. His disposition will be notably spiritual." I felt certain that the coming child would bear these resemblances to Kashi.

Later I visited the child, whose parents had given him his old name of Kashi. Even in infancy he was strikingly similar in appearance to my dear Ranchi student. The child showed me an instantaneous affection; the attraction of the past awoke with redoubled intensity.

Years later the teen-age boy wrote me, during my stay in America. He explained his deep longing to follow the path of a renunciate. I directed him to a Himalayan master who, to this day, guides the reborn Kashi.

29

Rabindranath Tagore and I Compare Schools

"Rabindranath Tagore taught us to sing, as a natural form of self-expression, like the birds."

Bhola Nath, a bright fourteen-year-old lad at my Ranchi school, gave me this explanation after I had complimented him one morning on his melodious outbursts. With or without provocation, the boy poured forth a tuneful stream. He had previously attended the famous Tagore school of "Santiniketan" (Haven of Peace) at Bolpur.

"The songs of Rabindranath have been on my lips since early youth," I told my companion. "All Bengal, even the unlettered peasants, delights in his lofty verse."

"I met Rabindranath soon after he had received the Nobel Prize for literature," I remarked after our vocalizing. "I was drawn to visit him because I admired his undiplomatic courage in disposing of his literary critics." I chuckled.

Bhola curiously inquired the story.

"The scholars severely flayed Tagore for introducing a new style into Bengali poetry," I began. "He mixed colloquial and classical expressions, ignoring all the prescribed limitations dear to the pundits' hearts. His songs embody deep philosophic truth in emotionally appealing terms, with little regard for the accepted literary forms.

"One influential critic slightingly referred to Rabindranath as a 'pigeon-poet who sold his cooings in print for a rupee.' But Tagore's revenge was at hand; the whole Western world paid homage at his feet soon after he had translated into English his GITANJALI ('Song Offerings'). A trainload of pundits, including his one-time critics, went to Santiniketan to offer their congratulations.

"Rabindranath received his guests only after an intentionally long delay, and then heard their praise in stoic silence. Finally he turned against them their own habitual weapons of criticism.

"'Gentlemen,' he said, 'the fragrant honors you here bestow are incongruously mingled with the putrid odors of your past contempt. Is there possibly any connection between my award of the Nobel Prize, and your suddenly acute powers of appreciation? I am still the same poet who displeased you when I first offered my humble flowers at the shrine of Bengal.'"

I went on. "I was introduced to Rabindranath in Calcutta by his secretary, Mr. C. F. Andrews, who was simply attired in a Bengali DHOTI. He referred lovingly to Tagore as his GURUDEVA. "Rabindranath received me graciously. He emanated a soothing aura of charm, culture, and courtliness. Replying to my question about his literary background, Tagore told me that one ancient source of his inspiration, besides our religious epics, had been the classical poet, Bidyapati."

Inspired by these memories, I began to sing Tagore's version of an old Bengali song, "Light the Lamp of Thy Love." Bhola and I chanted joyously as we strolled over the VIDYALAYA grounds.

About two years after founding the Ranchi school, I received an invitation from Rabindranath to visit him at Santiniketan in order to discuss our educational ideals. I went gladly. The poet was seated in his study when I entered. Tagore and I were soon deep in a comparative study of our schools, both founded along unorthodox lines. We discovered many identical features – outdoor instruction, simplicity, ample scope for the child's creative spirit. Rabindranath, however, laid considerable stress on the study of literature and poetry, and the self-expression through music and song which I had already noted in the case of Bhola. The Santiniketan children observed periods of silence, but were given no special yoga training.

The poet listened with flattering attention to my description of the energizing "Yogoda" exercises and the yoga concentration techniques which are taught to all students at Ranchi.

Tagore told me of his own early educational struggles. "I fled from school after the fifth grade," he said, laughing. I could readily understand how his innate poetic delicacy had been affronted by the dreary, disciplinary atmosphere of a schoolroom.

"That is why I opened Santiniketan under the shady trees and the glories of the sky." He motioned eloquently to a little group studying in the beautiful garden. "A child is in his natural setting amidst the flowers and songbirds. Only thus may he fully express the hidden wealth of his individual endowment. True education can never be crammed and pumped from without; rather it must aid in bringing spontaneously to the surface the infinite hoards of wisdom within."

I agreed.

The poet spoke lovingly of his father, Devendranath, who had inspired the Santiniketan beginnings.

"Father presented me with this fertile land, where he had already built a guest house and temple," Rabindranath told me. "I started my educational experiment here in 1901, with only ten boys. The eight thousand pounds which came with the Nobel Prize all went for the upkeep of the school." The elder Tagore, Devendranath, known far and wide as "Maharishi," was a very remarkable man, as one may discover from his AUTOBIOGRAPHY. Two years of his manhood were spent in meditation in the Himalayas.

Rabindranath invited me to stay overnight in the guest house. It was indeed a charming spectacle, in the evening, to see the poet seated with a group in the patio. In his melodious voice, Rabindranath read to us a few of his exquisite poems, newly created.

The following day, after lunch, I bade the poet a reluctant farewell. I rejoice that his little school has now grown to an international university, "Viswa-Bharati," where scholars of all lands have found an ideal setting.

30

The Law of Miracles

The great novelist Leo Tolstoy wrote a delightful story, THE THREE HERMITS. His friend Nicholas Roerich has summarized the tale, as follows:

"On an island there lived three old hermits. They were so simple that the only prayer they used was: 'We are three; Thou art Three – have mercy on us!' Great miracles were manifested during this naïve prayer.

"The local bishop came to hear about the three hermits and their inadmissible prayer, and decided to visit them in order to teach them the canonical invocations. He arrived on the island, told the hermits that their heavenly petition was undignified, and taught them many of the customary prayers. The bishop then left on a boat. He saw, following the ship, a radiant light. As it approached, he discerned the three hermits, who were holding hands and running upon the waves in an effort to overtake the vessel.

"'We have forgotten the prayers you taught us,' they cried as they reached the bishop, 'and have hastened to ask you to repeat them.' The awed bishop shook his head.

"'Dear ones,' he replied humbly, 'continue to live with your old prayer!'"

How did the three saints walk on the water?

How did Christ resurrect his crucified body?

How did Lahiri Mahasaya and Sri Yukteswar perform their miracles?

Modern science has, as yet, no answer; though with the advent of the atomic bomb and the wonders of radar, the scope of the world-mind has been abruptly enlarged. The word "impossible" is becoming less prominent in the scientific vocabulary.

The ancient Vedic scriptures declare that the physical world operates under one fundamental law of MAYA, the principle of relativity and duality. God, the Sole Life, is an Absolute Unity; He cannot appear as the separate and diverse manifestations of a creation except under a false or unreal veil. That cosmic illusion is MAYA. Every great scientific discovery of modern times has served as a confirmation of this simple pronouncement of the rishis.

Newton's Law of Motion is a law of MAYA: "To every action there is always an equal and contrary reaction; the mutual actions of any two bodies are always equal and oppositely directed." Action and reaction are thus exactly equal. "To have a single force is impossible. There must be, and always is, a pair of forces equal and opposite."

Fundamental natural activities all betray their mayic origin. Electricity, for example, is a phenomenon of repulsion and attraction; its electrons and protons are electrical opposites. Another example: the atom or final particle of matter is, like the earth itself, a magnet with positive and negative poles. The entire phenomenal world is under the inexorable sway of polarity; no law of physics, chemistry, or any other science is ever found free from inherent opposite or contrasted principles.

Physical science, then, cannot formulate laws outside of MAYA, the very texture and structure of creation. Nature herself is MAYA; natural science must perforce deal with her ineluctable quiddity. In her own domain, she is eternal and inexhaustible; future scientists can do no more than probe one aspect after another of her varied infinitude. Science thus remains in a perpetual flux, unable to reach finality; fit indeed to formulate the laws of an already existing and functioning cosmos, but powerless to detect the Law Framer and Sole Operator. The majestic manifestations of gravitation and electricity have become known, but what gravitation and electricity are, no mortal knoweth.

To surmount MAYA was the task assigned to the human race by the millennial prophets. To rise above the duality of creation and perceive the unity of the Creator was conceived of as man's highest goal. Those who cling to the cosmic illusion must accept its essential law of polarity: flow and ebb, rise and fall, day and night, pleasure and pain, good and evil, birth and death. This cyclic pattern assumes a certain anguishing monotony, after man has gone through a few thousand human births; he begins to cast a hopeful eye beyond the compulsions of MAYA.

To tear the veil of MAYA is to pierce the secret of creation. The yogi who thus denudes the universe is the only true monotheist. All others are worshiping heathen images. So long as man remains subject to the dualistic delusions of nature, the Janus-faced MAYA is his goddess; he cannot know the one true God.

The world illusion, MAYA, is individually called AVIDYA, literally, "not-knowledge," ignorance, delusion. MAYA or AVIDYA can never be destroyed through intellectual conviction or analysis, but solely through attaining the interior state of NIRBIKALPA SAMADHI. The Old Testament prophets, and seers of all lands and ages, spoke from that state of consciousness. Ezekiel says (43:1-2): "Afterwards he brought me to the gate, even the gate that looketh toward the east: and, behold, the glory of the God of Israel came from the way of the east: and his voice was like a noise of many waters: and the earth shined with his glory." Through the divine eye in the forehead (east), the yogi sails his consciousness into omnipresence, hearing the Word or Aum, divine sound of many waters or vibrations which is the sole reality of creation.

Among the trillion mysteries of the cosmos, the most phenomenal is light. Unlike sound-waves, whose transmission requires air or other material media, light-waves pass freely through the vacuum of interstellar space. Even the hypothetical ether, held as the interplanetary medium of light in the undulatory theory, can be discarded on the Einsteinian grounds that the geometrical properties of space render the theory of ether unnecessary. Under either hypothesis, light remains the most subtle, the freest from material dependence, of any natural manifestation.

In the gigantic conceptions of Einstein, the velocity of light-186,000 miles per second-dominates the whole Theory of Relativity. He proves mathematically that the velocity of light is, so far as man's finite mind is concerned, the only CONSTANT in a universe of unstayable flux. On the sole absolute of light-velocity depend all human standards of time and space. Not abstractly eternal as hitherto considered, time and space are relative and finite factors, deriving their measurement validity only in reference to the yardstick of light-velocity. In joining space as a dimensional relativity, time has surrendered age-old claims to a changeless value. Time is now stripped to its rightful nature – a simple essence of ambiguity! With a few equational strokes of his pen, Einstein has banished from the cosmos every fixed reality except that of light.

In a later development, his Unified Field Theory, the great physicist embodies in one mathematical formula the laws of gravitation and of electromagnetism. Reducing the cosmical structure to variations on a single law, Einstein reaches across the ages to the rishis who proclaimed a sole texture of creation – that of a protean MAYA.

On the epochal Theory of Relativity have arisen the mathematical possibilities of exploring the ultimate atom. Great scientists are now boldly asserting not only that the atom is energy rather than matter, but that atomic energy is essentially mind-stuff.

With the recent discovery of the electron microscope came definite proof of the light-essence of atoms and of the inescapable duality of nature. The New York Times gave the following report of a 1937 demonstration of the electron microscope before a meeting of the American Association for the Advancement of Science:

"The crystalline structure of tungsten, hitherto known only indirectly by means of X-rays, stood outlined boldly on a fluorescent screen, showing nine atoms in their correct positions in the space lattice, a cube, with one atom in each corner and one in the center. The atoms in the crystal lattice of the tungsten appeared on the fluorescent screen as points of light, arranged in geometric pattern. Against this crystal cube of light the bombarding molecules of air could be observed as dancing points of light, similar to points of sunlight shimmering on moving waters. . . .

"The principle of the electron microscope was first discovered in 1927 by Drs. Clinton J. Davisson and Lester H. Germer of the Bell Telephone Laboratories, New York City, who found that the electron had a dual personality partaking of the characteristic of both a particle and a wave. The wave quality gave the electron the characteristic of light, and a search was begun to devise means for 'focusing' electrons in a manner similar to the focusing of light by means of a lens.

"For his discovery of the Jekyll-Hyde quality of the electron, which corroborated the prediction made in 1924 by De Broglie, French Nobel Prize winning physicist, and showed that the entire realm of physical nature had a dual personality, Dr. Davisson also received the Nobel Prize in physics."

"The stream of knowledge," Sir James Jeans writes in THE MYSTERIOUS UNIVERSE, "is heading towards a non-mechanical reality; the universe begins to look more like a great thought than like a great machine." Twentieth-century science is thus sounding like a page from the hoary VEDAS.

From science, then, if it must be so, let man learn the philosophic truth that there is no material universe; its warp and woof is MAYA, illusion. Its mirages of reality all break down under analysis. As one by one the reassuring props of a physical cosmos crash beneath him, man dimly perceives his idolatrous reliance, his past transgression of the divine command: "Thou shalt have no other gods before Me."

This Conception Brings Us to the Law of Miracles.

The masters who are able to materialize and dematerialize their bodies or any other object, and to move with the velocity of light, and to utilize the creative light-rays in bringing into instant visibility any physical manifestation, have fulfilled the necessary Einsteinian condition: their mass is infinite.

The consciousness of a perfected yogi is effortlessly identified, not with a narrow body, but with the universal structure. Gravitation, whether the "force" of Newton or the Einsteinian "manifestation of inertia," is powerless to COMPEL a master to exhibit the property of "weight" which is the distinguishing gravitational condition of all material objects. He who knows himself as the omnipresent Spirit is subject no longer to the rigidities of a body in time and space. Their imprisoning "rings-pass-not" have yielded to the solvent: "I am He."

A yogi who through perfect meditation has merged his consciousness with the Creator perceives the cosmical essence as light; to him there is no difference between the light rays composing water and the light rays composing land. Free from matter-consciousness, free from the three dimensions of space and the fourth dimension of time, a master transfers his body of light with equal ease over the light rays of earth, water, fire, or air. Long concentration on the liberating spiritual eye has enabled the yogi to destroy all delusions concerning matter and its gravitational weight; thenceforth he sees the universe as an essentially undifferentiated mass of light.

"Optical images," Dr. L. T. Troland of Harvard tells us, "are built up on the same principle as the ordinary 'half-tone' engravings; that is, they are made up of minute dottings or stripplings far too small to be detected by the eye. . . . The sensitiveness of the retina is so great that a visual sensation can be produced by relatively few Quanta of the right kind of light." Through a master's divine knowledge of light phenomena, he can instantly project into perceptible manifestation the ubiquitous light atoms. The actual form of the projection — whether it be a tree, a medicine, a human body – is in conformance with a yogi's powers of will and of visualization.

In man's dream-consciousness, where he has loosened in sleep his clutch on the egoistic limitations that daily hem him round, the omnipotence of his mind has a nightly demonstration. Lo! there in the dream stand the long-dead friends, the remotest continents, the resurrected scenes of his childhood. With that free and unconditioned consciousness, known to all men in the phenomena of dreams, the God-tuned master has forged a never-severed link. Innocent of all personal motives, and employing the creative will bestowed on him by the Creator, a yogi rearranges the light atoms of the universe to satisfy any sincere prayer of a devotee. For this purpose were man and creation made: that he should rise up as master of MAYA, knowing his dominion over the cosmos.

In 1915, shortly after I had entered the Swami Order, I witnessed a vision of violent contrasts. In it the relativity of human consciousness was vividly established; I clearly perceived the unity of the Eternal Light behind the painful dualities of MAYA. The vision descended on me as I sat one morning in my little attic room in Father's Gurpar Road home. For months World War I had been raging in Europe; I reflected sadly on the vast toll of death.

As I closed my eyes in meditation, my consciousness was suddenly transferred to the body of a captain in command of a battleship. The thunder of guns split the air as shots were exchanged between shore batteries and the ship's cannons. A huge shell hit the powder magazine and tore my ship asunder. I jumped into the water, together with the few sailors who had survived the explosion.

Heart pounding, I reached the shore safely. But alas! a stray bullet ended its furious flight in my chest. I fell groaning to the ground. My whole body was paralyzed, yet I was aware of possessing it as one is conscious of a leg gone to sleep.

"At last the mysterious footstep of Death has caught up with me," I thought. With a final sigh, I was about to sink into unconsciousness when lo! I found myself seated in the lotus posture in my Gurpar Road room.

Hysterical tears poured forth as I joyfully stroked and pinched my regained possession – a body free from any bullet hole in the breast. I rocked to and fro, inhaling and exhaling to assure myself that I was alive. Amidst these self-congratulations, again I found my consciousness transferred to the captain's dead body by the gory shore. Utter confusion of mind came upon me.

"Lord," I prayed, "am I dead or alive?"

A dazzling play of light filled the whole horizon. A soft rumbling vibration formed itself into words:

"What has life or death to do with Light? In the image of My Light I have made you. The relativities of life and death belong to the cosmic dream. Behold your dreamless being! Awake, my child, awake!"

As steps in man's awakening, the Lord inspires scientists to discover, at the right time and place, the secrets of His creation. Many modern discoveries help men apprehend the cosmos as a varied expression of one power-light, guided by divine intelligence. The wonders of the motion picture, of radio, of television, of radar, of the photo-electric cell-the all-seeing "electric eye," of atomic energies, are all based on the electromagnetic phenomenon of light.

The motion picture art can portray any miracle. From the impressive visual standpoint, no marvel is barred to trick photography. A man's transparent astral body can be seen rising from his gross physical form, he can walk on the water, resurrect the dead, reverse the natural sequence of developments, and play havoc with time and space. Assembling the light images as he pleases, the photographer achieves optical wonders which a true master produces with actual light rays.

A cinema audience can look up and see that all screen images are appearing through the instrumentality of one imageless beam of light. The colorful universal drama is similarly issuing from the single white light of a Cosmic Source. With inconceivable ingenuity God is staging an entertainment for His human children, making them actors as well as audience in His planetary theater.

As I finished writing this chapter, I sat on my bed in the lotus posture. My room was dimly lit by two shaded lamps. Lifting my gaze, I noticed that the ceiling was dotted with small mustard-colored lights, scintillating and quivering with a radiumlike luster.Myriads of pencilled rays, like sheets of rain, gathered into a transparent shaft and poured silently upon me.

At once my physical body lost its grossness and became metamorphosed into astral texture. I felt a floating sensation as, barely touching the bed, the weightless body shifted slightly and alternately to left and right. I looked around the room; the furniture and walls were as usual, but the little mass of light had so multiplied that the ceiling was invisible. I was wonderstruck.

"This is the cosmic motion picture mechanism." A voice spoke as though from within the light. "Shedding its beam on the white screen of your bed sheets, it is producing the picture of your body. Behold, your form is nothing but light!"

I gazed at my arms and moved them back and forth, yet could not feel their weight. An ecstatic joy overwhelmed me. For a long time I experienced this motion picture of my body in the dimly lighted theater of my own bedroom. Despite the many visions I have had, none was ever more singular. As my illusion of a solid body was completely dissipated, and my realization deepened that the essence of all objects is light, I looked up to the throbbing stream of lifetrons and spoke entreatingly.

"Divine Light, please withdraw this, my humble bodily picture, into Thyself."

This prayer was evidently startling; the beam disappeared. My body resumed its normal weight and sank on the bed; the swarm of dazzling ceiling lights flickered and vanished. My time to leave this earth had apparently not arrived.

31

An Interview with the Sacred Mother

"Reverend Mother, I was baptized in infancy by your prophet-husband. He was the guru of my parents and of my own guru Sri Yukteswarji. Will you therefore give me the privilege of hearing a few incidents in your sacred life?"

I was addressing Srimati Kashi Moni, the life-companion of Lahiri Mahasaya. Finding myself in Benares for a short period, I was fulfilling a long-felt desire to visit the venerable lady. She received me graciously at the old Lahiri homestead in the Garudeswar Mohulla section of Benares.

"Son, you are welcome here. Come upstairs."

Kashi Moni led the way to a very small room where, for a time, she had lived with her husband. I felt honored to witness the shrine in which the peerless master had condescended to play the human drama of matrimony.

"It was years before I came to realize the divine stature of my husband," she began. "One night, in this very room, I had a vivid dream. Glorious angels floated in unimaginable grace above me. So realistic was the sight that I awoke at once; the room was strangely enveloped in dazzling light.

"My husband, in lotus posture, was levitated in the center

of the room, surrounded by angels who were worshiping him with the supplicating dignity of palm-folded hands. Astonished beyond measure, I was convinced that I was still dreaming.

"'Woman,' Lahiri Mahasaya said, 'you are not dreaming. Forsake your sleep forever and forever.' As he slowly descended to the floor, I prostrated myself at his feet.

"'Master,' I cried, 'again and again I bow before you! Will you pardon me for having considered you as my husband? I die with shame to realize that I have remained asleep in ignorance by the side of one who is divinely awakened. From this night, you are no longer my husband, but my guru. Will you accept my insignificant self as your disciple?'

"The master touched me gently. 'Sacred soul, arise. You are accepted.' He motioned toward the angels. 'Please bow in turn to each of these holy saints.'

"When I had finished my humble genuflections, the angelic voices sounded together, like a chorus from an ancient scripture.

"'Consort of the Divine One, thou art blessed. We salute thee.' They bowed at my feet and lo! their refulgent forms vanished. The room darkened.

"My guru asked me to receive initiation into KRIYA YOGA.

"'Of course,' I responded. 'I am sorry not to have had its blessing earlier in my life.'

"'The time was not ripe.' Lahiri Mahasaya smiled consolingly. 'Much of your karma I have silently helped you to work out. Now you are willing and ready.'

"'Penetrate your consciousness through the star into the kingdom of the Infinite.' My guru's voice had a new note, soft like distant music.

"Vision after vision broke as oceanic surf on the shores of my soul. The panoramic spheres finally melted in a sea of bliss. I lost myself in ever-surging blessedness. When I returned hours later to awareness of this world, the master gave me the technique of KRIYA YOGA.

"From that night on, Lahiri Mahasaya never slept in my room again. Nor, thereafter, did he ever sleep. He remained in the front room downstairs, in the company of his disciples both by day and by night."

The illustrious lady fell into silence. And I realized the uniqueness of her relationship with the sublime yogi. I thanked Kashi Moni for sharing with me her wondrous experiences.

On the following day I returned to her home and enjoyed several hours of philosophical discussion with Tincouri and Ducouri Lahiri. These two saintly sons of India's great yogi followed closely in his ideal footsteps.

Lahiri Mahasaya performed two miracles in connection with a woman disciple, Abhoya. She and her husband, a Calcutta lawyer, started one day for Benares to visit the guru. Their carriage was delayed by heavy traffic; they reached the Howrah main station only to hear the Benares train whistling for departure.

Abhoya, near the ticket office, stood quietly.

"Lahiri Mahasaya, I beseech thee to stop the train!" she silently prayed. "I cannot suffer the pangs of delay in waiting another day to see thee."

The wheels of the snorting train continued to move round and round, but there was no onward progress. The engineer and passengers descended to the platform to view the phenomenon. An English railroad guard approached Abhoya and her husband. Contrary to all precedent, he volunteered his services.

"Babu," he said, "give me the money. I will buy your tickets while you get aboard."

As soon as the couple was seated and had received the tickets, the train slowly moved forward. In panic, the engineer and passengers clambered again to their places, knowing neither how the train started, nor why it had stopped in the first place.

Arriving at the home of Lahiri Mahasaya in Benares, Abhoya silently prostrated herself before the master, and tried to touch his feet.

"Compose yourself, Abhoya," he remarked. "How you love to bother me! As if you could not have come here by the next train!"

Abhoya visited Lahiri Mahasaya on another memorable occasion. This time she wanted his intercession, not with a train, but with the stork.

"I pray you to bless me that my ninth child may live," she said. "Eight babies have been born to me; all died soon after birth."

The master smiled sympathetically. "Your coming child will live. Please follow my instructions carefully. The baby, a girl, will be born at night. See that the oil lamp is kept burning until dawn. Do not fall asleep and thus allow the light to become extinguished."

Abhoya's child was a daughter, born at night, exactly as foreseen by the omniscient guru. The mother instructed her nurse to keep the lamp filled with oil. Both women kept the urgent vigil far into the early morning hours, but finally fell asleep. The lamp oil was almost gone; the light flickered feebly.

The bedroom door unlatched and flew open with a violent sound. The startled women awoke. Their astonished eyes beheld the form of Lahiri Mahasaya.

"Abhoya, behold, the light is almost gone!" He pointed to the lamp, which the nurse hastened to refill. As soon as it burned again brightly, the master vanished. The door closed; the latch was affixed without visible agency.

Abhoya's ninth child survived; in 1935, when I made inquiry, she was still living.

Lahiri Mahasaya had a very famous friend, Swami Trailanga, who was reputed to be over three hundred years old. The two yogis often sat together in meditation. Trailanga's fame is so widespread that few Hindus would deny the possibility of truth in any story of his astounding miracles. If Christ returned to earth and walked the streets of New York, displaying his divine powers, it would cause the same excitement that was created by Trailanga decades ago as he passed through the crowded lanes of Benares.

On many occasions the swami was seen to drink, with no ill effect, the most deadly poisons. Thousands of people, including a few who are still living, have seen Trailanga floating on the Ganges. For days together he would sit on top of the water, or remain hidden for very long periods under the waves. A common sight at the Benares bathing GHATS was the swami's motionless body on the blistering stone slabs, wholly exposed to the merciless Indian sun. By these feats Trailanga sought to teach men that a yogi's life does not depend upon oxygen or ordinary conditions and precautions. Whether he were above water or under it, and whether or not his body lay exposed to the fierce solar rays, the master proved that he lived by divine consciousness: death could not touch him.

Trailanga always remained completely nude. The harassed police of Benares came to regard him as a baffling problem child. The natural swami, like the early Adam in the garden of Eden, was utterly unconscious of his nakedness. The police were quite conscious of it, however, and unceremoniously committed him to jail. General embarrassment ensued; the enormous body of Trailanga was soon seen, in its usual entirety, on the prison roof. His cell, still securely locked, offered no clue to his mode of escape.

The great yogi preserved a habitual silence. In spite of his round face and huge, barrel-like stomach, Trailanga ate only occasionally. After weeks without food, he would break his fast with potfuls of clabbered milk offered to him by devotees. A skeptic once determined to expose Trailanga as a charlatan. A large bucket of calcium-lime mixture, used in whitewashing walls, was placed before the swami.

"Master," the materialist said, in mock reverence, "I have brought you some clabbered milk. Please drink it."

Trailanga unhesitatingly drained, to the last drop, the containerful of burning lime. In a few minutes the evildoer fell to the ground in agony.

"Help, swami, help!" he cried. "I am on fire! Forgive my wicked test!"

The great yogi broke his habitual silence. "Scoffer," he said, "you did not realize when you offered me poison that my life is one with your own. Except for my knowledge that God is present in my stomach, as in every atom of creation, the lime would have killed me. Now that you know the divine meaning of boomerang, never again play tricks on anyone."

The well-purged sinner, healed by Trailanga's words, slunk feebly away.

The grace of the Christlike yogi, Trailanga, was once bestowed on my SAJO MAMA (maternal uncle). One morning

Uncle saw the master surrounded by a crowd of devotees at a Benares ghat. He managed to edge his way close to Trailanga, whose feet he touched humbly. Uncle was astonished to find himself instantly freed from a painful chronic disease.

The only known living disciple of the great yogi is a woman, Shankari Mai Jiew. Daughter of one of Trailanga's disciples, she received the swami's training from her early childhood. She lived for forty years in a series of lonely Himalayan caves near Badrinath, Kedarnath, Amarnath, and Pasupatinath. The BRAHMACHARINI (woman ascetic), born in 1826, is now well over the century mark. Not aged in appearance, however, she has retained her black hair, sparkling teeth, and amazing energy. She comes out of her seclusion every few years to attend the periodical MELAS or religious fairs.

32

Rama Is Raised from the Dead

"Now a certain man was sick, named Lazarus.... When Jesus heard that, he said, "This sickness is not unto death, but for the glory of God, that the Son of God might be glorified thereby.""

Sri Yukteswar was expounding the Christian scriptures one sunny morning on the balcony of his Serampore hermitage. Besides a few of Master's other disciples, I was present with a small group of my Ranchi students.

"In this passage Jesus calls himself the Son of God. Though he was truly united with God, his reference here has a deep impersonal significance," my guru explained. "The Son of God is the Christ or Divine Consciousness in man. No MORTAL can glorify God. The only honor that man can pay his Creator is to seek Him; man cannot glorify an Abstraction that he does not know. The 'glory' or nimbus around the head of the saints is a symbolic witness of their CAPACITY to render divine homage."

Sri Yukteswar went on to read the marvelous story of Lazarus' resurrection. At its conclusion Master fell into a long silence, the sacred book open on his knee.

"I too was privileged to behold a similar miracle." My

guru finally spoke with solemn unction. "Lahiri Mahasaya resurrected one of my friends from the dead."

The young lads at my side smiled with keen interest. There was enough of the boy in me, too, to enjoy not only the philosophy but, in particular, any story I could get Sri Yukteswar to relate about his wondrous experiences with his guru.

"My friend Rama and I were inseparable," Master began. "Because he was shy and reclusive, he chose to visit our guru Lahiri Mahasaya only during the hours of midnight and dawn, when the crowd of daytime disciples was absent. As Rama's closest friend, I served as a spiritual vent through which he let out the wealth of his spiritual perceptions."

"Rama was suddenly put to a severe test," Sri Yukteswar continued. "He contracted the disease of Asiatic cholera. As our master never objected to the services of physicians at times of serious illness, two specialists were summoned. Amidst the frantic rush of ministering to the stricken man, I was deeply praying to Lahiri Mahasaya for help. I hurried to his home and sobbed out the story.

"'The doctors are seeing Rama. He will be well.' My guru smiled jovially.

"I returned with a light heart to my friend's bedside, only to find him in a dying state.

"'He cannot last more than one or two hours,' one of the physicians told me with a gesture of despair. Once more I hastened to Lahiri Mahasaya.

"'The doctors are conscientious men. I am sure Rama will be well.' The master dismissed me blithely.

"At Rama's place I found both doctors gone. One had left me a note: 'We have done our best, but his case is hopeless.'

"My friend was indeed the picture of a dying man. I did not understand how Lahiri Mahasaya's words could fail to come true, yet the sight of Rama's rapidly ebbing life kept suggesting to my mind: 'All is over now.' Tossing thus on the seas of faith and apprehensive doubt, I ministered to my friend as best I could. He roused himself to cry out:

"'Yukteswar, run to Master and tell him I am gone. Ask him to bless my body before its last rites.' With these words Rama sighed heavily and gave up the ghost.

"I wept for an hour by his beloved form. Always a lover of quiet, now he had attained the utter stillness of death. Another disciple came in; I asked him to remain in the house until I returned. Half-dazed, I trudged back to my guru.

"'How is Rama now?' Lahiri Mahasaya's face was wreathed in smiles.

"'Sir, you will soon see how he is,' I blurted out emotionally. 'In a few hours you will see his body, before it is carried to the crematory grounds.' I broke down and moaned openly.

"'Yukteswar, control yourself. Sit calmly and meditate.' My guru retired into SAMADHI. The afternoon and night passed in unbroken silence; I struggled unsuccessfully to regain an inner composure.

"At dawn Lahiri Mahasaya glanced at me consolingly. 'I see you are still disturbed. Why didn't you explain yesterday that you expected me to give Rama tangible aid in the form of some medicine?' The master pointed to a cup-shaped lamp containing crude castor oil. 'Fill a little bottle from the lamp; put seven drops into Rama's mouth.'

"'Sir,' I remonstrated, 'he has been dead since yesterday noon. Of what use is the oil now?'

"'Never mind; just do as I ask.' Lahiri Mahasaya's cheerful

mood was incomprehensible; I was still in the unassuaged agony of bereavement. Pouring out a small amount of oil, I departed for Rama's house.

"I found my friend's body rigid in the death-clasp. Paying no attention to his ghastly condition, I opened his lips with my right finger and managed, with my left hand and the help of the cork, to put the oil drop by drop over his clenched teeth.

"As the seventh drop touched his cold lips, Rama shivered violently. His muscles vibrated from head to foot as he sat up wonderingly.

"'I saw Lahiri Mahasaya in a blaze of light,' he cried. 'He shone like the sun. 'Arise; forsake your sleep,' he commanded me. 'Come with Yukteswar to see me.'"

"I could scarcely believe my eyes when Rama dressed himself and was strong enough after that fatal sickness to walk to the home of our guru. There he prostrated himself before Lahiri Mahasaya with tears of gratitude.

"The master was beside himself with mirth. His eyes twinkled at me mischievously.

As Sri Yukteswar finished the awesome story, he motioned me to a blanket seat at his feet.

"Yogananda," he said with unusual gravity, "you have been surrounded from birth by direct disciples of Lahiri Mahasaya. The great master lived his sublime life in partial seclusion, and steadfastly refused to permit his followers to build any organization around his teachings. He made, nevertheless, a significant prediction.

"'About fifty years after my passing,' he said, 'my life will be written because of a deep interest in yoga which the West will manifest. The yogic message will encircle the globe, and aid in establishing that brotherhood of man which results from direct perception of the One Father.'

"My son Yogananda," Sri Yukteswar went on, "you must do your part in spreading that message, and in writing that sacred life."

Fifty years after Lahiri Mahasaya's passing in 1895 culminated in 1945, the year of completion of this present book. I cannot but be struck by the coincidence that the year 1945 has also ushered in a new age – the era of revolutionary atomic energies. All thoughtful minds turn as never before to the urgent problems of peace and brotherhood, lest the continued use of physical force banish all men along with the problems.

Toward realization of the world's highest ideal – peace through brotherhood – may yoga, the science of personal contact with the Divine, spread in time to all men in all lands.

Though India's civilization is ancient above any other, few historians have noted that her feat of national survival is by no means an accident, but a logical incident in the devotion to eternal verities which India has offered through her best men in every generation. India has proved herself not witless against the thousand cunnings of time. Self-realized masters in every century have hallowed her soil; modern Christlike sages, like Lahiri Mahasaya and his disciple Sri Yukteswar, rise up to proclaim that the science of yoga is more vital than any material advances to man's happiness and to a nation's longevity.

Very scanty information about the life of Lahiri Mahasaya and his universal doctrine has ever appeared in print. Nothing but one or two small pamphlets in English has been written on the guru's life. One biography in Bengali, SRI SRI SHYAMA

CHARAN LAHIRI MAHASAYA, appeared in 1941. It was written by my disciple, Swami Satyananda.

It was into a pious Brahmin family of ancient lineage that Lahiri Mahasaya was born on September 30, 1828. His birthplace was the village of Ghurni in the Nadia district near Krishnagar, Bengal. He was the youngest son of Muktakashi, the second wife of the esteemed Gaur Mohan Lahiri. His mother passed away during his childhood.

The boy Lahiri, whose given name was Shyama Charan, spent his early years in the ancestral home at Nadia. The Lahiri estate was destroyed in the winter of 1833, when the nearby Jalangi River changed its course and disappeared into the depths of the Ganges.

Gaur Mohan Lahiri and his family left Nadia and became residents of Benares. He conducted his household along the lines of Vedic discipline, with regular observance of ceremonial worship, acts of charity, and scriptural study. Just and open-minded, however, he did not ignore the beneficial current of modern ideas.

The boy Lahiri took lessons in Hindi and Urdu in Benares study-groups. He attended a school conducted by Joy Narayan Ghosal, receiving instruction in Sanskrit, Bengali, French, and English. Applying himself to a close study of the VEDAS, the young yogi listened eagerly to scriptural discussions by learned Brahmins, including a Marhatta pundit named Nag-Bhatta.

In 1846, Shyama Charan Lahiri was married to Srimati Kashi Moni, daughter of Sri Debnarayan Sanyal. A model Indian housewife, Kashi Moni cheerfully carried on her home duties and the traditional householder's obligation to serve guests and the poor. Two saintly sons, Tincouri and Ducouri, blessed the union.

At the age of 23, in 1851, Lahiri Mahasaya took the post of accountant in the Military Engineering Department of the English government. He received many promotions during the time of his service. As the offices of the Army Department were shifted, Lahiri Mahasaya was transferred to Gazipur, Mirjapur, Danapur, Naini Tal, Benares, and other localities.

It was in his thirty-third year that Lahiri Mahasaya saw fulfillment of the purpose for which he had been reincarnated on earth. He met his great guru, Babaji, near Ranikhet, and was initiated by him into KRIYA YOGA.

This auspicious event did not happen to him alone; it was a fortunate moment for all the human race, many of whom were later privileged to receive the soul-awakening gift of KRIYA. The lost, or long-vanished, highest art of yoga was again being brought to light.

33

Babaji, the Yogi-Christ of Modern India

The northern Himalayan crags near Badrinarayan are still blessed by the living presence of Babaji, guru of Lahiri Mahasaya. The secluded master has retained his physical form for centuries, perhaps for millenniums. The deathless Babaji is an AVATARA. This Sanskrit word means "descent"; its roots are AVA, "down," and TRI, "to pass." In the Hindu scriptures, AVATARA signifies the descent of Divinity into flesh.

The UPANISHADS have minutely classified every stage of spiritual advancement. A SIDDHA ("perfected being") has progressed from the state of a JIVANMUKTA ("freed while living") to that of a PARAMUKTA ("supremely free"- full power over death); the latter has completely escaped from the mayic thralldom and its reincarnational round. The PARAMUKTA therefore seldom returns to a physical body; if he does, he is an avatar, a divinely appointed medium of supernal blessings on the world.

Krishna, Rama, Buddha, and Patanjali were among the ancient Indian avatars. A considerable poetic literature in Tamil has grown up around Agastya, a South Indian avatar.

He worked many miracles during the centuries preceding and following the Christian era, and is credited with retaining his physical form even to this day.

Babaji's mission in India has been to assist prophets in carrying out their special dispensations. He thus qualifies for the scriptural classification of MAHAVATAR (Great Avatar). He has stated that he gave yoga initiation to Shankara, ancient founder of the Swami Order, and to Kabir, famous medieval saint. His chief nineteenth-century disciple was, as we know, Lahiri Mahasaya, revivalist of the lost KRIYA art.

The MAHAVATAR is in constant communion with Christ; together they send out vibrations of redemption, and have planned the spiritual technique of salvation for this age. The work of these two fully-illumined masters-one with the body, and one without it-is to inspire the nations to forsake suicidal wars, race hatreds, religious sectarianism, and the boomerang-evils of materialism. Babaji is well aware of the trend of modern times, especially of the influence and complexities of Western civilization, and realizes the necessity of spreading the self-liberations of yoga equally in the West and in the East.

Great prophets like Christ and Krishna come to earth for a specific and spectacular purpose; they depart as soon as it is accomplished. Other avatars, like Babaji, undertake work which is concerned more with the slow evolutionary progress of man during the centuries than with any one outstanding event of history. Such masters always veil themselves from the gross public gaze, and have the power to become invisible at will. For these reasons, and because they generally instruct their disciples to maintain silence about them, a number of towering spiritual figures remain world-unknown. I give in these pages on Babaji merely a hint of his life-only a few facts which he deems it fit and helpful to be publicly imparted.

No limiting facts about Babaji's family or birthplace, dear to the annalist's heart, have ever been discovered. His speech is generally in Hindi, but he converses easily in any language. He has adopted the simple name of Babaji (revered father); other titles of respect given him by Lahiri Mahasaya's disciples are Mahamuni Babaji Maharaj (supreme ecstatic saint), Maha Yogi (greatest of yogis), Trambak Baba and Shiva Baba (titles of avatars of Shiva). Does it matter that we know not the patronymic of an earth-released master?

The deathless guru bears no marks of age on his body; he appears to be no more than a youth of twenty-five. Fair-skinned, of medium build and height, Babaji's beautiful, strong body radiates a perceptible glow. His eyes are dark, calm, and tender; his long, lustrous hair is copper-colored. A very strange fact is that Babaji bears an extraordinarily exact resemblance to his disciple Lahiri Mahasaya..

Swami Kebalananda, my saintly Sanskrit tutor, spent some time with Babaji in the Himalayas.

"The peerless master moves with his group from place to place in the mountains," Kebalananda told me. "His small band contains two highly advanced American disciples. After Babaji has been in one locality for some time, he says: 'DERA DANDA UTHAO.' His words are the signal for moving with his group instantaneously to another place.

"Babaji can be seen or recognized by others only when he so desires. As his undecaying body requires no food, the master seldom eats. As a social courtesy to visiting disciples, he occasionally accepts fruits, or rice cooked in milk and clarified butter.

"Two amazing incidents of Babaji's life are known to me," Kebalananda went on. "His disciples were sitting one night around a huge fire which was blazing for a sacred Vedic ceremony. The master suddenly seized a burning log and lightly struck the bare shoulder of a chela who was close to the fire.

"'Sir, how cruel!' Lahiri Mahasaya, who was present, made this remonstrance.

"'Would you rather have seen him burned to ashes before your eyes, according to the decree of his past karma?'

"With these words Babaji placed his healing hand on the chela's disfigured shoulder. 'I have freed you tonight from painful death. The karmic law has been satisfied through your slight suffering by fire.'

"On another occasion Babaji's sacred circle was disturbed by the arrival of a stranger. He had climbed with astonishing skill to the nearly inaccessible ledge near the camp of the master.

"'Sir, you must be the great Babaji.' The man's face was lit with inexpressible reverence. 'For months I have pursued a ceaseless search for you among these forbidding crags. I implore you to accept me as a disciple.'

"When the great guru made no response, the man pointed to the rocky chasm at his feet.

"'If you refuse me, I will jump from this mountain. Life has no further value if I cannot win your guidance to the Divine.'

"'Jump then,' Babaji said unemotionally. 'I cannot accept you in your present state of development.'

"The man immediately hurled himself over the cliff. Babaji instructed the shocked disciples to fetch the stranger's body. When they returned with the mangled form, the master placed his divine hand on the dead man. Lo! he opened his eyes and prostrated himself humbly before the omnipotent one.

"'You are now ready for discipleship.' Babaji beamed lovingly on his resurrected chela. "You have courageously passed a difficult test. Death shall not touch you again; now you are one of our immortal flock."

For Babaji, there is no relativity of past, present, future; from the beginning he has known all phases of his life. Yet, accommodating himself to the limited understanding of men, he has played many acts of his divine life in the presence of one or more witnesses. Thus it came about that a disciple of Lahiri Mahasaya was present when Babaji deemed the time to be ripe for him to proclaim the possibility of bodily immortality. He uttered this promise before Ram Gopal Muzumdar, that it might finally become known for the inspiration of other seeking hearts. During my visit at Ranbajpur with Ram Gopal, "the sleepless saint," he related the wondrous story of his first meeting with Babaji.

"I sometimes left my isolated cave to sit at Lahiri Mahasaya's feet in Benares," Ram Gopal told me. "One midnight as I was silently meditating in a group of his disciples, the master made a surprising request.

"'Ram Gopal,' he said, 'go at once to the Dasasamedh bathing GHAT.'

"I soon reached the secluded spot. The night was bright with moonlight and the glittering stars. After I had sat in patient silence for awhile, my attention was drawn to a huge stone slab near my feet. It rose gradually, revealing an underground cave. As the stone remained balanced in some unknown manner, the draped form of a young and surpassingly lovely woman was levitated from the cave high into the air. Surrounded by a soft halo, she slowly descended in front of me and stood motionless, steeped in an inner state of ecstasy. She finally stirred, and spoke gently.

"'I am Mataji, the sister of Babaji. I have asked him and also Lahiri Mahasaya to come to my cave tonight to discuss a matter of great importance.'

"A nebulous light was rapidly floating over the Ganges; the strange luminescence was reflected in the opaque waters. It approached nearer and nearer until, with a blinding flash, it appeared by the side of Mataji and condensed itself instantly into the human form of Lahiri Mahasaya. He bowed humbly at the feet of the woman saint.

"Before I had recovered from my bewilderment, I was further wonderstruck to behold a circling mass of mystical light traveling in the sky. Descending swiftly, the flaming whirlpool neared our group and materialized itself into the body of a beautiful youth who, I understood at once, was Babaji.

"Lahiri Mahasaya, Mataji, and myself knelt at the guru's feet. An ethereal sensation of beatific glory thrilled every fiber of my being as I touched his divine flesh.

"'Blessed sister,' Babaji said, 'I am intending to shed my form and plunge into the Infinite Current.'

"'I have already glimpsed your plan, beloved master. I wanted to discuss it with you tonight. Why should you leave your body?' The glorious woman looked at him beseechingly.

"'What is the difference if I wear a visible or invisible wave on the ocean of my Spirit?'

"Mataji replied with a quaint flash of wit. 'Deathless guru, if it makes no difference, then please do not ever relinquish your form.'

"'Be it so,' Babaji said solemnly. 'I will never leave my physical body. It will always remain visible to at least a small number of people on this earth. The Lord has spoken His own wish through your lips.'

"As I listened in awe to the conversation between these exalted beings, the great guru turned to me with a benign gesture.

"'Fear not, Ram Gopal,' he said, 'you are blessed to be a witness at the scene of this immortal promise.'

"As the sweet melody of Babaji's voice faded away, his form and that of Lahiri Mahasaya slowly levitated and moved backward over the Ganges. An aureole of dazzling light templed their bodies as they vanished into the night sky. Mataji's form floated to the cave and descended; the stone slab closed of itself, as if working on an invisible leverage.

"Infinitely inspired, I wended my way back to Lahiri Mahasaya's place. As I bowed before him in the early dawn, my guru smiled at me understandingly.

"'I am happy for you, Ram Gopal,' he said. 'The desire of meeting Babaji and Mataji, which you have often expressed to me, has found at last a sacred fulfillment.'

"My fellow disciples informed me that Lahiri Mahasaya had not moved from his dais since early the preceding evening.

"Lahiri Mahasaya later explained to me many metaphysical points concerning the hidden divine plan for this earth," Ram Gopal concluded. "Babaji has been chosen by God to remain in his body for the duration of this particular world cycle. Ages shall come and go--still the deathless master, beholding the drama of the centuries, shall be present on this stage terrestrial."

34

Materializing a Palace in the Himalayas

"Babaji's first meeting with Lahiri Mahasaya is an enthralling story, and one of the few which gives us a detailed glimpse of the deathless guru."

These words were Swami Kebalananda's preamble to a wondrous tale. The first time he recounted it I was literally spellbound. On many other occasions I coaxed my gentle Sanskrit tutor to repeat the story, which was later told me in substantially the same words by Sri Yukteswar. Both these Lahiri Mahasaya disciples had heard the awesome tale direct from the lips of their guru.

"My first meeting with Babaji took place in my thirty-third year," Lahiri Mahasaya had said. "In the autumn of 1861 I was stationed in Danapur as a government accountant in the Military Engineering Department. One morning the office manager summoned me.

"'Lahiri,' he said, 'a telegram has just come from our main office. You are to be transferred to Ranikhet, where an army post is now being established.'

"With one servant, I set out on the 500-mile trip. Traveling by horse and buggy, we arrived in thirty days at the Himalayan site of Ranikhet.

"My office duties were not onerous; I was able to spend many hours roaming in the magnificent hills. A rumor reached me that great saints blessed the region with their presence; I felt a strong desire to see them. During a ramble one early afternoon, I was astounded to hear a distant voice calling my name. I continued my vigorous upward climb on Drongiri Mountain. A slight uneasiness beset me at the hought that I might not be able to retrace my steps before darkness had descended over the jungle.

"I finally reached a small clearing whose sides were dotted with caves. On one of the rocky ledges stood a smiling young man, extending his hand in welcome. I noticed with astonishment that, except for his copper-colored hair, he bore a remarkable resemblance to myself.

"'Lahiri, you have come!' The saint addressed me affectionately in Hindi. 'Rest here in this cave. It was I who called you.'

"I entered a neat little grotto which contained several woolen blankets and a few KAMANDULUS (begging bowls).

"'Lahiri, do you remember that seat?' The yogi pointed to a folded blanket in one corner.

"'No, sir.' Somewhat dazed at the strangeness of my adventure, I added, 'I must leave now, before nightfall. I have business in the morning at my office.'

"The mysterious saint replied in English, 'The office was brought for you, and not you for the office.'

"I was dumbfounded that this forest ascetic should not only speak English but also paraphrase the words of Christ.

"'I see my telegram took effect.' The yogi's remark was incomprehensible to me; I inquired his meaning.

"'I refer to the telegram that summoned you to these isolated parts. It was I who silently suggested to the mind of your superior officer that you be transferred to Ranikhet. When one feels his unity with mankind, all minds become transmitting stations through which he can work at will.' He added gently, 'Lahiri, surely this cave seems familiar to you?'

"As I maintained a bewildered silence, the saint approached and struck me gently on the forehead. At his magnetic touch, a wondrous current swept through my brain, releasing the sweet seed-memories of my previous life.

"'I remember!' My voice was half-choked with joyous sobs. 'You are my guru Babaji, who has belonged to me always! Scenes of the past arise vividly in my mind; here in this cave I spent many years of my last incarnation!' As ineffable recollections overwhelmed me, I tearfully embraced my master's feet.

"'For more than three decades I have waited for you here – waited for you to return to me!' Babaji's voice rang with celestial love. 'You slipped away and vanished into the tumultuous waves of the life beyond death. The magic wand of your karma touched you, and you were gone! Though you lost sight of me, never did I lose sight of you! I pursued you over the luminescent astral sea where the glorious angels sail. Through gloom, storm, upheaval, and light I followed you, like a mother bird guarding her young. Now you are with me! Lo, here is your cave, loved of yore! I have kept it ever clean and ready for you.'

"'My guru, what can I say?' I murmured brokenly. 'Where has one ever heard of such deathless love?' I gazed long and ecstatically on my eternal treasure, my guru in life and death.

"'Lahiri, you need purification. Drink the oil in this

bowl and lie down by the river.' Babaji's practical wisdom, I reflected with a quick, reminiscent smile, was ever to the fore.

"I obeyed his directions. Though the icy Himalayan night was descending, a comforting warmth, an inner radiation, began to pulsate in every cell of my body. I marveled. Was the unknown oil endued with a cosmical heat?

"Bitter winds whipped around me in the darkness, shrieking a fierce challenge. The chill wavelets of the Gogash River lapped now and then over my body, outstretched on the rocky bank. Tigers howled near-by, but my heart was free of fear; the radiant force newly generated within me conveyed an assurance of unassailable protection. Several hours passed swiftly; faded memories of another life wove themselves into the present brilliant pattern of reunion with my divine guru.

"My solitary musings were interrupted by the sound of approaching footsteps. In the darkness, a man's hand gently helped me to my feet, and gave me some dry clothing.

"'Come, brother,' my companion said. 'The master awaits you.'

"He led the way through the forest. The somber night was suddenly lit by a steady luminosity in the distance.

"'Can that be the sunrise?' I inquired. 'Surely the whole night has not passed?'

"'The hour is midnight.' My guide laughed softly. 'Yonder light is the glow of a golden palace, materialized here tonight by the peerless Babaji. In the dim past, you once expressed a desire to enjoy the beauties of a palace. Our master is now satisfying your wish, thus freeing you from the bonds of karma.' He added, 'The magnificent palace will be the scene of your initiation tonight into KRIYA YOGA. All your brothers here join in a paean of welcome, rejoicing at the end of your long exile. Behold!'

"A vast palace of dazzling gold stood before us. I followed my companion into a spacious reception hall. The odor of incense and of roses wafted through the air; dim lamps shed a multicolored glow. Small groups of devotees, some fair, some dark-skinned, chanted musically, or sat in the meditative posture, immersed in an inner peace. A vibrant joy pervaded the atmosphere.

"'Feast your eyes; enjoy the artistic splendors of this palace, for it has been brought into being solely in your honor.' My guide smiled sympathetically as I uttered a few ejaculations of wonderment.

"'Brother,' I said, 'the beauty of this structure surpasses the bounds of human imagination. Please tell me the mystery of its origin.'

"'I will gladly enlighten you.' My companion's dark eyes sparkled with wisdom. 'In reality there is nothing inexplicable about this materialization. The whole cosmos is a materialized thought of the Creator. This heavy, earthly clod, floating in space, is a dream of God. He made all things out of His consciousness, even as man in his dream consciousness reproduces and vivifies a creation with its creatures.

"'God first created the earth as an idea. Then He quickened it; energy atoms came into being. He coordinated the atoms into this solid sphere. All its molecules are held together by the will of God. When He withdraws His will, the earth again will disintegrate into energy. Energy will dissolve into consciousness; the earth-idea will disappear from objectivity.

"'The substance of a dream is held in materialization by the subconscious thought of the dreamer. When that cohesive thought is withdrawn in wakefulness, the dream and its elements dissolve. A man closes his eyes and erects a dream-creation which, on awakening, he effortlessly dematerializes. He follows the divine archetypal pattern. Similarly, when he awakens in cosmic consciousness, he will effortlessly dematerialize the illusions of the cosmic dream.

"'Being one with the infinite all-accomplishing Will, Babaji can summon the elemental atoms to combine and manifest themselves in any form. This golden palace, instantaneously created, is real, ven as this earth is real. Babaji created this palatial mansion out of his mind and is holding its atoms together by the power of his will, even as God created this earth and is maintaining it intact.' He added, 'When this structure has served its purpose, Babaji will dematerialize it.'

"My stately companion led me through ornate arches and corridors into a series of chambers richly furnished in the style of an emperor's palace. We entered an immense hall. In the center stood a golden throne, encrusted with jewels shedding a dazzling medley of colors. There, in lotus posture, sat the supreme Babaji. I knelt on the shining floor at his feet.

"'Lahiri, are you still feasting on your dream desires for a golden palace?' My guru's eyes were twinkling like his own sapphires. 'Wake! All your earthly thirsts are about to be quenched forever.' He murmured some mystic words of blessing. 'My son, arise. Receive your initiation into the kingdom of God through KRIYA YOGA.'

"Babaji stretched out his hand; a HOMA (sacrificial) fire appeared, surrounded by fruits and flowers. I received the liberating yogic technique before this flaming altar.

"The rites were completed in the early dawn. I felt no need for sleep in my ecstatic state, and wandered around the palace, filled on all sides with treasures and priceless OBJETS D'ART.

"'Lahiri, you are hungry.' Babaji added, 'Close your eyes.'

"When I reopened them, the enchanting palace and its picturesque gardens had disappeared. My own body and the forms of Babaji and the cluster of chelas were all now seated on the bare ground at the exact site of the vanished palace, not far from the sunlit entrances of the rocky grottos. I recalled that my guide had remarked that the palace would be dematerialized, its captive atoms released into the thought-essence from which it had sprung. Although stunned, I looked trustingly at my guru. I knew not what to expect next on this day of miracles.

"'The purpose for which the palace was created has now been served,' Babaji explained. He lifted an earthen vessel from the ground. 'Put your hand there and receive whatever food you desire.'

"'Beloved guru, last night you demonstrated for me the link of beauty in heaven and earth!' I smiled at memories of the vanished palace; surely no simple yogi had ever received initiation into the august mysteries of Spirit amidst surroundings of more impressive luxury! I gazed tranquilly at the stark contrast of the present scene. The gaunt ground, the skyey roof, the caves offering primitive shelter-all seemed a gracious natural setting for the seraphic saints around me.

"I sat that afternoon on my blanket, hallowed by associations of past-life realizations. My divine guru approached and passed his hand over my head. I entered the NIRBIKALPA SAMADHI state, remaining unbrokenly in its bliss for seven days. Crossing the successive strata of self-knowledge, I penetrated the deathless realms of reality. All delusive limitations dropped away; my soul was fully established on the eternal altar of the Cosmic Spirit. On the eighth day I fell at my guru's feet and implored him to keep me always near him in this sacred wilderness.

"'My son,' Babaji said, embracing me, 'your role in this incarnation must be played on an outward stage. Prenatally blessed by many lives of lonely meditation, you must now mingle in the world of men.

"'A deep purpose underlay the fact that you did not meet me this time until you were already a married man, with modest business responsibilities. You must put aside your thoughts of joining our secret band in the Himalayas; your life lies in the crowded marts, serving as an example of the ideal yogi-householder.'"

"How remote seemed my family, the office, the world, as I listened to my guru in the high Himalayan solitudes. Yet adamantine truth rang in his words; I submissively agreed to leave this blessed haven of peace. Babaji instructed me in the ancient rigid rules which govern the transmission of the yogic art from guru to disciple.

"'Bestow the KRIYA key only on qualified chelas,' Babaji said. 'He who vows to sacrifice all in the quest of the Divine is fit to unravel the final mysteries of life through the science of meditation.'

"'Angelic guru, as you have already favored mankind by resurrecting the lost KRIYA art, will you not increase that benefit by relaxing the strict requirements for discipleship?' I gazed beseechingly at Babaji. 'I pray that you permit me to communicate KRIYA to all seekers, even though at first they cannot vow themselves to complete inner renunciation. The tortured men and women of the world, pursued by the threefold suffering, need special encouragement. They may never attempt the road to freedom if KRIYA initiation be withheld from them.'

"'Be it so. The divine wish has been expressed through

you.' With these simple words, the merciful guru banished the rigorous safeguards that for ages had hidden KRIYA from the world. 'Give KRIYA freely to all who humbly ask for help.'

"After a silence, Babaji added, 'Repeat to each of your disciples this majestic promise from the BHAGAVAD GITA: "SWALPAMASYA DHARMASYA, TRAYATA MAHATO BHOYAT"--"Even a little bit of the practice of this religion will save you from dire fears and colossal sufferings."'

"As I knelt the next morning at my guru's feet for his farewell blessing, he sensed my deep reluctance to leave him.

"'There is no separation for us, my beloved child.' He touched my shoulder affectionately. 'Wherever you are, whenever you call me, I shall be with you instantly.'

"Consoled by his wondrous promise, and rich with the newly found gold of God-wisdom, I wended my way down the mountain. At the office I was welcomed by my fellow employees, who for ten days had thought me lost in the Himalayan jungles. A letter soon arrived from the head office.

"'Lahiri should return to the Danapur office,' it read. 'His transfer to Ranikhet occurred by error. Another man should have been sent to assume the Ranikhet duties.'

I smiled, reflecting on the hidden crosscurrents in the events which had led me to this furthermost spot of India.

35

The Christlike Life of Lahiri Mahasaya

"Thus it becometh us to fulfill all righteousness." In these words to John the Baptist, and in asking John to baptize him, Jesus was acknowledging the divine rights of his guru.

From a reverent study of the Bible from an Oriental viewpoint, and from intuitional perception, I am convinced that John the Baptist was, in past lives, the guru of Christ. There are numerous passages in the Bible which infer that John and Jesus in their last incarnations were, respectively, Elijah and his disciple Elisha.

The very end of the Old Testament is a prediction of the reincarnation of Elijah and Elisha: "Behold, I will send you Elijah the prophet before the coming of the great and dreadful day of the Lord." Thus John (Elijah), sent "before the coming . . . of the Lord," was born slightly earlier to serve as a herald for Christ. An angel appeared to Zacharias the father to testify that his coming son John would be no other than Elijah.

The roles became reversed, because Elijah-John was no longer needed to be the ostensible guru of Elisha-Jesus, now perfected in divine realization.

When Christ was transfigured on the mountain it was his

guru Elias, with Moses, whom he saw. Again, in his hour of extremity on the cross, Jesus cried out the divine name: "ELI, ELI, LAMA SABACHTHANI? that is to say, My God, my God, why hast thou forsaken me? Some of them that stood there, when they heard that, said, This man calleth for Elias. . . . Let us see whether Elias will come to save him."

The eternal bond of guru and disciple that existed between John and Jesus was present also for Babaji and Lahiri Mahasaya. With tender solicitude the deathless guru swam the Lethean waters that swirled between the last two lives of his chela, and guided the successive steps taken by the child and then by the man Lahiri Mahasaya. It was not until the disciple had reached his thirty-third year that Babaji deemed the time to be ripe to openly reestablish the never-severed link. Then, after their brief meeting near Ranikhet, the selfless master banished his dearly-beloved disciple from the little mountain group, releasing him for an outward world mission. "My son, I shall come whenever you need me." What mortal lover can bestow that infinite promise?

Unknown to society in general, a great spiritual renaissance began to flow from a remote corner of Benares. Just as the fragrance of flowers cannot be suppressed, so Lahiri Mahasaya, quietly living as an ideal householder, could not hide his innate glory. Slowly, from every part of India, the devotee-bees sought the divine nectar of the liberated master.

The English office superintendent was one of the first to notice a strange transcendental change in his employee, whom he endearingly called "Ecstatic Babu."

"Sir, you seem sad. What is the trouble?" Lahiri Mahasaya made this sympathetic inquiry one morning to his employer.

"My wife in England is critically ill. I am torn by anxiety."

"I shall get you some word about her." Lahiri Mahasaya left the room and sat for a short time in a secluded spot. On his return he smiled consolingly.

"Your wife is improving; she is now writing you a letter." The omniscient yogi quoted some parts of the missive.

"Ecstatic Babu, I already know that you are no ordinary man. Yet I am unable to believe that, at will, you can banish time and space!"

The promised letter finally arrived. The astounded superintendent found that it contained not only the good news of his wife's recovery, but also the same phrases which, weeks earlier, Lahiri Mahasaya had repeated.

The wife came to India some months later. She visited the office, where Lahiri Mahasaya was quietly sitting at his desk. The woman approached him reverently.

"Sir," she said, "it was your form, haloed in glorious light, that I beheld months ago by my sickbed in London. At that moment I was completely healed! Soon after, I was able to undertake the long ocean voyage to India."

Day after day, one or two devotees besought the sublime guru for KRIYA initiation. In addition to these spiritual duties, and to those of his business and family life, the great master took an enthusiastic interest in education.

Though ensconced in the seat of the Supreme One, Lahiri Mahasaya showed reverence to all men, irrespective of their differing merits. When his devotees saluted him, he bowed in turn to them. With a childlike humility, the master often touched the feet of others, but seldom allowed them to pay him similar honor, even though such obeisance toward the guru is an ancient Oriental custom.

A significant feature of Lahiri Mahasaya's life was his gift of

KRIYA initiation to those of every faith. Not Hindus only, but Moslems and Christians were among his foremost disciples. One of his highly advanced chelas was Abdul Gufoor Khan, a Mohammedan. It shows great courage on the part of Lahiri Mahasaya that, although a high-caste Brahmin, he tried his utmost to dissolve the rigid caste bigotry of his time.

The great guru encouraged his various students to adhere to the good traditional discipline of their own faith. Stressing the all-inclusive nature of KRIYA as a practical technique of liberation, Lahiri Mahasaya then gave his chelas liberty to express their lives in conformance with environment and up bringing.

With wise discernment the guru guided his followers into the paths of BHAKTI (devotion), KARMA (action), JNANA (wisdom), or RAJA (royal or complete) YOGAS, according to each man's natural tendencies. The master, who was slow to give his permission to devotees wishing to enter the formal path of monkhood, always cautioned them to first reflect well on the austerities of the monastic life.

The great guru taught his disciples to avoid theoretical discussion of the scriptures. "He only is wise who devotes himself to realizing, not reading only, the ancient revelations," he said. "Solve all your problems through meditation. Exchange unprofitable religious speculations for actual God-contact. Clear your mind of dogmatic theological debris; let in the fresh, healing waters of direct perception. Attune yourself to the active inner Guidance; the Divine Voice has the answer to every dilemma of life. Though man's ingenuity for getting himself into trouble appears to be endless, the Infinite Succor is no less resourceful."

The distant disciples of Lahiri Mahasaya were often made

aware of his enfolding presence. "I am ever with those who practice KRIYA," he said consolingly to chelas who could not remain near him. "I will guide you to the Cosmic Home through your enlarging perceptions."

Swami Satyananda was told by a devotee that, unable to go to Benares, the man had nevertheless received precise KRIYA initiation in a dream. Lahiri Mahasaya had appeared to instruct the chela in answer to his prayers.

If a disciple neglected any of his worldly obligations, the master would gently correct and discipline him.

Lahiri Mahasaya carefully graded KRIYA into four progressive initiations. He bestowed the three higher techniques only after the devotee had manifested definite spiritual progress. One day a certain chela, convinced that his worth was not being duly evaluated, gave voice to his discontent.

"Master," he said, "surely I am ready now for the second initiation."

At this moment the door opened to admit a humble disciple, Brinda Bhagat. He was a Benares postman.

"Brinda, sit by me here." The great guru smiled at him affectionately. "Tell me, are you ready for the second technique of KRIYA?"

The little postman folded his hands in supplication. "Gurudeva," he said in alarm, "no more initiations, please! How can I assimilate any higher teachings? I have come today to ask your blessings, because the first divine KRIYA has filled me with such intoxication that I cannot deliver my letters!"

"Already Brinda swims in the sea of Spirit." At these words from Lahiri Mahasaya, his other disciple hung his head.

"Master," he said, "I see I have been a poor workman, finding fault with my tools."

The postman, who was an uneducated man, later developed his insight through KRIYA to such an extent that scholars occasionally sought his interpretation on involved scriptural points. Innocent alike of sin and syntax, little Brinda won renown in the domain of learned pundits.

Among many saints who received KRIYA from Lahiri Mahasaya may be mentioned the illustrious Swami Vhaskarananda Saraswati of Benares, and the Deogarh ascetic of high stature, Balananda Brahmachari. For a time Lahiri Mahasaya served as private tutor to the son of Maharaja Iswari Narayan Sinha Bahadur of Benares. Recognizing the master's spiritual attainment, the maharaja, as well as his son, sought KRIYA initiation, as did the Maharaja Jotindra Mohan Thakur.

Although the great master did not adopt the system of preaching through the modern medium of an organization, or through the printing press, he knew that the power of his message would rise like a resistless flood, inundating by its own force the banks of human minds. The changed and purified lives of devotees were the simple guarantees of the deathless vitality of KRIYA.

In 1886, twenty-five years after his Ranikhet initiation, Lahiri Mahasaya was retired on a pension. With his availability in the daytime, disciples sought him out in ever-increasing numbers. The great guru now sat in silence most of the time, locked in the tranquil lotus posture. He seldom left his little parlor, even for a walk or to visit other parts of the house. A quiet stream of chelas arrived, almost ceaselessly, for a DARSHAN (holy sight) of the guru.

To the awe of all beholders, Lahiri Mahasaya's habitual physiological state exhibited the superhuman features of breathlessness, sleeplessness, cessation of pulse and heartbeat, calm eyes unblinking for hours, and a profound aura of peace. No visitors departed without upliftment of spirit; all knew they had received the silent blessing of a true man of God.

The master now permitted his disciple, Panchanon Bhattacharya, to open an "Arya Mission Institution" in Calcutta. Here the saintly disciple spread the message of KRIYA YOGA, and prepared for public benefit certain yogic herbal medicines.

The Arya Mission Institution undertook the publication of many of the guru's scriptural commentaries. Like Jesus and other great prophets, Lahiri Mahasaya himself wrote no books, but his penetrating interpretations were recorded and arranged by various disciples. Some of these voluntary amanuenses were more discerning than others in correctly conveying the profound insight of the guru; yet, on the whole, their efforts were successful. Through their zeal, the world possesses unparalleled commentaries by Lahiri Mahasaya on twenty-six ancient scriptures.

Sri Ananda Mohan Lahiri, a grandson of the master, has written an interesting booklet on KRIYA. "The text of the BHAGAVAD GITA is a part of the great epic, the MAHABHARATA, which possesses several knot-points (VYAS-KUTAS)," Sri Ananda wrote. "Keep those knot-points unquestioned, and we find nothing but mythical stories of a peculiar and easily-misunderstood type. Keep those knot-points unexplained, and we have lost a science which the East has preserved with superhuman patience after a quest of thousands of years of experiment. It was the commentaries of Lahiri Mahasaya which brought to light, clear of allegories, the very science of religion that had been so cleverly put out of sight in the riddle of scriptural letters and imagery. No longer a mere unintelligible jugglery of words, the otherwise unmeaning formulas of Vedic worship have been proved by the master to be full of scientific significance. . . .

"Our eagerness for worldly activity kills in us the sense of spiritual awe. We cannot comprehend the Great Life behind all names and forms, just because science brings home to us how we can use the powers of nature; this familiarity has bred a contempt for her ultimate secrets. Our relation with nature is one of practical business. We tease her, so to speak, to know how she can be used to serve our purposes; we make use of her energies, whose Source yet remains unknown. In science our relation with nature is one that exists between a man and his servant, or in a philosophical sense she is like a captive in the witness box. We cross-examine her, challenge her, and minutely weigh her evidence in human scales which cannot measure her hidden values. On the other hand, when the self is in communion with a higher power, nature automatically obeys, without stress or strain, the will of man. This effortless command over nature is called 'miraculous' by the uncomprehending materialist.

"The life of Lahiri Mahasaya set an example which changed the erroneous notion that yoga is a mysterious practice. Every man may find a way through KRIYA to understand his proper relation with nature, and to feel spiritual reverence for all phenomena, whether mystical or of everyday occurrence, in spite of the matter-of-factness of physical science. We must bear in mind that what was mystical a thousand years ago is no longer so, and what is mysterious now may become lawfully intelligible a hundred years hence. It is the Infinite, the Ocean of Power, that is at the back of all manifestations.

"The law of KRIYA YOGA is eternal. It is true like mathematics; like the simple rules of addition and subtraction, the law of KRIYA can never be destroyed. Burn to ashes all the books on mathematics, the logically-minded will always rediscover such truths; destroy all the sacred books on yoga, its fundamental laws will come out whenever there appears a true yogi who comprises within himself pure devotion and consequently pure knowledge."

Just as Babaji is among the greatest of avatars, a MAHAVATAR, and Sri Yukteswar a JNANAVATAR or Incarnation of Wisdom, so Lahiri Mahasaya may justly be called YOGAVATAR, or Incarnation of Yoga. By the standards of both qualitative and quantitative good, he elevated the spiritual level of society. In his power to raise his close disciples to Christlike stature and in his wide dissemination of truth among the masses, Lahiri Mahasaya ranks among the saviors of mankind.

His uniqueness as a prophet lies in his practical stress on a definite method, KRIYA, opening for the first time the doors of yoga freedom to all men. Apart from the miracles of his own life, surely the YOGAVATAR reached the zenith of all wonders in reducing the ancient complexities of yoga to an effective simplicity not beyond the ordinary grasp.

Through use of the KRIYA key, persons who cannot bring themselves to believe in the divinity of any man will behold at last the full divinity of their own selves.

36

Babaji's Interest in the West

"Master, did you ever meet Babaji?"

It was a calm summer night in Serampore; the large stars of the tropics gleamed over our heads as I sat by Sri Yukteswar's side on the second-story balcony of the hermitage.

"Yes." Master smiled at my direct question; his eyes lit with reverence. "Three times I have been blessed by the sight of the deathless guru. Our first meeting was in Allahabad at a KUMBHA MELA.

"I was not a swami at the time I met Babaji," Sri Yukteswar went on. "But I had already received KRIYA initiation from Lahiri Mahasaya. He encouraged me to attend the MELA which was convening in January, 1894 at Allahabad. It was my first experience of a KUMBHA; I felt slightly dazed by the clamor and surge of the crowd. In my searching gazes around I saw no illumined face of a master. Passing a bridge on the bank of the Ganges, I noticed an acquaintance standing nearby, his begging bowl extended.

"'Oh, this fair is nothing but a chaos of noise and beggars,' I thought in disillusionment. 'I wonder if Western scientists, patiently enlarging the realms of knowledge for the practical good of mankind, are not more pleasing to God than these idlers who profess religion but concentrate on alms.'

"My smouldering reflections on social reform were interrupted by the voice of a tall sannyasi who halted before me.

"'Sir,' he said, 'a saint is calling you.'

"'Who is he?'

"'Come and see for yourself.'

"Hesitantly following this laconic advice, I soon found myself near a tree whose branches were sheltering a guru with an attractive group of disciples. The master, a bright unusual figure, with sparkling dark eyes, rose at my approach and embraced me.

"'Welcome, Swamiji,' he said affectionately.

"'Sir,' I replied emphatically, 'I am NOT a swami.'

"'Those on whom I am divinely directed to bestow the title of "swami" never cast it off.' The saint addressed me simply, but deep conviction of truth rang in his words; I was engulfed in an instant wave of spiritual blessing. Smiling at my sudden elevation into the ancient monastic order, I bowed at the feet of the obviously great and angelic being in human form who had thus honored me.

"Babaji – for it was indeed he – motioned me to a seat near him under the tree. He was strong and young, and looked like Lahiri Mahasaya; yet the resemblance did not strike me, even though I had often heard of the extraordinary similarities in the appearance of the two masters. Babaji possesses a power by which he can prevent any specific thought from arising in a person's mind. Evidently the great guru wished me to be perfectly natural in his presence, not overawed by knowledge of his identity.

"'What do you think of the KUMBHA MELA?'

"'I was greatly disappointed, sir.' I added hastily, 'Up until the time I met you. Somehow saints and this commotion don't seem to belong together.'

"'Child,' the master said, though apparently I was nearly twice his own age, 'for the faults of the many, judge not the whole. Everything on earth is of mixed character, like a mingling of sand and sugar. Be like the wise ant which seizes only the sugar, and leaves the sand untouched. Though many sadhus here still wander in delusion, yet the MELA is blessed by a few men of God-realization.'

"In view of my own meeting with this exalted master, I quickly agreed with his observation.

"'Sir,' I commented, 'I have been thinking of the scientific men of the West, greater by far in intelligence than most people congregated here, living in distant Europe and America, professing different creeds, and ignorant of the real values of such MELAS as the present one. They are the men who could benefit greatly by meetings with India's masters. But, although high in intellectual attainments, many Westerners are wedded to rank materialism. Others, famous in science and philosophy, do not recognize the essential unity in religion. Their creeds serve as insurmountable barriers that threaten to separate them from us forever.'

"'I saw that you are interested in the West, as well as the East.' Babaji's face beamed with approval. 'I felt the pangs of your heart, broad enough for all men, whether Oriental or Occidental. That is why I summoned you here.

"'East and West must establish a golden middle path of activity and spirituality combined,' he continued. 'India has much to learn from the West in material development; in return, India can teach the universal methods by which the West will be able to base its religious beliefs on the unshakable foundations of yogic science.

"'You, Swamiji, have a part to play in the coming harmonious exchange between Orient and Occident. Some years hence I shall send you a disciple whom you can train for yoga dissemination in the West. The vibrations there of many spiritually seeking souls come floodlike to me. I perceive potential saints in America and Europe, waiting to be awakened.'"

At this point in his story, Sri Yukteswar turned his gaze fully on mine.

"My son," he said, smiling in the moonlight, "you are the disciple that, years ago, Babaji promised to send me."

I was happy to learn that Babaji had directed my steps to Sri Yukteswar, yet it was hard for me to visualize myself in the remote West, away from my beloved guru and the simple hermitage peace.

"'At my request, Swamiji, please undertake another task,' Babaji said. 'Will you not write a short book on the underlying basic unity between the Christian and Hindu scriptures? Show by parallel references that the inspired sons of God have spoken the same truths, now obscured by men's sectarian differences.'

"'Maharaj,' I answered diffidently, 'what a command! Shall I be able to fulfill it?'

"Babaji laughed softly. 'My son, why do you doubt?' he said reassuringly. 'Indeed, Whose work is all this, and Who is the Doer of all actions? Whatever the Lord has made me say is bound to materialize as truth.'

"I deemed myself empowered by the blessings of the saint, and agreed to write the book. Feeling reluctantly that the parting-hour had arrived, I rose from my leafy seat.

"'Do you know Lahiri?' the master inquired. 'He is a great

soul, isn't he? Tell him of our meeting.' He then gave me a message for Lahiri Mahasaya.

"After I had bowed humbly in farewell, the saint smiled benignly. 'When your book is finished, I shall pay you a visit,' he promised. 'Good-by for the present.'

"I left Allahabad the following day and entrained for Benares. Reaching my guru's home, I poured out the story of the wonderful saint at the KUMBHA MELA.

"'Oh, didn't you recognize him?' Lahiri Mahasaya's eyes were dancing with laughter. 'I see you couldn't, for he prevented you. He is my incomparable guru, the celestial Babaji!'

"'Babaji!' I repeated, awestruck. 'The Yogi-Christ Babaji! The invisible-visible savior Babaji! Oh, if I could just recall the past and be once more in his presence, to show my devotion at his lotus feet!'

"'Never mind,' Lahiri Mahasaya said consolingly. 'He has promised to see you again.'

"'Gurudeva, the divine master asked me to give you a message. "Tell Lahiri," he said, "that the stored-up power for this life now runs low; it is nearly finished."'

"At my utterance of these enigmatic words, Lahiri Mahasaya's figure trembled as though touched by a lightning current. In an instant everything about him fell silent; his smiling countenance turned incredibly stern. Like a wooden statue, somber and immovable in its seat, his body became colorless. I was alarmed and bewildered. Never in my life had I seen this joyous soul manifest such awful gravity. The other disciples present stared apprehensively.

"Three hours passed in utter silence. Then Lahiri Mahasaya resumed his natural, cheerful demeanor, and spoke affectionately to each of the chelas. Everyone sighed in relief.

"I realized by my master's reaction that Babaji's message had been an unmistakable signal by which Lahiri Mahasaya understood that his body would soon be untenanted. His awesome silence proved that my guru had instantly controlled his being, cut his last cord of attachment to the material world, and fled to his ever-living identity in Spirit. Babaji's remark had been his way of saying: 'I shall be ever with you.'

"I soon left Benares, and set to work in Serampore on the scriptural writings requested by Babaji," Sri Yukteswar continued. "No sooner had I begun my task than I was able to compose a poem dedicated to the deathless guru. The melodious lines flowed effortlessly from my pen, though never before had I attempted Sanskrit poetry.

"In the quiet of night I busied myself over a comparison of the Bible and the scriptures of SANATAN DHARMA. Quoting the words of the blessed Lord Jesus, I showed that his teachings were in essence one with the revelations of the VEDAS. To my relief, my book was finished in a short time; I realized that this speedy blessing was due to the grace of my PARAM-GURU-MAHARAJ. The chapters first appeared in the SADHUSAMBAD journal; later they were privately printed as a book by one of my Kidderpore disciples.

"The morning after I had concluded my literary efforts," Master continued, "I went to the Rai Ghat here to bathe in the Ganges. The ghat was deserted; I stood still for awhile, enjoying the sunny peace. After a dip in the sparkling waters, I started for home. As I passed beyond the site of the large banyan tree near the river bank, a strong impulse urged me to look back. There, under the shade of the banyan, and surrounded by a few disciples, sat the great Babaji!

"'Greetings, Swamiji!' The beautiful voice of the master rang out to assure me I was not dreaming. 'I see you have successfully completed your book. As I promised, I am here to thank you.'

"With a fast-beating heart, I prostrated myself fully at his feet. 'Param-guruji,' I said imploringly, 'will you and your chelas not honor my near-by home with your presence?'

"The supreme guru smilingly declined. 'No, child,' he said, 'we are people who like the shelter of trees; this spot is quite comfortable.'

"'Please tarry awhile, Master.' I gazed entreatingly at him. 'I shall be back at once with some special sweetmeats.'

"When I returned in a few minutes with a dish of delicacies, lo! The lordly banyan no longer sheltered the celestial troupe. I searched all around the ghat, but in my heart I knew the little band had already fled on etheric wings.

"A few months later I visited Lahiri Mahasaya in Benares. As I entered his little parlor, my guru smiled in greeting.

"That was one of my last visits to Benares to see my guru," Sri Yukteswar concluded. "Even as Babaji had foretold at the KUMBHA MELA, the householder-incarnation of Lahiri Mahasaya was drawing to a close. During the summer of 1895 his stalwart body developed a small boil on the back. He protested against lancing; he was working out in his own flesh the evil karma of some of his disciples. Finally a few chelas became very insistent; the master replied cryptically:

"'The body has to find a cause to go; I will be agreeable to whatever you want to do.'

"A short time later the incomparable guru gave up his body in Benares. No longer need I seek him out in his little parlor; I find every day of my life blessed by his omnipresent guidance."

Lahiri Mahasaya's beautiful body, so dear to the devotees, was cremated with solemn householder rites at Manikarnika Ghat by the holy Ganges.

37

I Go to America

"America! Surely these people are Americans!" This was my thought as a panoramic vision of Western faces passed before my inward view.

Immersed in meditation, I was sitting behind some dusty boxes in the storeroom of the Ranchi school. A private spot was difficult to find during those busy years with the youngsters!

The storeroom door opened; as usual, one of the young lads had discovered my hiding place.

"Come here, Bimal," I cried gaily. "I have news for you: the Lord is calling me to America!"

"To America?" The boy echoed my words in a tone that implied I had said "to the moon."

"Yes! I am going forth to discover America, like Columbus. He thought he had found India; surely there is a karmic link between those two lands!"

Bimal scampered away; soon the whole school was informed by the two-legged newspaper. I summoned the bewildered faculty and gave the school into its charge.

"I know you will keep Lahiri Mahasaya's yoga ideals of education ever to the fore," I said. "I shall write you frequently; God willing, someday I shall be back."

I entrained for Calcutta a few hours after my vision. The

following day I received an invitation to serve as the delegate from India to an International Congress of Religious Liberals in America. It was to convene that year in Boston, under the auspices of the American Unitarian Association.

My head in a whirl, I sought out Sri Yukteswar in Serampore.

"Guruji, I have just been invited to address a religious congress in America. Shall I go?"

"All doors are open for you," Master replied simply. "It is now or never."

"But, sir," I said in dismay, "what do I know about public speaking? Seldom have I given a lecture, and never in English."

"English or no English, your words on yoga shall be heard in the West."

I laughed. "Well, dear guruji, I hardly think the Americans will learn Bengali! Please bless me with a push over the hurdles of the English language."

When I broke the news of my plans to Father, he was utterly taken aback. To him America seemed incredibly remote; he feared he might never see me again.

"How can you go?" he asked sternly. "Who will finance you?"

"The Lord will surely finance me." I replied. Without very much guile, I added, "Father, perhaps God will put it into your mind to help me."

"No, never!" He glanced at me piteously.

I was astounded, therefore, when Father handed me, the following day, a check made out for a large amount.

"I give you this money," he said, "not in my capacity as a father, but as a faithful disciple of Lahiri Mahasaya. Go then to that far Western land; spread there the creedless teachings of KRIYA YOGA."

As I went about my preparations to leave Master and my native land for the unknown shores of America, I experienced not a little trepidation. I had heard many stories about the materialistic Western atmosphere, one very different from the spiritual background of India, pervaded with the centuried aura of saints.

One early morning I began to pray, with an adamant determination to continue, to even die praying, until I heard the voice of God. I wanted His blessing and assurance that I would not lose myself in the fogs of modern utilitarianism. My heart was set to go to America, but even more strongly was my resolve to hear the solace of divine permission.

I prayed and prayed, muffling my sobs. No answer came. My silent petition increased in excruciating crescendo until, at noon, I had reached a zenith; my brain could no longer withstand the pressure of my agonies. If I cried once more with an increased depth of my inner passion, I felt as though my brain would split. At that moment there came a knock outside the vestibule adjoining the Gurpar Road room in which I was sitting. Opening the door, I saw a young man in the scanty garb of a renunciate. He came in, closed the door behind him and, refusing my request to sit down, indicated with a gesture that he wished to talk to me while standing.

"He must be Babaji!" I thought, dazed, because the man before me had the features of a younger Lahiri Mahasaya.

He answered my thought. "Yes, I am Babaji." He spoke melodiously in Hindi. "Our Heavenly Father has heard your prayer. He commands me to tell you: Follow the behests of your guru and go to America. Fear not; you will be protected."

After a vibrant pause, Babaji addressed me again. "You are the one I have chosen to spread the message of KRIYA

YOGA in the West. Long ago I met your guru Yukteswar at a KUMBHA MELA; I told him then I would send you to him for training."

I was speechless, choked with devotional awe at his presence, and deeply touched to hear from his own lips that he had guided me to Sri Yukteswar. I lay prostrate before the deathless guru. He graciously lifted me from the floor. Telling me many things about my life, he then gave me some personal instruction, and uttered a few secret prophecies.

"KRIYA YOGA, the scientific technique of God-realization," he finally said with solemnity, "will ultimately spread in all lands, and aid in harmonizing the nations through man's personal, transcendental perception of the Infinite Father."

With a gaze of majestic power, the master electrified me by a glimpse of his cosmic consciousness. In a short while he started toward the door.

"Do not try to follow me," he said. "You will not be able to do so."

"Please, Babaji, don't go away!" I cried repeatedly. "Take me with you!"

Looking back, he replied, "Not now. Some other time."

Overcome by emotion, I disregarded his warning. As I tried to pursue him, I discovered that my feet were firmly rooted to the floor. From the door, Babaji gave me a last affectionate glance. He raised his hand by way of benediction and walked away, my eyes fixed on him longingly.

After a few minutes my feet were free. I sat down and went into a deep meditation, unceasingly thanking God not only for answering my prayer but for blessing me by a meeting with Babaji. My whole body seemed sanctified through the touch of the ancient, ever-youthful master. Long had it been my burning desire to behold him.

The eve of my departure for the United States found me in Sri Yukteswar's holy presence.

"Forget you were born a Hindu, and don't be an American. Take the best of them both," Master said in his calm way of wisdom. "Be your true self, a child of God. Seek and incorporate into your being the best qualities of all your brothers, scattered over the earth in various races."

Then he blessed me.

I left India in August, 1920, on THE CITY OF SPARTA, the first passenger boat sailing for America after the close of World War I. During the two-months' voyage a fellow passenger found out that I was the Indian delegate to the Boston congress.

"Swami Yogananda," he said, with the first of many quaint pronunciations by which I was later to hear my name spoken by the Americans, "please favor the passengers with a lecture next Thursday night. I think we would all benefit by a talk on 'The Battle of Life and How to Fight It.'"

Alas! I had to fight the battle of my own life, I discovered on Wednesday. Desperately trying to organize my ideas into a lecture in English, I finally abandoned all preparations. Fully trusting in Master's past assurances, however, I appeared before my Thursday audience in the saloon of the steamer. No eloquence rose to my lips; speechlessly I stood before the assemblage. After an endurance contest lasting ten minutes, the audience realized my predicament and began to laugh.

The situation was not funny to me at the moment; indignantly I sent a silent prayer to Master.

"You CAN! Speak!" His voice sounded instantly within my consciousness.

My thoughts fell at once into a friendly relation with the English language. Forty-five minutes later the audience was still attentive. The talk won me a number of invitations to lecture later before various groups in America.

Once in awhile, during the remainder of the ocean trip, I experienced a few apprehensive twinges about the coming English-lecture ordeal at the Boston congress.

THE CITY OF SPARTA docked near Boston in late September. On the sixth of October I addressed the congress with my maiden speech in America. It was well received; I sighed in relief. The magnanimous secretary of the American Unitarian Association wrote the following comment in a published account of the congress proceedings:

"Swami Yogananda, delegate from the Brahmacharya Ashram of Ranchi, India, brought the greetings of his Association to the Congress. In fluent English and a forcible delivery he gave an address of a philosophical character on 'The Science of Religion,' which has been printed in pamphlet form for a wider distribution. Religion, he maintained, is universal and it is one. We cannot possibly universalize particular customs and convictions, but the common element in religion can be universalized, and we can ask all alike to follow and obey it."

Four happy years were spent in humble circumstances in Boston. I gave public lectures, taught classes, and wrote a book of poems, SONGS OF THE SOUL, with a preface by Dr. Frederick B. Robinson, president of the College of the City of New York.

Starting a transcontinental tour in the summer of 1924, I spoke before thousands in the principal cities, ending my western trip with a vacation in the beautiful Alaskan north.

With the help of large-hearted students, by the end of 1925 I had established an American headquarters on the Mount Washington Estates in Los Angeles. The building is the one I had seen years before in my vision at Kashmir.

Years sped by. I lectured in every part of my new land, and addressed hundreds of clubs, colleges, churches, and groups of every denomination. Tens of thousands of Americans received yoga initiation. To them all I dedicated a new book of prayer thoughts in 1929-WHISPERS FROM ETERNITY, with a preface by Amelita Galli-Curci.

Sometimes-usually on the first of the month when the bills rolled in for upkeep of the Mount Washington and other Self-Realization Fellowship centers!-I thought longingly of the simple peace of India. But daily I saw a widening understanding between West and East; my soul rejoiced.

I have found the great heart of America expressed in the wondrous lines by Emma Lazarus, carved at the base of the Statue of Liberty, the "Mother of Exiles":

From her beacon-hand Glows world-wide welcome; her mild eyes command The air-bridged harbor that twin cities frame. Keep, ancient lands, your storied pomp!" cries she With silent lips. "Give me your tired, your poor, Your huddled masses yearning to breathe free, The wretched refuse of your teeming shore. Send these, the homeless, tempest-tost to me, I lift my lamp beside the golden door.

38

Luther Burbank:
A Saint amidst the Roses

"The secret of improved plant breeding, apart from scientific knowledge, is love." Luther Burbank uttered this wisdom as I walked beside him in his Santa Rosa garden. We halted near a bed of edible cacti.

"While I was conducting experiments to make 'spineless' cacti," he continued, "I often talked to the plants to create a vibration of love. 'You have nothing to fear,' I would tell them. 'You don't need your defensive thorns. I will protect you.' Gradually the useful plant of the desert emerged in a thornless variety."

I was charmed at this miracle. "Please, dear Luther, give me a few cacti leaves to plant in my garden at Mount Washington."

A workman standing near-by started to strip off some leaves; Burbank prevented him.

"I myself will pluck them for the swami." He handed me three leaves, which later I planted, rejoicing as they grew to huge estate.

The great horticulturist told me that his first notable triumph was the large potato, now known by his name. With the indefatigability of genius, he went on to present the world with hundreds of crossed improvements on nature – his new Burbank varieties of tomato, corn, squash, cherries, plums, nectarines, berries, poppies, lilies, roses.

I focused my camera as Luther led me before the famous walnut tree by which he had proved that natural evolution can be telescopically hastened.

"In only sixteen years," he said, "this walnut tree reached a state of abundant nut production to which an unaided nature would have brought the tree in twice that time."

Burbank's little adopted daughter came romping with her dog into the garden.

"She is my human plant." Luther waved to her affectionately.

"Luther, you would delight in my Ranchi school, with its outdoor classes, and atmosphere of joy and simplicity."

My words touched the chord closest to Burbank's heart–child education. He plied me with questions, interest gleaming from his deep, serene eyes.

"Swamiji," he said finally, "schools like yours are the only hope of a future millennium. I am in revolt against the educational systems of our time, severed from nature and stifling of all individuality. I am with you heart and soul in your practical ideals of education."

As I was taking leave of the gentle sage, he autographed a small volume and presented it to me. "Here is my book on THE TRAINING OF THE HUMAN PLANT," he said.

I read his little book that night with intense interest. His eye envisioning a glorious future for the race, he wrote: "The most stubborn living thing in this world, the most difficult to swerve, is a plant once fixed in certain habits. . . . Remember that this plant has preserved its individuality all through the ages; perhaps it is one which can be traced backward through eons of time in the very rocks themselves, never having varied to any great extent in all these vast periods. Do you suppose, after all these ages of repetition, the plant does not become possessed of a will, if you so choose to call it, of unparalleled tenacity? Indeed, there are plants, like certain of the palms, so persistent that no human power has yet been able to change them. The human will is a weak thing beside the will of a plant. But see how this whole plant's lifelong stubbornness is broken simply by blending a new life with it, making, by crossing, a complete and powerful change in its life. Then when the break comes, fix it by these generations of patient supervision and selection, and the new plant sets out upon its new way never again to return to the old, its tenacious will broken and changed at last.

"When it comes to so sensitive and pliable a thing as the nature of a child, the problem becomes vastly easier."

Magnetically drawn to this great American, I visited him again and again. One morning I arrived at the same time as the postman, who deposited in Burbank's study about a thousand letters. Horticulturists wrote him from all parts of the world.

"Swamiji, your presence is just the excuse I need to get out into the garden," Luther said gaily. He opened a large desk-drawer containing hundreds of travel folders.

"See," he said, "this is how I do my traveling. Tied down by my plants and correspondence, I satisfy my desire for foreign lands by a glance now and then at these pictures."

My car was standing before his gate; Luther and I drove along the streets of the little town, its gardens bright with his own varieties of Santa Rosa, Peachblow, and Burbank roses.

"My friend Henry Ford and I both believe in the ancient theory of reincarnation," Luther told me. "It sheds light on aspects of life otherwise inexplicable. Memory is not a test of truth; just because man fails to remember his past lives does not prove he never had them. Memory is blank concerning his womb-life and infancy, too; but he probably passed through them!" He chuckled.

The great scientist had received KRIYA initiation during one of my earlier visits. "I practice the technique devoutly, Swamiji," he said. After many thoughtful questions to me about various aspects of yoga, Luther remarked slowly:

"The East indeed possesses immense hoards of knowledge which the West has scarcely begun to explore."

We drove back reluctantly toward his home and those waiting thousand letters.

"Luther," I remarked, "next month I am starting a magazine to present the truth-offerings of East and West. Please help me decide on a good name for the journal."

We discussed titles for awhile, and finally agreed on EAST-WEST. After we had reentered his study, Burbank gave me an article he had written on "Science and Civilization."

"This will go in the first issue of EAST-WEST," I said gratefully.

As our friendship grew deeper, I called Burbank my "American saint." "Behold a man," I quoted, "in whom there is no guile!" His heart was fathomlessly deep, long acquainted with humility, patience, sacrifice. His little home amidst the roses was austerely simple; he knew the worthlessness of luxury, the joy of few possessions. The modesty with which he wore his scientific fame repeatedly reminded me of the trees that bend low with the burden of ripening fruits; it is the barren tree that lifts its head high in an empty boast.

I was in New York when, in 1926, my dear friend passed away. In tears I thought, "Oh, I would gladly walk all the way from here to Santa Rosa for one more glimpse of him!" Locking myself away from secretaries and visitors, I spent the next twenty-four hours in seclusion.

The following day I conducted a Vedic memorial rite around a large picture of Luther. A group of my American students, garbed in Hindu ceremonial clothes, chanted the ancient hymns as an offering was made of flowers, water, and fire – symbols of the bodily elements and their release in the Infinite Source.

39

Therese Neumann,
the Catholic Stigmatist

"Return to India. I have waited for you patiently for fifteen years. Soon I shall swim out of the body and on to the Shining Abode. Yogananda, come!"

Sri Yukteswar's voice sounded startlingly in my inner ear as I sat in meditation at my Mt. Washington headquarters. Traversing ten thousand miles in the twinkling of an eye, his message penetrated my being like a flash of lightning.

Fifteen years! Yes, I realized, now it is 1935; I have spent fifteen years in spreading my guru's teachings in America. Now he recalls me.

I made arrangements to sail, via Europe, for India. Busy weeks of preparations at Mount Washington! In March, 1935 I had the Self-Realization Fellowship chartered under the laws of the State of California as a non-profit corporation. To this educational institution go all public donations as well as the revenue from the sale of my books, magazine, written courses, class tuition, and every other source of income.

"I shall be back," I told my students. "Never shall I forget America."

At a farewell banquet given to me in Los Angeles by loving

friends, I looked long at their faces and thought gratefully, "Lord, he who remembers Thee as the Sole Giver will never lack the sweetness of friendship among mortals."

I sailed from New York on June 9, 1935 in the EUROPA. Two students accompanied me: my secretary, C. Richard Wright, and an elderly lady from Cincinnati, Ettie Bletch. We enjoyed the days of ocean peace, a welcome contrast to the past hurried weeks.

Like any other group of inquisitive tourists, we walked around the huge and ancient city of London. The following day I was invited to address a large meeting in Caxton Hall, at which I was introduced to the London audience by Sir Francis Younghusband. Our party spent a pleasant day as guests of Sir Harry Lauder at his estate in Scotland. We soon crossed the English Channel to the continent, for I wanted to make a special pilgrimage to Bavaria. This would be my only chance, I felt, to visit the great Catholic mystic, Therese Neumann of Konnersreuth.

Years earlier I had read an amazing account of Therese. Information given in the article was as follows:

(1) Therese, born in 1898, had been injured in an accident at the age of twenty; she became blind and paralyzed.

(2) She miraculously regained her sight in 1923 through prayers to St. Teresa, "The Little Flower." Later Therese Neumann's limbs were instantaneously healed.

(3) From 1923 onward, Therese has abstained completely from food and drink, except for the daily swallowing of one small consecrated wafer.

(4) The stigmata, or sacred wounds of Christ, appeared in 1926 on Therese's head, breast, hands, and feet. On

Friday of every week thereafter, she has passed through the Passion of Christ, suffering in her own body all his historic agonies.

(5) Knowing ordinarily only the simple German of her village, during her Friday trances Therese utters phrases which scholars have identified as ancient Aramaic. At appropriate times in her vision, she speaks Hebrew or Greek.

(6) By ecclesiastical permission, Therese has several times been under close scientific observation. Dr. Fritz Gerlick, editor of a Protestant German newspaper, went to Konnersreuth to "expose the Catholic fraud," but ended up by reverently writing her biography.

As always, whether in East or West, I was eager to meet a saint. I rejoiced as our little party entered, on July 16th, the quaint village of Konnersreuth. The Bavarian peasants exhibited lively interest in our Ford automobile (brought with us from America) and its assorted group – an American young man, an elderly lady, and an olive-hued Oriental with long hair tucked under his coat collar.

Therese's little cottage, clean and neat, with geraniums blooming by a primitive well, was alas! silently closed. The neighbors, and even the village postman who passed by, could give us no information. Rain began to fall; my companions suggested that we leave.

"No," I said stubbornly, "I will stay here until I find some clue leading to Therese."

Two hours later we were still sitting in our car amidst the dismal rain. "Lord," I sighed complainingly, "why didst Thou lead me here if she has disappeared?"

An English-speaking man halted beside us, politely offering his aid.

"I don't know for certain where Therese is," he said, "but she often visits at the home of Professor Wurz, a seminary master of Eichstatt, eighty miles from here."

The following morning our party motored to the quiet village of Eichstatt, narrowly lined with cobblestoned streets. Dr. Wurz greeted us cordially at his home; "Yes, Therese is here." He sent her word of the visitors. A messenger soon appeared with her reply.

"Though the bishop has asked me to see no one without his permission, I will receive the man of God from India."

Deeply touched at these words, I followed Dr. Wurz upstairs to the sitting room. Therese entered immediately, radiating an aura of peace and joy. She wore a black gown and spotless white head dress. Although her age was thirty-seven at this time, she seemed much younger, possessing indeed a childlike freshness and charm. Healthy, well-formed, rosy-cheeked, and cheerful, this is the saint that does not eat!

Therese greeted me with a very gentle handshaking. We both beamed in silent communion, each knowing the other to be a lover of God.

Dr. Wurz kindly offered to serve as interpreter. As we seated ourselves, I noticed that Therese was glancing at me with naïve curiosity; evidently Hindus had been rare in Bavaria.

"Don't you eat anything?" I wanted to hear the answer from her own lips.

"No, except a consecrated rice-flour wafer, once every morning at six o'clock."

"How large is the wafer?"

"It is paper-thin, the size of a small coin." She added, "I

take it for sacramental reasons; if it is unconsecrated, I am unable to swallow it."

"Certainly you could not have lived on that, for twelve whole years?"

"I live by God's light." How simple her reply, how Einsteinian!

"I see you realize that energy flows to your body from the ether, sun, and air."

A swift smile broke over her face. "I am so happy to know you understand how I live."

"Your sacred life is a daily demonstration of the truth uttered by Christ: 'Man shall not live by bread alone, but by every word that proceedeth out of the mouth of God.'"

Again she showed joy at my explanation. "It is indeed so. One of the reasons I am here on earth today is to prove that man can live by God's invisible light, and not by food only."

"Can you teach others how to live without food?"

She appeared a trifle shocked. "I cannot do that; God does not wish it."

As my gaze fell on her strong, graceful hands, Therese showed me a little, square, freshly healed wound on each of her palms. On the back of each hand, she pointed out a smaller, crescent-shaped wound, freshly healed. Each wound went straight through the hand. The sight brought to my mind distinct recollection of the large square iron nails with crescent-tipped ends, still used in the Orient, but which I do not recall having seen in the West.

The saint told me something of her weekly trances. "As a helpless onlooker, I observe the whole Passion of Christ." Each week, from Thursday midnight until Friday afternoon at one o'clock, her wounds open and bleed; she loses ten pounds of her ordinary 121-pound weight. Suffering intensely in her sympathetic love, Therese yet looks forward joyously to these weekly visions of her Lord.

I realized at once that her strange life is intended by God to reassure all Christians of the historical authenticity of Jesus' life and crucifixion as recorded in the New Testament, and to dramatically display the ever-living bond between the Galilean Master and his devotees.

At the time of parting, I expressed to Therese my desire to be present at her trance.

"Yes, please come to Konnersreuth next Friday," she said graciously. "The bishop will give you a permit. I am very happy you sought me out in Eichstatt."

Therese shook hands gently, many times, and walked with our party to the gate.

On Thursday afternoon our party drove to the home of the bishop, who looked at my flowing locks with some surprise. He readily wrote out the necessary permit. There was no fee; the rule made by the Church is simply to protect Therese from the onrush of casual tourists, who in previous years had flocked on Fridays by the thousands.

We arrived Friday morning about nine-thirty in Konnersreuth. I noticed that Therese's little cottage possesses a special glass-roofed section to afford her plenty of light. We were glad to see the doors no longer closed, but wide-open in hospitable cheer. There was a line of about twenty visitors, armed with their permits. Many had come from great distances to view the mystic trance.

Therese had passed my first test at the professor's house by her intuitive knowledge that I wanted to see her for spiritual reasons, and not just to satisfy a passing curiosity.

My second test was connected with the fact that, just before I went upstairs to her room, I put myself into a yogic trance state in order to be one with her in telepathic and televisic rapport. I entered her chamber, filled with visitors; she was lying in a white robe on the bed. With Mr. Wright following closely behind me, I halted just inside the threshold, awestruck at a strange and most frightful spectacle.

Blood flowed thinly and continuously in an inch-wide stream from Therese's lower eyelids. Her gaze was focused upward on the spiritual eye within the central forehead. The cloth wrapped around her head was drenched in blood from the stigmata wounds of the crown of thorns. The white garment was redly splotched over her heart from the wound in her side at the spot where Christ's body, long ages ago, had suffered the final indignity of the soldier's spear-thrust.

As I was in attunement with her, I began to see the scenes of her vision. She was watching Jesus as he carried the cross amidst the jeering multitude. Suddenly she lifted her head in consternation: the Lord had fallen under the cruel weight. The vision disappeared. In the exhaustion of fervid pity, Therese sank heavily against her pillow.

Remembering the patiently waiting line of pilgrims, Mr. Wright and I silently bade farewell to Therese and left her sacred presence.

The following day our little group motored south, thankful that we were not dependent on trains, but could stop the Ford wherever we chose throughout the countryside. In Italy we made a special trip to Assisi to honor the apostle of humility, St. Francis. The European tour ended in Greece, where we viewed the Athenian temples, and saw the prison in which the gentle Socrates had drunk his death potion.

We took ship over the sunny Mediterranean, disembarking at Palestine. The spirit of Christ is all-pervasive in Palestine; I walked reverently by his side at Bethlehem, Gethsemane, Calvary, the holy Mount of Olives, and by the River Jordan and the Sea of Galilee. Our little party visited the Birth Manger, Joseph's carpenter shop, the tomb of Lazarus, the house of Martha and Mary, the hall of the Last Supper.

On to Egypt, with its modern Cairo and ancient pyramids. Then a boat down the narrow Red Sea, over the vasty Arabian Sea; lo, India!

40

I Return to India

Gratefully I was inhaling the blessed air of India. Our boat RAJPUTANA docked on August 22, 1935 in the huge harbor of Bombay. Even this, my first day off the ship, was a foretaste of the year ahead-twelve months of ceaseless activity. Friends had gathered at the dock with garlands and greetings; soon, at our suite in the Taj Mahal Hotel, there was a stream of reporters and photographers.

Bombay was a city new to me; I found it energetically modern, with many innovations from the West. I was impatient, eager to see my beloved guru and other dear ones. Consigning the Ford to a baggage car, our party was soon speeding eastward by train toward Calcutta.

Our arrival at Howrah Station found such an immense crowd assembled to greet us that for awhile we were unable to dismount from the train. The young Maharaja of Kasimbazar and my brother Bishnu headed the reception committee; I was unprepared for the warmth and magnitude of our welcome.

Preceded by a line of automobiles and motorcycles, and amidst the joyous sound of drums and conch shells, Miss Bletch, Mr. Wright, and myself, flower-garlanded from head to foot, drove slowly to my father's home.

My aged parent embraced me as one returning from

the dead; long we gazed on each other, speechless with joy. Brothers and sisters, uncles, aunts, and cousins, students and friends of years long past were grouped around me, not a dry eye among us. Passed now into the archives of memory, the scene of loving reunion vividly endures, unforgettable in my heart.

As for my meeting with Sri Yukteswar, words fail me; let the following description from my secretary suffice.

"Today, filled with the highest anticipations, I drove Yoganandaji from Calcutta to Serampore," Mr. Wright recorded in his travel diary. "We passed by quaint shops, one of them the favorite eating haunt of Yoganandaji during his college days, and finally entered a narrow, walled lane. A sudden left turn, and there before us towered the simple but inspiring two-story ashram, its Spanish-style balcony jutting from the upper floor. The pervasive impression was that of peaceful solitude.

"In grave humility I walked behind Yoganandaji into the courtyard within the hermitage walls. Hearts beating fast, we proceeded up some old cement steps, trod, no doubt, by myriads of truth-seekers. The tension grew keener and keener as on we strode. Before us, near the head of the stairs, quietly appeared the Great One, Swami Sri Yukteswarji, standing in the noble pose of a sage.

"My heart heaved and swelled as I felt myself blessed by the privilege of being in his sublime presence. Tears blurred my eager sight when Yoganandaji dropped to his knees, and with bowed head offered his soul's gratitude and greeting, touching with his hand his guru's feet and then, in humble obeisance, his own head. He rose then and was embraced on both sides of the bosom by Sri Yukteswarji.

"No words passed at the beginning, but the most intense feeling was expressed in the mute phrases of the soul. How their eyes sparkled and were fired with the warmth of renewed soul-union! A tender vibration surged through the quiet patio, and even the sun eluded the clouds to add a sudden blaze of glory.

"Swami Sri Yukteswarji's joy is obviously intense at the return of his 'product' (and he seems to be somewhat inquisitive about the 'product's product'). However, predominance of the wisdom-aspect in the Great One's nature hinders his outward expression of feeling.

"Yoganandaji presented him with some gifts, as is the custom when the disciple returns to his guru. We sat down later to a simple but well-cooked meal. All the dishes were vegetable and rice combinations. Sri Yukteswarji was pleased at my use of a number of Indian customs, 'finger-eating' for example.

"After several hours of flying Bengali phrases and the exchange of warm smiles and joyful glances, we paid obeisance at his feet, bade adieu with a PRONAM, and departed for Calcutta with an everlasting memory of a sacred meeting and greeting. Although I write chiefly of my external impressions of him, yet I was always conscious of the true basis of the saint-his spiritual glory. I felt his power, and shall carry that feeling as my divine blessing."

From America, Europe, and Palestine I had brought many presents for Sri Yukteswar. He received them smilingly, but without remark.

As soon as I could tear myself away from Serampore and Calcutta, I set out, with Mr. Wright, for Ranchi. What a welcome there, a veritable ovation! Tears stood in my eyes as

I embraced the selfless teachers who had kept the banner of the school flying during my fifteen years' absence. The bright faces and happy smiles of the residential and day students were ample testimony to the worth of their many-sided school and yoga training.

Yet, alas! the Ranchi institution was in dire financial difficulties. Sir Manindra Chandra Nundy, the old Maharaja whose Kasimbazar Palace had been converted into the central school building, and who had made many princely donations was now dead. Many free, benevolent features of the school were now seriously endangered for lack of sufficient public support.

For one week I remained in Ranchi, wrestling with critical problems. Then came interviews in Calcutta with prominent leaders and educators, a long talk with the young Maharaja of Kasimbazar, a financial appeal to my father, and lo! the shaky foundations of Ranchi began to be righted. Many donations including one huge check arrived in the nick of time from my American students.

Within a few months after my arrival in India, I had the joy of seeing the Ranchi school legally incorporated. My lifelong dream of a permanently endowed yoga educational center stood fulfilled. That vision had guided me in the humble beginnings in 1917 with a group of seven boys.

The school, or Yogoda Sat-Sanga Brahmacharya Vidyalaya, conducts outdoor classes in grammar and high school subjects. The residential students and day scholars also receive vocational training of some kind. Sports and games are encouraged. Instruction in primary subjects is given in Hindi to the KOLS, SANTALS, and MUNDAS, aboriginal tribes of the province. Classes for girls only have been organized in near-by villages.

The unique feature at Ranchi is the initiation into KRIYA YOGA. The boys daily practice their spiritual exercises, engage in GITA chanting, and are taught by precept and example the virtues of simplicity, self-sacrifice, honor, and truth.

A guest house is hospitably open for Western visitors. The Ranchi library contains numerous magazines, and about a thousand volumes in English and Bengali, donations from the West and the East. There is a collection of the scriptures of the world. A well-classified museum displays archeological, geological, and anthropological exhibits; trophies, to a great extent, of my wanderings over the Lord's varied earth.

The charitable hospital and dispensary of the Lahiri Mahasaya Mission, with many outdoor branches in distant villages, have already ministered to 150,000 of India's poor. The Ranchi students are trained in first aid, and have given praiseworthy service to their province at tragic times of flood or famine.

A stately Yogoda Math was dedicated in 1939 at Dakshineswar, directly on the Ganges. The activities of the Yogoda Math include a fortnightly mailing of Self-Realization Fellowship teachings to students in various parts of India.

It is needless to say that all these educational and humanitarian activities have required the self-sacrificing service and devotion of many teachers and workers. I do not list their names here, because they are so numerous; but in my heart each one has a lustrous niche. Inspired by the ideals of Lahiri Mahasaya, these teachers have abandoned promising worldly goals to serve humbly, to give greatly.

41

An Idyl in South India

"You are the first Westerner, Dick, ever to enter that shrine. Many others have tried in vain."

At my words Mr. Wright looked startled, then pleased. We had just left the beautiful Chamundi Temple in the hills overlooking Mysore in southern India. There we had bowed before the gold and silver altars of the Goddess Chamundi, patron deity of the family of the reigning maharaja.

"As a souvenir of the unique honor," Mr. Wright said, carefully stowing away a few blessed rose petals, "I will always preserve this flower, sprinkled by the priest with rose water."

My companion and I were spending the month of November, 1935, as guests of the State of Mysore. The Maharaja, H.H. Sri Krishnaraja Wadiyar IV, is a model prince with intelligent devotion to his people. A pious Hindu, the Maharaja has empowered a Mohammedan, the able Mirza Ismail, as his Dewan or Premier. Popular representation is given to the seven million inhabitants of Mysore in both an Assembly and a Legislative Council.

The heir to the Maharaja, H.H. the Yuvaraja, Sir Sri Krishna Narasingharaj Wadiyar, had invited my secretary and me to visit his enlightened and progressive realm. During the past fortnight I had addressed thousands of Mysore citizens and students, at the Town Hall, the Maharajah's College, the University Medical School; and three mass meetings in Bangalore, at the National High School, the Intermediate College, and the Chetty Town Hall where over three thousand persons had assembled. Whether the eager listeners had been able to credit the glowing picture I drew of America, I know not; but the applause had always been loudest when I spoke of the mutual benefits that could flow from exchange of the best features in East and West.

Mr. Wright and I were now relaxing in the tropical peace.

Southern India, rich with historical and archaeological remains, is a land of definite and yet indefinable charm. To the north of Mysore is the largest native state in India, Hyderabad, a picturesque plateau cut by the mighty Godavari River. Broad fertile plains, the lovely Nilgiris or "Blue Mountains," other regions with barren hills of limestone or granite. Hyderabad history is a long, colorful story, starting three thousand years ago under the Andhra kings, and continuing under Hindu dynasties until A.D. 1294, when it passed to a line of Moslem rulers who reign to this day.

The most breath-taking display of architecture, sculpture, and painting in all India is found at Hyderabad in the ancient rock-sculptured caves of Ellora and Ajanta. The Kailasa at Ellora, a huge monolithic temple, possesses carved figures of gods, men, and beasts in the stupendous proportions of a Michelangelo. Ajanta is the site of five cathedrals and twenty-five monasteries, all rock excavations maintained by tremendous frescoed pillars on which artists and sculptors have immortalized their genius.

Hyderabad City is graced by the Osmania University and by the imposing Mecca Masjid Mosque, where ten thousand Mohammedans may assemble for prayer.

Mysore State too is a scenic wonderland, three thousand feet above sea level, abounding in dense tropical forests, the home of wild elephants, bison, bears, panthers, and tigers. Its two chief cities, Bangalore and Mysore, are clean, attractive, with many parks and public gardens.

The rock pillars found in northern Mysore date from the third century B.C., illuminating the memory of King Asoka. He succeeded to the throne of the Maurya dynasty then prevailing; his empire included nearly all of modern India, Afghanistan, and Baluchistan. This illustrious emperor, considered even by Western historians to have been an incomparable ruler, has left the following wisdom on a rock memorial:

This religious inscription has been engraved in order that our sons and grandsons may not think a new conquest is necessary; that they may not think conquest by the sword deserves the name of conquest; that they may see in it nothing but destruction and violence; that they may consider nothing as true conquest save the conquest of religion. Such conquests have value in this world and in the next.

Asoka was a grandson of the formidable Chandragupta Maurya (known to the Greeks as Sandrocottus), who in his youth had met Alexander the Great. Later Chandragupta destroyed the Macedonian garrisons left in India, defeated the invading Greek army of Seleucus in the Punjab, and then received at his Patna court the Hellenic ambassador Megasthenes.

Intensely interesting stories have been minutely recorded by Greek historians and others who accompanied or followed after Alexander in his expedition to India. The narratives of Arrian, Diodoros, Plutarch, and Strabo the geographer have been translated by Dr. J. W. M'Crindle to throw a shaft of light on ancient India. The most admirable feature of Alexander's unsuccessful invasion was the deep interest he displayed in Hindu philosophy and in the yogis and holy men whom he encountered from time to time and whose society he eagerly sought. Shortly after the Greek warrior had arrived in Taxila in northern India, he sent a messenger, Onesikritos, a disciple of the Hellenic school of Diogenes, to fetch an Indian teacher, Dandamis, a great sannyasi of Taxila.

"Hail to thee, O teacher of Brahmins!" Onesikritos said after seeking out Dandamis in his forest retreat. "The son of the mighty God Zeus, being Alexander who is the Sovereign Lord of all men, asks you to go to him, and if you comply, he will reward you with great gifts, but if you refuse, he will cut off your head!"

The yogi received this fairly compulsive invitation calmly, and "did not so much as lift up his head from his couch of leaves."

"I also am a son of Zeus, if Alexander be such," he commented. "I want nothing that is Alexander's, for I am content with what I have, while I see that he wanders with his men over sea and land for no advantage, and is never coming to an end of his wanderings.

"Go and tell Alexander that God the Supreme King is never the Author of insolent wrong, but is the Creator of light, of peace, of life, of water, of the body of man and of souls; He receives all men when death sets them free, being in no way subject to evil disease. He alone is the God of my homage, who abhors slaughter and instigates no wars.

"Alexander is no god, since he must taste of death," continued the sage in quiet scorn. "How can such as he be the world's master, when he has not yet seated himself on a throne of inner universal dominion? Neither as yet has he entered living into Hades, nor does he know the course of the sun through the central regions of the earth, while the nations on its boundaries have not so much as heard his name!"

After this chastisement, surely the most caustic ever sent to assault the ears of the "Lord of the World," the sage added ironically, "If Alexander's present dominions be not capacious enough for his desires, let him cross the Ganges River; there he will find aregion able to sustain all his men, if the country on this side be too narrow to hold him.

"Know this, however, that what Alexander offers and the gifts he promises are things to me utterly useless; the things I prize and find of real use and worth are these leaves which are my house, these blooming plants which supply me with daily food, and the water which is my drink; while all other possessions which are amassed with anxious care are wont to prove ruinous to those who gather them, and cause only sorrow and vexation, with which every poor mortal is fully fraught. As for me, I lie upon the forest leaves, and having nothing which requires guarding, close my eyes in tranquil slumber; whereas had I anything to guard, that would banish sleep. The earth supplies me with everything, even as a mother her child with milk. I go wherever I please, and there are no cares with which I am forced to cumber myself.

"Should Alexander cut off my head, he cannot also destroy my soul. My head alone, then silent, will remain, leaving the body like a torn garment upon the earth, whence also it was taken. I then, becoming Spirit, shall ascend to my God, who enclosed us all in flesh and left us upon earth to prove whether, when here below, we shall live obedient to His ordinances and who also will require of us all, when we depart hence to His presence, an account of our life, since He is Judge of all proud wrongdoing; for the groans of the oppressed become the punishment of the oppressor.

"Let Alexander then terrify with these threats those who wish for wealth and who dread death, for against us these weapons are both alike powerless; the Brahmins neither love gold nor fear death. Go then and tell Alexander this: Dandamis has no need of aught that is yours, and therefore will not go to you, and if you want anything from Dandamis, come you to him."

With close attention Alexander received through Onesikritos the message from the yogi, and "felt a stronger desire than ever to see Dandamis who, though old and naked, was the only antagonist in whom he, the conqueror of many nations, had met more than his match."

Alexander invited to Taxila a number of Brahmin ascetics noted for their skill in answering philosophical questions with pithy wisdom. An account of the verbal skirmish is given by Plutarch; Alexander himself framed all the questions.

"Which be the more numerous, the living or the dead?"

"The living, for the dead are not."

"Which breeds the larger animals, the sea or the land?"

"The land, for the sea is only a part of land."

"Which is the cleverest of beasts?"

"That one with which man is not yet acquainted." (Man fears the unknown.)

"Which existed first, the day or the night?"

"The day was first by one day." This reply caused Alexander to betray surprise; the Brahmin added: "Impossible questions require impossible answers."

"How best may a man make himself beloved?"

"A man will be beloved if, possessed with great power, he still does not make himself feared."

"How may a man become a god?"

"By doing that which it is impossible for a man to do."

"Which is stronger, life or death?"

"Life, because it bears so many evils."

Alexander succeeded in taking out of India, as his teacher, a true yogi. This man was Swami Sphines, called "Kalanos" by the Greeks because the saint, a devotee of God in the form of Kali, greeted everyone by pronouncing Her auspicious name.

Kalanos accompanied Alexander to Persia. On a stated day, at Susa in Persia, Kalanos gave up his aged body by entering a funeral pyre in view of the whole Macedonian army. The historians record the astonishment of the soldiers who observed that the yogi had no fear of pain or death, and who never once moved from his position as he was consumed in the flames. Before leaving for his cremation, Kalanos had embraced all his close companions, but refrained from bidding farewell to Alexander, to whom the Hindu sage had merely remarked:

"I shall see you shortly in Babylon."

Alexander left Persia, and died a year later in Babylon. His Indian guru's words had been his way of saying he would be present with Alexander in life and death.

The Emperor Chandragupta who in 305 B.C. had defeated Alexander's general, Seleucus, decided seven years later to hand over the reins of India's government to his son. Traveling to South India, Chandragupta spent the last twelve years of his life as a penniless ascetic, seeking self-realization in a rocky cave at Sravanabelagola, now honored as a Mysore shrine. Near-by stands the world's largest statue, carved out of an immense boulder by the Jains in A.D. 983 to honor the saint Comateswara.

In the beautiful and fertile State of Travancore in the extreme south of India, where traffic is conveyed over rivers and canals, the Maharaja assumes every year a hereditary obligation to expiate the sin incurred by wars and the annexation in the distant past of several petty states to Travancore.

Madras Presidency on the southeast coast of India contains the flat, spacious, sea-girt city of Madras, and Conjeeveram, the Golden City, capital site of the Pallava dynasty whose kings ruled during the early centuries of the Christian era. In modern Madras Presidency, the nonviolent ideals of Mahatma Gandhi have made great headway; the white distinguishing "Gandhi caps" are seen everywhere. In the south generally the Mahatma has effected many important temple reforms for "untouchables" as well as caste-system reforms.

The origin of the caste system, formulated by the great legislator Manu, was admirable. He saw clearly that men are distinguished by natural evolution into four great classes: those capable of offering service to society through their bodily labor (SUDRAS); those who serve through mentality, skill, agriculture, trade, commerce, business life in general (VAISYAS); those whose talents are administrative, executive, and protective-rulers and warriors (KSHATRIYAS); those of contemplative nature, spiritually inspired and inspiring (BRAHMINS). "Neither birth nor sacraments nor tudy nor ancestry can decide whether a person is twice-born (i.e., a BRAHMIN);" the MAHABHARATA declares, "character and conduct only can decide."

Serious evils arose when the caste system became hardened through the centuries into a hereditary halter. Social reformers like Gandhi and the members of very numerous societies in India today are making slow but sure progress in restoring the ancient values of caste, based solely on natural qualification and not on birth. Every nation on earth has its own distinctive misery-producing karma to deal with and remove; India, too, with her versatile and invulnerable spirit, shall prove herself equal to the task of caste-reformation.

So entrancing is southern India that Mr. Wright and I yearned to prolong our idyl. But time, in its immemorial rudeness, dealt us no courteous extensions. I was scheduled soon to address the concluding session of the Indian Philosophical Congress at Calcutta University.

At the end of the visit to Mysore, I enjoyed a talk with Sir C. V. Raman, president of the Indian Academy of Sciences. This brilliant Hindu physicist was awarded the Nobel Prize in 1930 for his important discovery in the diffusion of light – the "Raman Effect" now known to every schoolboy.

Waving a reluctant farewell to a crowd of Madras students and friends, Mr. Wright and I set out for the north. On the way we stopped before a little shrine sacred to the memory of Sadasiva Brahman, in whose eighteenth-century life story miracles cluster thickly. A larger Sadasiva shrine at Nerur, erected by the Raja of Pudukkottai, is a pilgrimage spot which has witnessed numerous divine healings.

42

Last Days with My Guru

"Guruji, I am glad to find you alone this morning." I had just arrived at the Serampore hermitage, carrying a fragrant burden of fruit and roses. Sri Yukteswar glanced at me meekly.

"What is your question?" Master looked about the room as though he were seeking escape.

"Guruji, I came to you as a high-school youth; now I am a grown man, even with a gray hair or two. Though you have showered me with silent affection from the first hour to this, do you realize that once only, on the day of meeting, have you ever said, 'I love you'?" I looked at him pleadingly.

Master lowered his gaze. "Yogananda, must I bring out into the cold realms of speech the warm sentiments best guarded by the wordless heart?"

"Guruji, I know you love me, but my mortal ears ache to hear you say so."

"Be it as you wish. During my married life I often yearned for a son, to train in the yogic path. But when you came into my life, I was content; in you I have found my son." Two clear teardrops stood in Sri Yukteswar's eyes. "Yogananda, I love you always."

"Your answer is my passport to heaven." I felt a weight lift from my heart, dissolved forever at his words.

A few days later, when I spoke before a huge audience at Albert Hall in Calcutta, Sri Yukteswar consented to sit beside me on the platform, with the Maharaja of Santosh and the Mayor of Calcutta. Though Master made no remark to me, I glanced at him from time to time during my address, and thought I detected a pleased twinkle in his eyes.

Then came a talk before the alumni of Serampore College. As I gazed upon my old classmates, and as they gazed on their own "Mad Monk," tears of joy showed unashamedly. My silver-tongued professor of philosophy, Dr. Ghoshal, came forward to greet me, all our past misunderstandings dissolved by the alchemist Time.

A Winter Solstice Festival was celebrated at the end of December in the Serampore hermitage. As always, Sri Yukteswar's disciples gathered from far and near. Devotional SANKIRTANS, solos in the nectar-sweet voice of Kristo-da, a feast served by young disciples, Master's profoundly moving discourse under the stars in the thronged courtyard of the ashram-memories, memories! Joyous festivals of years long past! Tonight, however, there was to be a new feature.

"Yogananda, please address the assemblage in English." Master's eyes were twinkling as he made this doubly unusual request; was he thinking of the shipboard predicament that had preceded my first lecture in English? I told the story to my audience of brother disciples, ending with a fervent tribute to our guru.

"His omnipresent guidance was with me not alone on the ocean steamer," I concluded, "but daily throughout my fifteen years in the vast and hospitable land of America."

After the guests had departed, Sri Yukteswar called me to the same bedroom where – once only, after a festival of my early years – I had been permitted to sleep on his wooden bed. Tonight my guru was sitting there quietly, a semicircle of disciples at his feet. He smiled as I quickly entered the room.

"Yogananda, are you leaving now for Calcutta? Please return here tomorrow. I have certain things to tell you."

The next afternoon, with a few simple words of blessing, Sri Yukteswar bestowed on me the further monastic title of PARAMHANSA.

"It now formally supersedes your former title of SWAMI," he said as I knelt before him. With a silent chuckle I thought of the struggle which my American students would undergo over the pronunciation of PARAMHANSAJI.

"My task on earth is now finished; you must carry on." Master spoke quietly, his eyes calm and gentle. My heart was palpitating in fear.

"Please send someone to take charge of our ashram at Puri," Sri Yukteswar went on. "I leave everything in your hands. You will be able to successfully sail the boat of your life and that of the organization to the divine shores."

In tears, I was embracing his feet; he rose and blessed me endearingly.

The following day I summoned from Ranchi a disciple, Swami Sebananda, and sent him to Puri to assume the hermitage duties. Later my guru discussed with me the legal details of settling his estate; he was anxious to prevent the possibility of litigation by relatives, after his death, for possession of his two hermitages and other properties, which he wished to be deeded over solely for charitable purposes.

"Arrangements were recently made for Master to visit Kidderpore, but he failed to go." Amulaya Babu, a brother disciple, made this remark to me one afternoon; I felt a cold wave of premonition. To my pressing inquiries, Sri Yukteswar only replied, "I shall go to Kidderpore no more." For a moment, Master trembled like a frightened child.

"Guruji," I entreated him with a sob, "don't say that! Never utter those words to me!"

Sri Yukteswar's face relaxed in a peaceful smile. Though nearing his eighty-first birthday, he looked well and strong.

Basking day by day in the sunshine of my guru's love, unspoken but keenly felt, I banished from my conscious mind the various hints he had given of his approaching passing.

"Sir, the KUMBHA MELA is convening this month at Allahabad." I showed Master the MELA dates in a Bengali almanac.

"Do you really want to go?"

Not sensing Sri Yukteswar's reluctance to have me leave him, I went on, "Once you beheld the blessed sight of Babaji at an Allahabad KUMBHA. Perhaps this time I shall be fortunate enough to see him."

"I do not think you will meet him there." My guru then fell into silence, not wishing to obstruct my plans.

When I set out for Allahabad the following day with a small group, Master blessed me quietly in his usual manner. Apparently I was remaining oblivious to implications in Sri Yukteswar's attitude because the Lord wished to spare me the experience of being forced, helplessly, to witness my guru's passing. It has always happened in my life that, at the death of those dearly beloved by me, God has compassionately arranged that I be distant from the scene.

Our party reached the KUMBHA MELA on January 23, 1936. The surging crowd of nearly two million persons was an impressive sight, even an overwhelming one.. Westerners who were viewing the vast spectacle had a unique opportunity to feel the pulse of the land, the spiritual ardor to which India owes her quenchless vitality before the blows of time.

Here and there under the trees, around huge piles of burning logs, were picturesque sadhus, their hair braided and massed in coils on top of their heads. Some wore beards several feet in length, curled and tied in a knot. They meditated quietly, or extended their hands in blessing to the passing throng-beggars, maharajas on elephants, women in multicolored SARIS--their bangles and anklets tinkling, FAKIRS with thin arms held grotesquely aloft, BRAHMACHARIS carrying meditation elbow-props, humble sages whose solemnity hid an inner bliss. High above the din we heard the ceaseless summons of the temple bells.

On our second MELA day my companions and I entered various ashrams and temporary huts, offering PRONAMS to saintly personages. We received the blessing of the leader of the GIRI branch of the Swami Order. Our next visit took us to a hermitage whose guru had observed for the past nine years the vows of silence and a strict fruitarian diet. On the central dais in the ashram hall sat a blind sadhu, Pragla Chakshu, profoundly learned in the SHASTRAS and highly revered by all sects.

After I had given a brief discourse in Hindi on VEDANTA, our group left the peaceful hermitage to greet a near-by swami, Krishnananda. Reclining near him was a tame lioness. Succumbing to the monk's spiritual charm--not, I am sure, to his powerful physique!-the jungle animal refuses all meat in favor of rice and milk. The swami has taught the tawny-haired beast to utter "AUM" in a deep, attractive growl-a cat devotee!

Our next encounter, an interview with a learned young sadhu, is well described in Mr. Wright's sparkling travel diary.

"We rode in the Ford across the very low Ganges on a creaking pontoon bridge, crawling snakelike through the crowds and over narrow, twisting lanes, passing the site on the river bank which Yoganandaji pointed out to me as the meeting place of Babaji and Sri Yukteswarji. Alighting from the car a short time later, we walked some distance and halted in front of one of these insignificant temporary dwellings, with a pygmy doorless entrance, the shelter of Kara Patri, a young wandering sadhu noted for his exceptional intelligence. There he sat, cross-legged on a pile of straw, his only covering-and incidentally his only possession-being an ocher cloth draped over his shoulders.

"Truly a divine face smiled at us after we had crawled on all fours into the hut and PRONAMED at the feet of this enlightened soul. His face, especially his eyes and perfect teeth, beamed and glistened.

"Imagine the happy life of one unattached to the material world; free of the clothing problem; free of food craving, never begging, never touching cooked food except on alternate days, never carrying a begging bowl; free of all money entanglements, never handling money, never storing things away, always trusting in God; free of transportation worries, never riding in vehicles, but always walking on the banks of the sacred rivers; never remaining in one place longer than a week in order to avoid any growth of attachment.

"Such a modest soul! unusually learned in the VEDAS, and possessing an M.A. degree and the title of SHASTRI (master of scriptures) from Benares University. A sublime feeling pervaded me as I sat at his feet; it all seemed to be an answer to my desire to see the real, the ancient India, for he is a true representative of this land of spiritual giants."

I questioned Kara Patri about his wandering life. "Don't you have any extra clothes for winter?"

"No, this is enough."

"Do you carry any books?"

"No, I teach from memory those people who wish to hear me."

"What else do you do?"

"I roam by the Ganges."

At these quiet words, I was overpowered by a yearning for the simplicity of his life. I remembered America, and all the responsibilities that lay on my shoulders.

"No, Yogananda," I thought, sadly for a moment, "in this life roaming by the Ganges is not for you."

After the sadhu had told me a few of his spiritual realizations, I shot an abrupt question.

"Are you giving these descriptions from scriptural lore, or from inward experience?"

"Half from book learning," he answered with a straightforward smile, "and half from experience."

We sat happily awhile in meditative silence. After we had left his sacred presence, I said to Mr. Wright, "He is a king sitting on a throne of golden straw."

Two more days of the fascinating KUMBHA; then northwest along the Jumna banks to Agra. Once again I gazed on the Taj Mahal; in memory Jitendra stood by my side, awed by the dream in marble. Then on to the Brindaban ashram of Swami Keshabananda.

My object in seeking out Keshabananda was connected with this book. I had never forgotten Sri Yukteswar's request that I write the life of Lahiri Mahasaya. During my stay in India I was taking every opportunity of contacting direct disciples and relatives of the Yogavatar. Recording their conversations in voluminous notes, I verified facts and dates, and collected photographs, old letters, and documents. My Lahiri Mahasaya portfolio began to swell; I realized with dismay that ahead of me lay arduous labors in authorship. I prayed that I might be equal to my role as biographer of the colossal guru. Several of his disciples feared that in a written account their master might be belittled or misinterpreted.

Nevertheless, mindful of Lahiri Mahasaya's prediction about his biography, I spared no effort to secure and substantiate the facts of his outward life.

Swami Keshabananda greeted our party warmly at Brindaban in his Katayani Peith Ashram. He ushered us at once into a sitting room adorned with an enlargement of Lahiri Mahasaya's picture. The swami was approaching the age of ninety, but his muscular body radiated strength and health. I informed him that I wanted to mention his name in my book on India's masters.

"Please tell me about your earlier life." I smiled entreatingly; great yogis are often uncommunicative.

Keshabananda made a gesture of humility. "There is little of external moment. Practically my whole life has been spent in the Himalayan solitudes, traveling on foot from one quiet cave to another. For a while I maintained a small ashram outside Hardwar, surrounded on all sides by a grove of tall trees. It was a peaceful spot little visited by travelers, owing to the ubiquitous presence of cobras." Keshabananda chuckled. "Later a Ganges flood washed away the hermitage and cobras alike. My disciples then helped me to build this Brindaban ashram.

"Occasionally I left my seclusion to visit my guru in

Benares. He used to joke with me over my ceaseless travels in the Himalayan wilderness.

"'You have the mark of wanderlust on your foot,' he told me once. 'I am glad that the sacred Himalayas are extensive enough to engross you.'

"Many times," Keshabananda went on, "both before and after his passing, Lahiri Mahasaya has appeared bodily before me. For him no Himalayan height is inaccessible!"

Two hours later he led us to a dining patio. I sighed in silent dismay. Another fifteen-course meal! Less than a year of Indian hospitality, and I had gained fifty pounds! Yet it would have been considered the height of rudeness to refuse any of the dishes, carefully prepared for the endless banquets in my honor. In India (nowhere else, alas!) a well-padded swami is considered a delightful sight.

After dinner, Keshabananda led me to a secluded nook.

"Your arrival is not unexpected," he said. "I have a message for you."

I was surprised; no one had known of my plan to visit Keshabananda.

"While roaming last year in the northern Himalayas near Badrinarayan," the swami continued, "I lost my way. Shelter appeared in a spacious cave, which was empty, though the embers of a fire glowed in a hole in the rocky floor. Wondering about the occupant of this lonely retreat, I sat near the fire, my gaze fixed on the sunlit entrance to the cave.

"'Keshabananda, I am glad you are here.' These words came from behind me. I turned, startled, and was dazzled to behold Babaji! The great guru had materialized himself in a recess of the cave. Overjoyed to see him again after many years, I prostrated myself at his holy feet.

"'I called you here,' Babaji went on. 'That is why you lost your way and were led to my temporary abode in this cave. It is a long time since our last meeting; I am pleased to greet you once more.'

"The deathless master blessed me with some words of spiritual help, then added: 'I give you a message for Yogananda. He will pay you a visit on his return to India. Many matters connected with his guru and with the surviving disciples of Lahiri will keep Yogananda fully occupied. Tell him, then, that I won't see him this time, as he is eagerly hoping; but I shall see him on some other occasion.'"

I was deeply touched to receive from Keshabananda's lips this consoling promise from Babaji. A certain hurt in my heart vanished; I grieved no longer that, even as Sri Yukteswar had hinted, Babaji did not appear at the KUMBHA MELA.

Spending one night as guests of the ashram, our party set out the following afternoon for Calcutta.

In a few days our little group reached Calcutta. Eager to see Sri Yukteswar, I was disappointed to hear that he had left Serampore and was now in Puri, about three hundred miles to the south.

"Come to Puri ashram at once." This telegram was sent on March 8th by a brother disciple to Atul Chandra Roy Chowdhry, one of Master's chelas in Calcutta. News of the message reached my ears; anguished at its implications, I dropped to my knees and implored God that my guru's life be spared. As I was about to leave Father's home for the train, a divine voice spoke within.

"Do not go to Puri tonight. Thy prayer cannot be granted."

"Lord," I said, grief-stricken, "Thou dost not wish to engage with me in a 'tug of war' at Puri, where Thou wilt have to deny my incessant prayers for Master's life. Must he, then, depart for higher duties at Thy behest?"

In obedience to the inward command, I did not leave that night for Puri. The following evening I set out for the train; on the way, at seven o'clock, a black astral cloud suddenly covered the sky. Later, while the train roared toward Puri, a vision of Sri Yukteswar appeared before me. He was sitting, very grave of countenance, with a light on each side.

"Is it all over?" I lifted my arms beseechingly.

He nodded, then slowly vanished.

As I stood on the Puri train platform the following morning, still hoping against hope, an unknown man approached me.

"Have you heard that your Master is gone?" He left me without another word; I never discovered who he was nor how he had known where to find me.

Stunned, I swayed against the platform wall, realizing that in diverse ways my guru was trying to convey to me the devastating news. By the time I reached the Puri hermitage I was nearing collapse. The inner voice was tenderly repeating: "Collect yourself. Be calm."

I entered the ashram room where Master's body, unimaginably lifelike, was sitting in the lotus posture – a picture of health and loveliness. A short time before his passing, my guru had been slightly ill with fever, but before the day of his ascension into the Infinite, his body had become completely well. No matter how often I looked at his dear form I could not realize that its life had departed. His skin was smooth and soft; in his face was a beatific expression of tranquillity. He had consciously relinquished his body at the hour of mystic summoning.

"The Lion of Bengal is gone!" I cried in a daze.

I conducted the solemn rites on March 10. Sri Yukteswar was buried with the ancient rituals of the swamis in the garden of his Puri ashram. His disciples later arrived from far and near to honor their guru at a vernal equinox memorial service.

"Never again may you see him in the old Serampore mansion," my heart lamented. "No longer may you bring your friends to meet him, or proudly say: 'Behold, there sits India's JNANAVATAR!'"

Mr. Wright made arrangements for our party to sail from Bombay for the West in early June. After a fortnight in May of farewell banquets and speeches at Calcutta, Miss Bletch, Mr. Wright and myself left in the Ford for Bombay. On our arrival, the ship authorities asked us to cancel our passage, as no room could be found for the Ford, which we would need again in Europe.

"Never mind," I said gloomily to Mr. Wright. "I want to return once more to Puri." I silently added, "Let my tears once again water the grave of my guru."

43

The Resurrection of Sri Yukteswar

"Lord Krishna!" The glorious form of the avatar appeared in a shimmering blaze as I sat in my room at the Regent Hotel in Bombay. Shining over the roof of a high building across the street, the ineffable vision had suddenly burst on my sight as I gazed out of my long open third-story window.

The divine figure waved to me, smiling and nodding in greeting. When I could not understand the exact message of Lord Krishna, he departed with a gesture of blessing. Wondrously uplifted, I felt that some spiritual event was presaged.

Sitting on my bed in the Bombay hotel at three o'clock in the afternoon of June 19, 1936, one week after the vision of Krishna, I was roused from my meditation by a beatific light. Before my open and astonished eyes, the whole room was transformed into a strange world, the sunlight transmuted into supernal splendor.

Waves of rapture engulfed me as I beheld the flesh and blood form of Sri Yukteswar!

"My son!" Master spoke tenderly, on his face an angel-bewitching smile.

For the first time in my life I did not kneel at his feet in greeting but instantly advanced to gather him hungrily in my arms. Moment of moments! The anguish of past months was toll I counted weightless against the torrential bliss now descending.

"Master mine, beloved of my heart, why did you leave me?" I was incoherent in an excess of joy. "Why did you let me go to the KUMBHA MELA? How bitterly have I blamed myself for leaving you!"

"I did not want to interfere with your happy anticipation of seeing the pilgrimage spot where first I met Babaji. I left you only for a little while; am I not with you again?"

"But is it YOU, Master, the same Lion of God? Are you wearing a body like the one I buried beneath the cruel Puri sands?"

"Yes, my child, I am the same. This is a flesh and blood body. Though I see it as ethereal, to your sight it is physical. From the cosmic atoms I created an entirely new body, exactly like that cosmic-dream physical body which you laid beneath the dream-sands at Puri in your dream-world. I am in truth resurrected – not on earth but on an astral planet. Its inhabitants are better able than earthly humanity to meet my lofty standards. There you and your exalted loved ones shall someday come to be with me."

"Deathless guru, tell me more!"

Master gave a quick, mirthful chuckle. "Please, dear one," he said, "won't you relax your hold a little?"

"Only a little!" I had been embracing him with an octopus grip. I could detect the same faint, fragrant, natural odor which had been characteristic of his body before.

"As prophets are sent on earth to help men work out their

physical karma, so I have been directed by God to serve on an astral planet as a savior," Sri Yukteswar explained. "It is called HIRANYALOKA or 'Illumined Astral Planet.' There I am aiding advanced beings to rid themselves of astral karma and thus attain liberation from astral rebirths. The dwellers on Hiranyaloka are highly developed spiritually; all of them had acquired, in their last earth-incarnation, the meditation-given power of consciously leaving their physical bodies at death. No one can enter Hiranyaloka unless he has passed on earth beyond the state of SABIKALPA SAMADHI into the higher state of NIRBIKALPA SAMADHI. None but advanced beings can perform such redemptive work effectually in the astral worlds. Then, in order to free their souls more fully from the cocoon of karmic traces lodged in their astral bodies, these higher beings were drawn by cosmic law to be reborn with new astral bodies on Hiranyaloka where I have resurrected to help them."

My mind was now in such perfect attunement with my guru's that he was conveying his word-pictures to me partly by speech and partly by thought-transference. I was thus quickly receiving his idea-tabloids.

"You have read in the scriptures," Master went on, "that God encased the human soul successively in three bodies – the idea, or causal, body; the subtle astral body, seat of man's mental and emotional natures; and the gross physical body. On earth a man is equipped with his physical senses. An astral being works with his consciousness and feelings and a body made of lifetrons. A causal-bodied being remains in the blissful realm of ideas. My work is with those astral beings who are preparing to enter the causal world."

"Adorable Master, please tell me more about the astral

cosmos." Though I had slightly relaxed my embrace at Sri Yukteswar's request, my arms were still around him.

"There are many astral planets, teeming with astral beings," Master began. "The inhabitants use astral planes, or masses of light, to travel from one planet to another, faster than electricity and radioactive energies.

"The astral universe, made of various subtle vibrations of light and color, is hundreds of times larger than the material cosmos. The entire physical creation hangs like a little solid basket under the huge luminous balloon of the astral sphere. Just as many physical suns and stars roam in space, so there are also countless astral solar and stellar systems. Their planets have astral suns and moons, more beautiful than the physical ones. The astral luminaries resemble the aurora borealis-the sunny astral aurora being more dazzling than the mild-rayed moon-aurora. The astral day and night are longer than those of earth.

"The astral world is infinitely beautiful, clean, pure, and orderly. There are no dead planets or barren lands. The terrestrial blemishes--weeds, bacteria, insects, snakes-are absent.

"The ordinary astral universe – not the subtler astral heaven of Hiranyaloka – is peopled with millions of astral beings who have come, more or less recently, from the earth, and also with myriads of fairies, mermaids, fishes, animals, goblins, gnomes, demigods and spirits, all residing on different astral planets in accordance with karmic qualifications.

"In the vast realms above the dark astral prison, all is shining and beautiful. The astral cosmos is more naturally attuned than the earth to the divine will and plan of perfection. Every astral object is manifested primarily by the will of God, and partially by the will-call of astral beings. They possess the power of modifying or enhancing the grace and form of anything already created by the Lord. He has given His astral children the freedom and privilege of changing or improving at will the astral cosmos.

"The earth is dark with warfare and murder in the sea, land, and air," my guru continued, "but the astral realms know a happy harmony and equality. Astral beings dematerialize or materialize their forms at will. Flowers or fish or animals can metamorphose themselves, for a time, into astral men. All astral beings are free to assume any form, and can easily commune together. Certain karmic restrictions are present, but there are no distinctions in the astral world about desirability of various forms. Everything is vibrant with God's creative light.

"No one is born of woman; offspring are materialized by astral beings through the help of their cosmic will into specially patterned, astrally condensed forms. The recently physically disembodied being arrives in an astral family through invitation, drawn by similar mental and spiritual tendencies.

"The astral body is not subject to cold or heat or other natural conditions. The anatomy includes an astral brain, or the thousand-petaled lotus of light, and six awakened centers in the SUSHUMNA, or astral cerebro-spinal axis. The heart draws cosmic energy as well as light from the astral brain, and pumps it to the astral nerves and body cells, or lifetrons. Astral beings can affect their bodies by lifetronic force or by MANTRIC vibrations.

"The astral body is an exact counterpart of the last physical form. Astral beings retain the same appearance which they possessed in youth in their previous earthly sojourn; occasionally an astral being chooses, like myself, to retain his old age appearance." Master, emanating the very essence of youth, chuckled merrily.

"Unlike the spacial, three-dimensional physical world cognized only by the five senses, the astral spheres are visible to the all-inclusive sixth sense-intuition," Sri Yukteswar went on. "By sheer intuitional feeling, all astral beings see, hear, smell, taste, and touch. They possess three eyes, two of which are partly closed. The third and chief astral eye, vertically placed on the forehead, is open. Astral beings have all the outer sensory organs – ears, eyes, nose, tongue, and skin – but they employ the intuitional sense to experience sensations through any part of the body; they can see through the ear, or nose, or skin. They are able to hear through the eyes or tongue, and can taste through the ears or skin, and so forth.

"Man's physical body is exposed to countless dangers, and is easily hurt or maimed; the ethereal astral body may occasionally be cut or bruised but is healed at once by mere willing."

"Gurudeva, are all astral persons beautiful?"

"Beauty in the astral world is known to be a spiritual quality, and not an outward conformation," Sri Yukteswar replied.

"The intuition of astral beings pierces through the veil and observes human activities on earth, but man cannot view the astral world unless his sixth sense is somewhat developed. Thousands of earth-dwellers have momentarily glimpsed an astral being or an astral world.

"Inhabitants in all parts of the astral worlds are still subject to mental agonies. The sensitive minds of the higher beings on planets like Hiranyaloka feel keen pain if any mistake is made in conduct or perception of truth. These advanced beings endeavor to attune their every act and thought with the perfection of spiritual law.

"Communication among the astral inhabitants is held entirely by astral telepathy and television; there is none of the confusion and misunderstanding of the written and spoken word which earth-dwellers must endure. Man depends upon solids, liquids, gases, and energy for sustenance; astral beings sustain themselves principally by cosmic light."

"Master mine, do astral beings eat anything?" I was drinking in his marvelous elucidations with the receptivity of all my faculties-mind, heart, soul.

"Luminous raylike vegetables abound in the astral soils," he answered. "The astral beings consume vegetables, and drink a nectar flowing from glorious fountains of light and from astral brooks and rivers. Although dwellers on the heavenly planets like Hiranyaloka are almost freed from any necessity of eating, still higher is the unconditioned existence of almost completely liberated souls in the causal world, who eat nothing save the manna of bliss.

"The earth-liberated astral being meets a multitude of relatives, fathers, mothers, wives, husbands, and friends, acquired during different incarnations on earth, as they appear from time to time in various parts of the astral realms. He is therefore at a loss to understand whom to love especially; he learns in this way to give a divine and equal love to all, as children and individualized expressions of God.

"The span of life in the astral world is much longer than on earth. A normal advanced astral being's average life period is from five hundred to one thousand years, measured in accordance with earthly standards of time. As certain redwood trees outlive most trees by millenniums, or as some yogis live several hundred years though most men die before the age of sixty, so some astral beings live much longer than the usual span of astral existence. Visitors to the astral world dwell there for a longer or shorter period in accordance with the weight of their physical karma, which draws them back to earth within a specified time.

"Physical death is attended by the disappearance of breath and the disintegration of fleshly cells. Astral death consists of the dispersement of lifetrons, those manifest units of energy which constitute the life of astral beings. At physical death a being loses his consciousness of flesh and becomes aware of his subtle body in the astral world. Experiencing astral death in due time, a being thus passes from the consciousness of astral birth and death to that of physical birth and death."

"Beloved Master," I asked, "will you please describe more in detail the difference between rebirth on the earth and in the astral and causal spheres?"

"Man as an individualized soul is essentially causal-bodied," my guru explained. "That body is a matrix of the thirty-five IDEAS required by God as the basic or causal thought forces from which He later formed the subtle astral body of nineteen elements and the gross physical body of sixteen elements.

"The nineteen elements of the astral body are mental, emotional, and lifetronic. The nineteen components are intelligence; ego; feeling; mind (sense-consciousness); five instruments of KNOWLEDGE, the subtle counterparts of the senses of sight, hearing, smell, taste, touch; five instruments of ACTION, the mental correspondence for the executive abilities to procreate, excrete, talk, walk, and exercise manual skill; and five instruments of LIFE FORCE, those empowered to perform the crystallizing, assimilating, eliminating, metabolizing, and circulating functions of the body. This subtle astral encasement of nineteen elements survives the death of the physical body, which is made of sixteen gross metallic and nonmetallic elements.

"Physical desires are rooted in egotism and sense pleasures. The compulsion or temptation of sensory experience is more powerful than the desire-force connected with astral attachments or causal perceptions.

"Astral desires center around enjoyment in terms of vibration. Astral beings enjoy the ethereal music of the spheres and are entranced by the sight of all creation as exhaustless expressions of changing light. The astral beings also smell, taste, and touch light. Astral desires are thus connected with an astral being's power to precipitate all objects and experiences as forms of light or as condensed thoughts or dreams.

"Causal desires are fulfilled by perception only. The nearly-free beings who are encased only in the causal body see the whole universe as realizations of the dream-ideas of God; they can materialize anything and everything in sheer thought. Causal beings therefore consider the enjoyment of physical sensations or astral delights as gross and suffocating to the soul's fine sensibilities. Causal beings work out their desires by materializing them instantly.

"A soul, being invisible by nature, can be distinguished only by the presence of its body or bodies. The mere presence of a body signifies that its existence is made possible by unfulfilled desires.

"So long as the soul of man is encased in one, two, or three body-containers, sealed tightly with the corks of ignorance and desires, he cannot merge with the sea of Spirit. When the gross physical receptacle is destroyed by the hammer of death, the other two coverings-astral and causal-still remain to prevent the soul from consciously joining the Omnipresent Life. When desirelessness is attained through wisdom, its power disintegrates the two remaining vessels. The tiny human soul emerges, free at last; it is one with the Measureless Amplitude.

"Both death and rebirth in the causal world are in thought. Causal-bodied beings feast only on the ambrosia of eternally new knowledge. They drink from the springs of peace, roam on the trackless soil of perceptions, swim in the ocean-endlessness of bliss. Lo! see their bright thought-bodies zoom past trillions of Spirit-created planets, fresh bubbles of universes, wisdom-stars, spectral dreams of golden nebulae, all over the skiey blue osom of Infinity!

"Many beings remain for thousands of years in the causal cosmos. By deeper ecstasies the freed soul then withdraws itself from the little causal body and puts on the vastness of the causal cosmos. All the separate eddies of ideas, particularized waves of power, love, will, joy, peace, intuition, calmness, self-control, and concentration melt into the ever-joyous Sea of Bliss. No longer does the soul have to experience its joy as an individualized wave of consciousness, but is merged in the One Cosmic Ocean, with all its waves-eternal laughter, thrills, throbs.

"When a soul is out of the cocoon of the three bodies it escapes forever from the law of relativity and becomes the ineffable Ever-Existent. Behold the butterfly of Omnipresence, its wings etched with stars and moons and suns! The soul expanded into Spirit remains alone in the region of lightless light, darkles dark, thoughtless thought, intoxicated with its ecstasy of joy in God's dream of cosmic creation."

"A free soul!" I ejaculated in awe.

"When a soul finally gets out of the three jars of bodily delusions," Master continued, "it becomes one with the Infinite without any loss of individuality. Christ had won this final freedom even before he was born as Jesus. In three stages of his past, symbolized in his earth-life as the three days of his experience of death and resurrection, he had attained the power to fully arise in Spirit.

"The undeveloped man must undergo countless earthly and astral and causal incarnations in order to emerge from his three bodies. A master who achieves this final freedom may elect to return to earth as a prophet to bring other human beings back to God, or like myself he may choose to reside in the astral cosmos. There a savior assumes some of the burden of the inhabitants' karma } and thus helps them to terminate their cycle of reincarnation in the astral cosmos and go on permanently to the causal spheres. Or a freed soul may enter the causal world to aid its beings to shorten their span in the causal body and thus attain the Absolute Freedom."

"Resurrected One, I want to know more about the karma which forces souls to return to the three worlds." I could listen forever, I thought, to my omniscient Master.

"The physical karma or desires of man must be completely worked out before his permanent stay in astral worlds becomes possible," my guru elucidated in his thrilling voice. "Two kinds of beings live in the astral spheres. Those who still have earthly karma to dispose of and who must therefore reinhabit a gross physical body in order to pay their karmic debts could be classified, after physical death, as temporary visitors to the astral world rather than as permanent residents.

"Beings with unredeemed earthly karma are not permitted after astral death to go to the high causal sphere of cosmic ideas, but must shuttle to and fro from the physical and astral worlds only, conscious successively of their physical body of sixteen gross elements, and of their astral body of nineteen subtle elements. After each loss of his physical body, however, an undeveloped being from the earth remains for the most part in the deep stupor of the death-sleep and is hardly conscious of the beautiful astral sphere. After the astral rest, such a man returns to the material plane for further lessons, gradually accustoming himself, through repeated journeys, to the worlds of subtle astral texture.

"Normal or long-established residents of the astral universe, on the other hand, are those who, freed forever from all material longings, need return no more to the gross vibrations of earth. Such beings have only astral and causal karma to work out. At astral death these beings pass to the infinitely finer and more delicate causal world. Shedding the thought-form of the causal body at the end of a certain span, determined by cosmic law, these advanced beings then return to Hiranyaloka or a similar high astral planet, reborn in a new astral body to work out their unredeemed astral karma.

"My son, you may now comprehend more fully that I am resurrected by divine decree," Sri Yukteswar continued, "as a savior of astrally reincarnating souls coming back from the causal sphere, in particular, rather than of those astral beings who are coming up from the earth. Those from the earth, if they still retain vestiges of material karma, do not rise to the very high astral planets like Hiranyaloka.

"Only when a being has no further desires for experiences in the pleasing-to-the-eye astral cosmos, and cannot be tempted to go back there, does he remain in the causal world. Completing there the work of redeeming all causal karma or seeds of past desires, the confined soul thrusts out the last of the three corks of ignorance and, emerging from the final jar of the causal body, commingles with the Eternal.

"Now do you understand?" Master smiled so enchantingly!

"Yes, through your grace. I am speechless with joy and gratitude."

I had been lovingly observing Sri Yukteswar while he gave his wondrous exposition.

"O Master, I was grieving so deeply about your death!"

"Ah, wherein did I die? Isn't there some contradiction?" Sri Yukteswar's eyes were twinkling with love and amusement.

"You were only dreaming on earth; on that earth you saw my dream-body," he went on. "Later you buried that dream-image. Now my finer fleshly body-which you behold and are even now embracing rather closely!-is resurrected on another finer dream-planet of God. Someday that finer dream-body and finer dream-planet will pass away; they too are not forever. All dream-bubbles must eventually burst at a final wakeful touch. Differentiate, my son Yogananda, between dreams and Reality!"

This idea of VEDANTIC resurrection struck me with wonder. I was ashamed that I had pitied Master when I had seen his lifeless body at Puri. I comprehended at last that my guru had always been fully awake in God, perceiving his own life and passing on earth, and his present resurrection, as nothing more than relativities of divine ideas in the cosmic dream.

"I have now told you, Yogananda, the truths of my life, death, and resurrection. Grieve not for me; rather broadcast everywhere the story of my resurrection from the God-dreamed earth of men to another God-dreamed planet of astrally garbed souls! New hope will be infused into the hearts of misery-mad, death-fearing dreamers of the world."

"Yes, Master!" How willingly would I share with others my joy at his resurrection!

Sri Yukteswar gave me light on certain matters which I cannot reveal here. During the two hours that he spent with me in the Bombay hotel room he answered my every question. A number of world prophecies uttered by him that June day in 1936 have already come to pass.

"I leave you now, beloved one!" At these words I felt Master melting away within my encircling arms.

"My child," his voice rang out, vibrating into my very soul-firmament, "whenever you enter the door of NIRBIKALPA SAMADHI and call on me, I shall come to you in flesh and blood, even as today."

With this celestial promise Sri Yukteswar vanished from my sight. A cloud-voice repeated in musical thunder: "Tell all! Whosoever knows by NIRBIKALPA realization that your earth is a dream of God can come to the finer dream-created planet of Hiranyaloka, and there find me resurrected in a body exactly like my earthly one. Yogananda, tell all!"

Gone was the sorrow of parting. The pity and grief for his death, long robber of my peace, now fled in stark shame. Bliss poured forth like a fountain through endless, newly opened soul-pores. Anciently clogged with disuse, they now widened in purity at the driving flood of ecstasy. Subconscious thoughts and feelings of my past incarnations shed their karmic taints, lustrously renewed by Sri Yukteswar's divine visit.

44

With Mahatma Gandhi at Wardha

"Welcome to Wardha!" Mahadev Desai, secretary to Mahatma Gandhi, greeted Miss Bletch, Mr. Wright, and myself with these cordial words and the gift of wreaths of KHADDAR (homespun cotton). Our little group had just dismounted at the Wardha station on an early morning in August, glad to leave the dust and heat of the train. Consigning our luggage to a bullock cart, we entered an open motor car with Mr. Desai and his companions, Babasaheb Deshmukh and Dr. Pingale. A short drive over the muddy country roads brought us to MAGANVADI, the ashram of India's political saint.

Mr. Desai led us at once to the writing room where, cross-legged, sat Mahatma Gandhi. Pen in one hand and a scrap of paper in the other, on his face a vast, winning, warm-hearted smile!

"Welcome!" he scribbled in Hindi; it was a Monday, his weekly day of silence.

Though this was our first meeting, we beamed on each other affectionately. In 1925 Mahatma Gandhi had honored the Ranchi school by a visit, and had inscribed in its guest-book a gracious tribute.

The tiny 100-pound saint radiated physical, mental, and spiritual health. His soft brown eyes shone with intelligence, sincerity, and discrimination; this statesman has matched wits and emerged the victor in a thousand legal, social, and political battles. No other leader in the world has attained the secure niche in the hearts of his people that Gandhi occupies for India's unlettered millions. Their spontaneous tribute is his famous title-MAHATMA, "great soul." For them alone Gandhi confines his attire to the widely-cartooned loincloth, symbol of his oneness with the downtrodden masses who can afford no more.

"The ashram residents are wholly at your disposal; please call on them for any service." With characteristic courtesy, the Mahatma handed me this hastily-written note as Mr. Desai led our party from the writing room toward the guest house.

Observing Mr. Wright's travel diary, Mr. Desai opened a page and wrote on it a list of SATYAGRAHA vows taken by all the Mahatma's strict followers (SATYAGRAHIS):

"Nonviolence; Truth; Non-Stealing; Celibacy; Non-Possession; Body-Labor; Control of the Palate; Fearlessness; Equal Respect for all Religions; SWADESHI (use of home manufactures); Freedom from Untouchability. These eleven should be observed as vows in a spirit of humility."

(Gandhi himself signed this page on the following day, giving the date also-August 27, 1935.)

Two hours after our arrival my companions and I were summoned to lunch. The Mahatma was already seated under the arcade of the ashram porch, across the courtyard from his study. About twenty-five barefooted SATYAGRAHIS were squatting before brass cups and plates. A community chorus of prayer; then a meal served from large brass pots containing CHAPATIS (whole-wheat unleavened bread) sprinkled with GHEE; TALSARI (boiled and diced vegetables), and a lemon jam.

The Mahatma ate CHAPATIS, boiled beets, some raw vegetables, and oranges. On the side of his plate was a large lump of very bitter NEEM leaves, a notable blood cleanser. With his spoon he separated a portion and placed it on my dish. I bolted it down with water, remembering childhood days when Mother had forced me to swallow the disagreeable dose. Gandhi, however, bit by bit was eating the NEEM paste with as much relish as if it had been a delicious sweetmeat.

In this trifling incident I noted the Mahatma's ability to detach his mind from the senses at will. I recalled the famous appendectomy performed on him some years ago. Refusing anesthetics, the saint had chatted cheerfully with his disciples throughout the operation, his infectious smile revealing his unawareness of pain.

The afternoon brought an opportunity for a chat with Gandhi's noted disciple, daughter of an English admiral, Miss Madeleine Slade, now called Mirabai. Her strong, calm face lit with enthusiasm as she told me, in flawless Hindi, of her daily activities.

"Rural reconstruction work is rewarding! A group of us go every morning at five o'clock to serve the near-by villagers and teach them simple hygiene. We make it a point to clean their latrines and their mud-thatched huts. The villagers are illiterate; they cannot be educated except by example!" She laughed gaily.

I looked in admiration at this highborn Englishwoman whose true Christian humility enables her to do the scavengering work usually performed only by "untouchables."

Gandhi has sound economic and cultural reasons for encouraging the revival of cottage industries, but he does not counsel a fanatical repudiation of all modern progress. Machinery, trains, automobiles, the telegraph have played important parts in his own colossal life! Fifty years of public service, in prison and out, wrestling daily with practical details and harsh realities in the political world, have only increased his balance, open-mindedness, sanity, and humorous appreciation of the quaint human spectacle.

Our trio enjoyed a six o'clock supper as guests of Babasaheb Deshmukh. The 7:00 P.M. prayer hour found us back at the MAGANVADI ashram, climbing to the roof where thirty SATYAGRAHIS were grouped in a semicircle around Gandhi. He was squatting on a straw mat, an ancient pocket watch propped up before him.

A solemn chant led by Mr. Desai, with responses from the group; then a GITA reading. The Mahatma motioned to me to give the concluding prayer. Such divine unison of thought and aspiration! A memory forever: the Wardha roof top meditation under the early stars.

Punctually at eight o'clock Gandhi ended his silence. The herculean labors of his life require him to apportion his time minutely.

"Welcome, Swamiji!" The Mahatma's greeting this time was not via paper. We had just descended from the roof to his writing room, simply furnished with square mats (no chairs), a low desk with books, papers, and a few ordinary pens (not fountain pens); a nondescript clock ticked in a corner. An all-pervasive aura of peace and devotion. Gandhi was bestowing one of his captivating, cavernous, almost toothless smiles.

"Years ago," he explained, "I started my weekly observance of a day of silence as a means for gaining time to look after my correspondence. But now those twenty-four hours have become a vital spiritual need. A periodical decree of silence is not a torture but a blessing."

I agreed wholeheartedly. The Mahatma questioned me

about America and Europe; we discussed India and world conditions.

"Mahadev," Gandhi said as Mr. Desai entered the room, "please make arrangements at Town Hall for Swamiji to speak there on yoga tomorrow night."

As I was bidding the Mahatma good night, he considerately handed me a bottle of citronella oil.

"The Wardha mosquitoes don't know a thing about AHIMSA, Swamiji!" he said, laughing.

The following morning our little group breakfasted early on a tasty wheat porridge with molasses and milk. At ten-thirty we were called to the ashram porch for lunch with Gandhi and the SATYAGRAHIS. Today the menu included brown rice, a new selection of vegetables, and cardamom seeds.

Noon found me strolling about the ashram grounds, on to the grazing land of a few imperturbable cows. The protection of cows is a passion with Gandhi.

"The cow to me means the entire sub-human world, extending man's sympathies beyond his own species," the Mahatma has explained. "Man through the cow is enjoined to realize his identity with all that lives. Why the ancient rishis selected the cow for apotheosis is obvious to me. The cow in India was the best comparison; she was the giver of plenty. Not only did she give milk, but she also made agriculture possible. The cow is a poem of pity; one reads pity in the gentle animal. She is the second mother to millions of mankind. Protection of the cow means protection of the whole dumb creation of God. The appeal of the lower order of creation is all the more forceful because it is speechless."

Three daily rituals are enjoined on the orthodox Hindu. One is BHUTA YAJNA, an offering of food to the animal kingdom. This ceremony symbolizes man's realization of his obligations to less evolved forms of creation, instinctively tied to bodily identifications which also corrode human life, but lacking in that quality of liberating reason which is peculiar to humanity. BHUTA YAJNA thus reinforces man's readiness to succor the weak, as he in turn is comforted by countless solicitudes of higher unseen beings.

The other two daily YAJNAS are PITRI and NRI. PITRI YAJNA is an offering of oblations to ancestors, as a symbol of man's acknowledgment of his debt to the past, essence of whose wisdom illumines humanity today. NRI YAJNA is an offering of food to strangers or the poor, symbol of the present responsibilities of man, his duties to contemporaries.

Reentering the guest house I was struck anew by the stark simplicity and evidences of self-sacrifice which are everywhere present. The Gandhi vow of non-possession came early in his married life. Renouncing an extensive legal practice which had been yielding him an annual income of more than $20,000, the Mahatma dispersed all his wealth to the poor.

Saints like Gandhi have made not only tangible material sacrifices, but also the more difficult renunciation of selfish motive and private goal, merging their inmost being in the stream of humanity as a whole.

The Mahatma's remarkable wife, Kasturabai, did not object when he failed to set aside any part of his wealth for the use of herself and their children. Married in early youth, Gandhi and his wife took the vow of celibacy after the birth of several sons. A tranquil heroine in the intense drama that has been their life together, Kasturabai has followed her husband to prison, shared his three-week fasts, and fully borne her share of his endless responsibilities. She has paid Gandhi the following tribute:

I thank you for having had the privilege of being your lifelong companion and helpmate. I thank you for the most perfect marriage in the world, based on BRAHMACHARYA (self-control) and not on sex. I thank you for having considered me your equal in your life work for India. I thank you for not being one of those husbands who spend their time in gambling, racing, women, wine, and song, tiring of their wives and children as the little boy quickly tires of his childhood toys. How thankful I am that you were not one of those husbands who devote their time to growing rich on the exploitation of the labor of others.

How thankful I am that you put God and country before bribes, that you had the courage of your convictions and a complete and implicit faith in God. How thankful I am for a husband that put God and his country before me. I am grateful to you for your tolerance of me and my shortcomings of youth, when I grumbled and rebelled against the change you made in our mode of living, from so much to so little.

For years Kasturabai performed the duties of treasurer of the public funds which the idolized Mahatma is able to raise by the millions. One day the public treasurer, Kasturabai, could not account for a disbursement of four rupees. Gandhi duly published an auditing in which he inexorably pointed out his wife's four rupee discrepancy.

At three o'clock that afternoon in Wardha, I betook myself, by previous appointment, to the writing room of the saint who had been able to make an unflinching disciple out of his own wife – rare miracle! Gandhi looked up with his unforgettable smile.

"Mahatmaji," I said as I squatted beside him on the uncushioned mat, "please tell me your definition of AHIMSA."

"The avoidance of harm to any living creature in thought or deed."

"Beautiful ideal! But the world will always ask: May one not kill a cobra to protect a child, or one's self?"

"I could not kill a cobra without violating two of my vows – fearlessness, and non-killing. I would rather try inwardly to calm the snake by vibrations of love. I cannot possibly lower my standards to suit my circumstances." With his amazing candor, Gandhi added, "I must confess that I could not carry on this conversation were I faced by a cobra!"

I remarked on several very recent Western books on diet which lay on his desk.

"Yes, diet is important in the SATYAGRAHA movement-as everywhere else," he said with a chuckle. "Because I advocate complete continence for SATYAGRAHIS, I am always trying to find out the best diet for the celibate. One must conquer the palate before he can control the procreative instinct. Semi-starvation or unbalanced diets are not the answer. After overcoming the inward GREED for food, a SATYAGRAHI must continue to follow a rational vegetarian diet with all necessary vitamins, minerals, calories, and so forth. By inward and outward wisdom in regard to eating, the SATYAGRAHI'S sexual fluid is easily turned into vital energy for the whole body."

"Eggs are a high-protein food; are they forbidden to SATYAGRAHIS?" I asked.

"Not unfertilized eggs." The Mahatma laughed reminiscently. "For years I would not countenance their use; even now I personally do not eat them. One of my daughters-in-law was once dying of malnutrition; her doctor insisted on eggs. I would not agree, and advised him to give her some egg-substitute.

"'Gandhiji,' the doctor said, 'unfertilized eggs contain no life sperm; no killing is involved.'

"I then gladly gave permission for my daughter-in-law to eat eggs; she was soon restored to health."

On the previous night Gandhi had expressed a wish to receive the KRIYA YOGA of Lahiri Mahasaya. I was touched by the Mahatma's open-mindedness and spirit of inquiry. The hour for my promised instruction had arrived; several SATYAGRAHIS now entered the room – Mr. Desai, Dr. Pingale, and a few others who desired the KRIYA technique.

I first taught the little class the physical YOGODA exercises. The body is visualized as divided into twenty parts; the will directs energy in turn to each section. Soon everyone was vibrating before me like a human motor. It was easy to observe the rippling effect on Gandhi's twenty body parts, at all times completely exposed to view! Though very thin, he is not unpleasingly so; the skin of his body is smooth and unwrinkled.

Later I initiated the group into the liberating technique of KRIYA YOGA.

The Mahatma has reverently studied all world religions. The Jain scriptures, the Biblical New Testament, and the sociological writings of Tolstoy are the three main sources of Gandhi's nonviolent convictions. He has stated his credo thus:

I believe like every Hindu in God and His oneness, in rebirth and salvation. . . . I can no more describe my feeling for Hinduism than for my own wife. She moves me as no other woman in the world can. Not that she has no faults; I daresay she has many more than I see myself. But the feeling of an indissoluble bond is there. Even so I feel for and about Hinduism with all its faults and limitations. Nothing delights me so much as the music of the GITA, or the RAMAYANA by Tulsidas. When I fancied I was taking my last breath, the GITA was my solace.

Hinduism is not an exclusive religion. In it there is room for the worship of all the prophets of the world. It is not a missionary religion in the ordinary sense of the term. It has no doubt absorbed many tribes in its fold, but this absorption has been of an evolutionary, imperceptible character. Hinduism tells each man to worship God according to his own faith or DHARMA, and so lives at peace with all religions.

Of Christ, Gandhi has written: "I am sure that if He were living here now among men, He would bless the lives of many who perhaps have never even heard His name . . . just as it is written: 'Not every one that saith unto me, Lord, Lord . . . but he that doeth the will of my Father.' In the lesson of His own life, Jesus gave humanity the magnificent purpose and the single objective toward which we all ought to aspire. I believe that He belongs not solely to Christianity, but to the entire world, to all lands and races."

On my last evening in Wardha I addressed the meeting which had been called by Mr. Desai in Town Hall. The room was thronged to the window sills with about 400 people assembled to hear the talk on yoga. I spoke first in Hindi, then in English. Our little group returned to the ashram in time for a good-night glimpse of Gandhi, enfolded in peace and correspondence.

Night was still lingering when I rose at 5:00 A.M. After breakfast our trio sought out Gandhi for farewell PRONAMS. The saint rises at four o'clock for his morning prayer.

"Mahatmaji, good-by!" I knelt to touch his feet. "India is safe in your keeping!"

Years have rolled by since the Wardha idyl; the earth,

oceans, and skies have darkened with a world at war. Alone among great leaders, Gandhi has offered a practical nonviolent alternative to armed might. To redress grievances and remove injustices, the Mahatma has employed nonviolent means which again and again have proved their effectiveness.

War and crime never pay. The billions of dollars that went up in the smoke of explosive nothingness would have been sufficient to have made a new world, one almost free from disease and completely free from poverty. Not an earth of fear, chaos, famine, pestilence, the DANSE MACABRE, but one broad land of peace, of prosperity, and of widening knowledge.

The nonviolent voice of Gandhi appeals to man's highest conscience. Let nations ally themselves no longer with death, but with life; not with destruction, but with construction; not with the Annihilator, but with the Creator.

"One should forgive, under any injury," says the MAHABHARATA. "It hath been said that the continuation of species is due to man's being forgiving. Forgiveness is holiness; by forgiveness the universe is held together. Forgiveness is the might of the mighty; forgiveness is sacrifice; forgiveness is quiet of mind. Forgiveness and gentleness are the qualities of the self-possessed. They represent eternal virtue."

Nonviolence is the natural outgrowth of the law of forgiveness and love. "If loss of life becomes necessary in a righteous battle," Gandhi proclaims, "one should be prepared, like Jesus, to shed his own, not others', blood. Eventually there will be less blood spilt in the world."

"I would wait, if need be for ages," Gandhi says, "rather than seek the freedom of my country through bloody means." Never does the Mahatma forget the majestic warning: "All they that take the sword shall perish with the sword." Gandhi has written:

I call myself a nationalist, but my nationalism is as broad as the universe. It includes in its sweep all the nations of the earth. My nationalism includes the well-being of the whole world. I do not want my India to rise on the ashes of other nations. I do not want India to exploit a single human being. I want India to be strong in order that she can infect the other nations also with her strength. Not so with a single nation in Europe today; they do not give strength to the others.

By the Mahatma's training of thousands of true SATYAGRAHIS, who in turn spread the message; by patiently educating the Indian masses to understand the spiritual and eventually material benefits of nonviolence; by arming his people with nonviolent weapons--non-cooperation with injustice, the willingness to endure indignities, prison, death itself rather than resort to arms; by enlisting world sympathy through countless examples of heroic martyrdom among SATYAGRAHIS, Gandhi has dramatically portrayed the practical nature of nonviolence, its solemn power to settle disputes without war.

Gandhi has already won through nonviolent means a greater number of political concessions for his land than have ever been won by any leader of any country except through bullets. Nonviolent methods for eradication of all wrongs and evils have been strikingly applied not only in the political arena but in the delicate and complicated field of Indian social reform. Gandhi and his followers have removed many longstanding feuds between Hindus and Mohammedans; hundreds of thousands of Moslems look to the Mahatma as their leader. The untouchables have found in him their fearless and triumphant champion. "If there be a rebirth in store for me," Gandhi wrote, "I wish to be born a pariah in the midst of pariahs, because thereby I would be able to render them more effective service."

The Mahatma is indeed a "great soul," but it was illiterate millions who had the discernment to bestow the title. This gentle prophet is honored in his own land. The lowly peasant has been able to rise to Gandhi's high challenge. The Mahatma wholeheartedly believes in the inherent nobility of man. The inevitable failures have never disillusioned him. "Even if the opponent plays him false twenty times," he writes, "the SATYAGRAHI is ready to trust him the twenty-first time, for an implicit trust in human nature is the very essence of the creed."

"I am fighting for nothing less than world peace," Gandhi has declared. "If the Indian movement is carried to success on a nonviolent SATYAGRAHA basis, it will give a new meaning to patriotism and, if I may say so in all humility, to life itself."

Before the West dismisses Gandhi's program as one of an impractical dreamer, let it first reflect on a definition of SATYAGRAHA by the Master of Galilee:

"Ye have heard that it hath been said, An eye for an eye, and a tooth for a tooth: but I say unto you, That ye resist not evil: but whosoever shall smite thee on thy right cheek, turn to him the other also."

Gandhi's epoch has extended, with the beautiful precision of cosmic timing, into a century already desolated and devastated by two World Wars. A divine handwriting appears on the granite wall of his life: a warning against the further shedding of blood among brothers.

45

The Bengali "Joy-Permeated" Mother

"Sir, please do not leave India without a glimpse of Nirmala Devi. Her sanctity is intense; she is known far and wide as Ananda Moyi Ma (Joy-Permeated Mother)." My niece, Amiyo Bose, gazed at me earnestly.

"Of course! I want very much to see the woman saint." I added, "I have read of her advanced state of God-realization. A little article about her appeared years ago in EAST-WEST."

A few days later I heard that the Blissful Mother was staying at the home of a disciple in the Bhowanipur section of Calcutta. Mr. Wright and I set out immediately from my father's Calcutta home. As the Ford neared the Bhowanipur house, my companion and I observed an unusual street scene.

Ananda Moyi Ma was standing in an open-topped automobile, blessing a throng of about one hundred disciples. She was evidently on the point of departure. Mr. Wright parked the Ford some distance away, and accompanied me on foot toward the quiet assemblage. The woman saint glanced in our direction; she alit from her car and walked toward us.

"Father, you have come!" With these fervent words she put her arm around my neck and her head on my shoulder.

Mr. Wright, to whom I had just remarked that I did not know the saint, was hugely enjoying this extraordinary demonstration of welcome. The eyes of the one hundred chelas were also fixed with some surprise on the affectionate tableau.

I had instantly seen that the saint was in a high state of SAMADHI. Utterly oblivious to her outward garb as a woman, she knew herself as the changeless soul; from that plane she was joyously greeting another devotee of God. She led me by the hand into her automobile.

"Ananda Moyi Ma, I am delaying your journey!" I protested.

"Father, I am meeting you for the first time in this life, after ages!" she said. "Please do not leave yet."

We sat together in the rear seats of the car. The Blissful Mother soon entered the immobile ecstatic state. Her beautiful eyes glanced heavenward and, half-opened, became stilled, gazing into the near-far inner Elysium. The disciples chanted gently: "Victory to Mother Divine!"

I had found many men of God-realization in India, but never before had I met such an .alted woman saint. Her gentle face was burnished with the ineffable joy that had given her the name of Blissful Mother. Long black tresses lay loosely behind her unveiled head. I put some questions to a near-by woman chela while Ananda Moyi Ma remained entranced.

"The Blissful Mother travels widely in India; in many parts she has hundreds of disciples," the chela told me. "Her courageous efforts have brought about many desirable social reforms. Although a Brahmin, the saint recognizes no caste distinctions. A group of us always travel with her, looking after her comforts. We have to mother her; she takes no notice of her body. If no one gave her food, she would not eat, or make any inquiries. Even when meals are placed before her, she does not touch them. To prevent her disappearance from this world, we disciples feed her with our own hands. For days together she often stays in the divine trance, scarcely breathing, her eyes unwinking. One of her chief disciples is her husband. Many years ago, soon after their marriage, he took the vow of silence."

The chela pointed to a broad-shouldered, fine-featured man with long hair and hoary beard. He was standing quietly in the midst of the gathering, his hands folded in a disciple's reverential attitude.

Refreshed by her dip in the Infinite, Ananda Moyi Ma was now focusing her consciousness on the material world.

"Father, please tell me where you stay." Her voice was clear and melodious.

"At present, in Calcutta or Ranchi; but soon I shall be returning to America."

"America?"

"Yes. An Indian woman saint would be sincerely appreciated there by spiritual seekers. Would you like to go?"

"If Father can take me, I will go."

This reply caused her near-by disciples to start in alarm.

"Twenty or more of us always travel with the Blissful Mother," one of them told me firmly. "We could not live without her. Wherever she goes, we must go."

Reluctantly I abandoned the plan, as possessing an impractical feature of spontaneous enlargement!

"Please come at least to Ranchi, with your disciples," I said on taking leave of the saint. "As a divine child yourself, you will enjoy the little ones in my school."

"Whenever Father takes me, I will gladly go."

A short time later the Ranchi VIDYALAYA was in gala array for the saint's promised visit. The youngsters looked forward to any day of festivity – no lessons, hours of music, and a feast for the climax!

"It is beautiful here," Ananda Moyi Ma said graciously as I led her into the main building. She seated herself with a childlike smile by my side. The closest of dear friends, she made one feel, yet an aura of remoteness was ever around her- the paradoxical isolation of Omnipresence.

"Please tell me something of your life."

"Father knows all about it; why repeat it?" She evidently felt that the factual history of one short incarnation was beneath notice.

I laughed, gently repeating my question.

"Father, there is little to tell." She spread her graceful hands in a deprecatory gesture. "My consciousness has never associated itself with this temporary body. Before I came on this earth, Father, 'I was the same.' As a little girl, 'I was the same.' I grew into womanhood, but still 'I was the same.' When the family in which I had been born made arrangements to have this body married, 'I was the same.' And when, passion-drunk, my husband came to me and murmured endearing words, lightly touching my body, he received a violent shock, as if struck by lightning, for even then 'I was the same.'

"My husband knelt before me, folded his hands, and implored my pardon.

"'Mother,' he said, 'because I have desecrated your bodily temple by touching it with the thought of lust, not knowing that within it dwelt not my wife but the Divine Mother, I take this solemn vow: I shall be your disciple, a celibate follower, ever caring for you in silence as a servant, never speaking to anyone again as long as I live. May I thus atone for the sin I have today committed against you, my guru.'

"Even when I quietly accepted this proposal of my husband's, 'I was the same.' And, Father, in front of you now, 'I am the same.' Ever afterward, though the dance of creation change around me in the hall of eternity, 'I shall be the same.'"

Ananda Moyi Ma sank into a deep meditative state. Her form was statue-still; she had fled to her ever-calling kingdom. The dark pools of her eyes appeared lifeless and glassy. This expression is often present when saints remove their consciousness from the physical body, which is then hardly more than a piece of soulless clay. We sat together for an hour in the ecstatic trance. She returned to this world with a gay little laugh.

"Please, Ananda Moyi Ma," I said, "come with me to the garden. Mr. Wright will take some pictures."

"Of course, Father. Your will is my will." Her glorious eyes retained the unchanging divine luster as she posed for many photographs.

Time for the feast! Ananda Moyi Ma squatted on her blanket-seat, a disciple at her elbow to feed her. Like an infant, the saint obediently swallowed the food after the chela had brought it to her lips. It was plain that the Blissful Mother did not recognize any difference between curries and sweetmeats!

As dusk approached, the saint left with her party amidst a shower of rose petals, her hands raised in blessing on the little lads. Their faces shone with the affection she had effortlessly awakened.

Casting aside every inferior attachment, Ananda Moyi Ma offers her sole allegiance to the Lord. Not by the hairsplitting distinctions of scholars but by the sure logic of faith, the childlike saint has solved the only problem in human life-establishment of unity with God. Man has forgotten this stark simplicity, now befogged by a million issues. Refusing a monotheistic love to God, the nations disguise their infidelity by punctilious respect before the outward shrines of charity. These humanitarian gestures are virtuous, because for a moment they divert man's attention from himself, but they do not free him from his single responsibility in life, referred to by Jesus as the first commandment. The uplifting obligation to love God is assumed with man's first breath of an air freely bestowed by his only Benefactor.

On one other occasion after her Ranchi visit I had opportunity to see Ananda Moyi Ma. She stood among her disciples some months later on the Serampore station platform, waiting for the train.

"Father, I am going to the Himalayas," she told me. "Generous disciples have built me a hermitage in Dehra Dun."

As she boarded the train, I marveled to see that whether amidst a crowd, on a train, feasting, or sitting in silence, her eyes never looked away from God. Within me I still hear her voice, an echo of measureless sweetness:

"Behold, now and always one with the Eternal, 'I am ever the same.'"

46

The Woman Yogi Who Never Eats

"Sir, whither are we bound this morning?" Mr. Wright was driving the Ford; he took his eyes off the road long enough to gaze at me with a questioning twinkle. From day to day he seldom knew what part of Bengal he would be discovering next.

"God willing," I replied devoutly, "we are on our way to see an eighth wonder of the world – a woman saint whose diet is thin air!"

"Sir, we would like to know more of the fasting saint."

"Her name is Giri Bala," I informed my companions. "I first heard about her years ago from a scholarly gentleman, Sthiti Lal Nundy. He often came to the Gurpar Road home to tutor my brother Bishnu."

"'I know Giri Bala well,' Sthiti Babu told me. 'She employs a certain yoga technique which enables her to live without eating. I was her close neighbor in Nawabganj near Ichapur. I made it a point to watch her closely; never did I find evidence that she was taking either food or drink. My interest finally mounted so high that I approached the Maharaja of Burdwan and asked him to conduct an investigation. Astounded at the story, he invited her to his palace. She agreed to a test and lived for two months locked up in a small section of his home.

Later she returned for a palace visit of twenty days; and then for a third test of fifteen days. The Maharaja himself told me that these three rigorous scrutinies had convinced him beyond doubt of her non-eating state.'

"She must be quite aged now. I do not even know where, or if, she lives. But in a few hours we shall reach Purulia; her brother has a home there."

By ten-thirty our little group was conversing with the brother, Lambadar Dey, a lawyer of Purulia.

"Yes, my sister is living. She sometimes stays with me here, but at present she is at our family home in Biur." Lambadar Babu glanced doubtfully at the Ford. "I hardly think, Swamiji, that any automobile has ever penetrated into the interior as far as Biur. May Ganesh go with you!" Lambadar Babu said, laughing. He added courteously, "If you ever get there, I am sure Giri Bala will be glad to see you. She is approaching her seventies, but continues in excellent health."

"Please tell me, sir, if it is absolutely true that she eats nothing?" I looked directly into his eyes, those telltale windows of the mind.

"It is true." His gaze was open and honorable. "In more than five decades I have never seen her eat a morsel. If the world suddenly came to an end, I could not be more astonished than by the sight of my sister's taking food!"

We chuckled together over the improbability of these two cosmic events.

"Giri Bala has never sought an inaccessible solitude for her yoga practices," Lambadar Babu went on. "She has lived her entire life surrounded by her family and friends. They are all well accustomed now to her strange state. Not one of them who would not be stupefied if Giri Bala suddenly decided to eat anything!."

The brother's sincerity was manifest. Our little party thanked him warmly and set out toward Biur. The road became more and more sickly: wrinkles of ruts, boils of hardened clay, the sad infirmities of old age! Our group dismounted occasionally to allow Mr. Wright to more easily maneuver the Ford, which the four of us pushed from behind. And finally, about 5:00 P.M., we were close to our destination, Biur. This minute village in the interior of Bankura District, hidden in the protection of dense foliage, is unapproachable by travelers during the rainy season, when the streams are raging torrents and the roads serpentlike spit the mud-venom.

Asking for a guide among a group of worshipers on their way home from a temple prayer, we were besieged by a dozen scantily clad lads who clambered on the sides of the car, eager to conduct us to Giri Bala.

Halting by a narrow lane we found ourselves within a hundred feet of Giri Bala's ancestral home. We felt the thrill of fulfillment after the long road struggle crowned by a rough finish. We approached a large, two-storied building of brick and plaster, dominating the surrounding adobe huts; the house was under the process of repair, for around it was the characteristically tropical framework of bamboos.

With feverish anticipation and suppressed rejoicing we stood before the open doors of the one blessed by the Lord's 'hungerless' touch. Soon a short figure came into view in the doorway – Giri Bala! She was swathed in a cloth of dull, goldish silk; in typically Indian fashion.

Meekly she approached and silently assented to our snapping a number of pictures with our 'still' and 'movie' cameras. Patiently and shyly she endured our photo techniques of posture adjustment and light arrangement. Finally we had recorded for posterity many photographs of the only woman in the world who is known to have lived without food or drink for over fifty years. A face of rare peace and innocent poise – a wide, childlike, quivering lip, a feminine nose, narrow, sparkling eyes, and a wistful smile.

She PRONAMED before me in the customary gesture of greeting from a householder to a monk. Her simple charm and quiet smile gave us a welcome beyond that of honeyed oratory; forgotten was our difficult, dusty trip.

The little saint seated herself cross-legged on the verandah. Though bearing the scars of age, she was not emaciated; her olive-colored skin had remained clear and healthy in tone.

"Mother," I said in Bengali, "for over twenty-five years I have thought eagerly of this very pilgrimage! I heard about your sacred life from Sthiti Lal Nundy Babu."

She nodded in acknowledgment. "Yes, my good neighbor in Nawabganj."

"During those years I have crossed the oceans, but I never forgot my early plan to someday see you. The sublime drama that you are here playing so inconspicuously should be blazoned before a world that has long forgotten the inner food divine."

The saint lifted her eyes for a minute, smiling with serene interest.

"Baba (honored father) knows best," she answered meekly.

I was happy that she had taken no offense; one never knows how great yogis or yoginis will react to the thought of publicity. They shun it, as a rule, wishing to pursue in silence the profound soul research. An inner sanction comes to them when the proper time arrives to display their lives openly for the benefit of seeking minds.

"Mother," I went on, "please forgive me, then, for burdening you with many questions. Kindly answer only those that please you; I shall understand your silence, also."

She spread her hands in a gracious gesture. "I am glad to reply, insofar as an insignificant person like myself can give satisfactory answers."

"Oh, no, not insignificant!" I protested sincerely. "You are a great soul."

"I am the humble servant of all." She added quaintly, "I love to cook and feed people."

A strange pastime, I thought, for a non-eating saint!

"Tell me, Mother, from your own lips – do you live without food?"

"That is true." She was silent for a few moments; her next remark showed that she had been struggling with mental arithmetic. "From the age of twelve years four months down to my present age of sixty-eight--a period of over fifty-six years--I have not eaten food or taken liquids."

"Are you never tempted to eat?"

"If I felt a craving for food, I would have to eat." Simply yet regally she stated this axiomatic truth, one known too well by a world revolving around three meals a day!

"But you do eat something!" My tone held a note of remonstrance.

"Of course!" She smiled in swift understanding.

"Your nourishment derives from the finer energies of the air and sunlight, and from the cosmic power which recharges your body through the medulla oblongata."

"Baba knows." Again she acquiesced, her manner soothing and unemphatic.

"Mother, please tell me about your early life. It holds a

deep interest for all of India, and even for our brothers and sisters beyond the seas."

Giri Bala put aside her habitual reserve, relaxing into a conversational mood.

"So be it." Her voice was low and firm. "I was born in these forest regions. My childhood was unremarkable save that I was possessed by an insatiable appetite. I had been betrothed in early years.

"'Child,' my mother often warned me, 'try to control your greed. When the time comes for you to live among strangers in your husband's family, what will they think of you if your days are spent in nothing but eating?'

"The calamity she had foreseen came to pass. I was only twelve when I joined my husband's people in Nawabganj. My mother-in-law shamed me morning, noon, and night about my gluttonous habits. Her scoldings were a blessing in disguise, however; they roused my dormant spiritual tendencies. One morning her ridicule was merciless.

"'I shall soon prove to you,' I said, stung to the quick, 'that I shall never touch food again as long as I live.'

"My mother-in-law laughed in derision. 'So!' she said, 'how can you live without eating, when you cannot live without overeating?'

"This remark was unanswerable! Yet an iron resolution scaffolded my spirit. In a secluded spot I sought my Heavenly Father.

"'Lord,' I prayed incessantly, 'please send me a guru, one who can teach me to live by Thy light and not by food.'

"A divine ecstasy fell over me. Led by a beatific spell, I set out for the Nawabganj GHAT on the Ganges. On the way I encountered the priest of my husband's family.

"'Venerable sir,' I said trustingly, 'kindly tell me how to live without eating.'

"He stared at me without reply. Finally he spoke in a consoling manner. 'Child,' he said, 'come to the temple this evening; I will conduct a special VEDIC ceremony for you.'

"This vague answer was not the one I was seeking; I continued toward the GHAT. The morning sun pierced the waters; I purified myself in the Ganges, as though for a sacred initiation. As I left the river bank, my wet cloth around me, in the broad glare of day my master materialized himself before me!

"'Dear little one,' he said in a voice of loving compassion, 'I am the guru sent here by God to fulfill your urgent prayer. He was deeply touched by its very unusual nature! From today you shall live by the astral light, your bodily atoms fed from the infinite current.'"

Giri Bala fell into silence. I took Mr. Wright's pencil and pad and translated into English a few items for his information.

The saint resumed the tale, her gentle voice barely audible. "The GHAT was deserted, but my guru cast round us an aura of guarding light, that no stray bathers later disturb us. He initiated me into a KRIA technique which frees the body from dependence on the gross food of mortals. The technique includes the use of a certain MANTRA and a breathing exercise more difficult than the average person could perform. No medicine or magic is involved; nothing beyond the KRIA."

In the manner of the American newspaper reporter, who had unknowingly taught me his procedure, I questioned Giri Bala on many matters which I thought would be of interest to the world. She gave me, bit by bit, the following information:

"I have never had any children; many years ago I became

a widow. I sleep very little, as sleep and waking are the same to me. I meditate at night, attending to my domestic duties in the daytime. I slightly feel the change in climate from season to season. I have never been sick or experienced any disease. I feel only slight pain when accidentally injured. I have no bodily excretions. I can control my heart and breathing. I often see my guru as well as other great souls, in vision."

"Mother," I asked, "why don't you teach others the method of living without food?"

My ambitious hopes for the world's starving millions were nipped in the bud.

"No." She shook her head. "I was strictly commanded by my guru not to divulge the secret. It is not his wish to tamper with God's drama of creation. The farmers would not thank me if I taught many people to live without eating! The luscious fruits would lie uselessly on the ground. It appears that misery, starvation, and disease are whips of our karma which ultimately drive us to seek the true meaning of life."

"Mother," I said slowly, "what is the use of your having been singled out to live without eating?"

"To prove that man is Spirit." Her face lit with wisdom. "To demonstrate that by divine advancement he can gradually learn to live by the Eternal Light and not by food."

The tropical darkness had fallen. The light of a small kerosene lamp flickered fitfully over the faces of a score of villagers squatting silently in the shadows. The darting glowworms and distant oil lanterns of the huts wove bright eerie patterns into the velvet night. It was the painful hour of parting; a slow, tedious journey lay before our little party.

"Giri Bala," I said as the saint opened her eyes, "please give me a keepsake – a strip of one of your SARIS."

She soon returned with a piece of Benares silk, extending it in her hand as she suddenly prostrated herself on the ground.

"Mother," I said reverently, "rather let me touch your own blessed feet!"

47

I Return to the West

It is September, 1936; I am in England to fulfill a promise, given sixteen months earlier, to lecture again in London.

England, too, is receptive to the timeless yoga message. Reporters and newsreel cameramen swarmed over my quarters at Grosvenor House. The British National Council of the World Fellowship of Faiths organized a meeting on September 29 at Whitefield's Congregational Church where I addressed the audience on the weighty subject of "How Faith in Fellowship may Save Civilization." The eight o'clock lectures at Caxton Hall attracted such crowds that on two nights the overflow waited in Windsor House auditorium for my second talk at nine-thirty.

Unforgettable weeks in England; days of sight-seeing in London, then over the beautiful countryside. Mr. Wright and I summoned the trusty Ford to visit the birthplaces and tombs of the great poets and heroes of British history.

Our little party sailed from Southampton for America in late October on the BREMEN. The majestic Statue of Liberty in New York harbor brought a joyous emotional gulp not only to the throats of Miss Bletch and Mr. Wright, but to my own. And in late 1936, we were at Mount Washington.

The year-end holidays are celebrated annually at the Los

Angeles center with an eight-hour group meditation on December 24th (Spiritual Christmas), followed the next day by a banquet (Social Christmas). The festivities this year were augmented by the presence of dear friends and students from distant cities who had arrived to welcome home the three world travelers.

The Christmas Day feast included delicacies brought fifteen thousand miles for this glad occasion: GUCCHI mushrooms from Kashmir, canned RASAGULLA and mango pulp, PAPAR biscuits, and an oil of the Indian KEORA flower which flavored our ice cream.

Gift-time! Presents from the earth's far corners-Palestine, Egypt, India, England, France, Italy. How laboriously had Mr. Wright counted the trunks at each foreign junction, that no pilfering hand receive the treasures intended for loved ones in America! Plaques of the sacred olive tree from the Holy Land, delicate laces and embroideries from Belgium and Holland, Persian carpets, finely woven Kashmiri shawls, everlastingly fragrant sandalwood trays from Mysore, Shiva "bull's eye" stones from Central Provinces, old Indian coins of dynasties long fled, bejeweled vases and cups, miniatures, tapestries, temple incense and perfumes, SWADESHI cotton prints, lacquer work, Mysore ivory carvings, Persian slippers with their inquisitive long toe, quaint old illuminated manuscripts, velvets, brocades, Gandhi caps, potteries, tiles, brasswork, prayer rugs-booty of three continents!

One by one I distributed the gaily wrapped packages from the immense pile under the tree.

"Sister Gyanamata!" I handed a long box to the saintly American lady of sweet visage and deep realization who, during my absence, had been in charge at Mt. Washington.

From the paper tissues she lifted a SARI of golden Benares silk.

"Thank you, sir; it brings the pageant of India before my eyes."

"Mr. Dickinson!" The next parcel contained a gift which I had bought in a Calcutta bazaar. "Mr. Dickinson will like this," I had thought at the time. A dearly beloved disciple, Mr. Dickinson had been present at every Christmas festivity since the 1925 founding of Mt. Washington. At this eleventh annual celebration, he was standing before me, untying the ribbons of his square little package.

"The silver cup!" Struggling with emotion, he stared at the present, a tall drinking cup. He seated himself some distance away, apparently in a daze. I smiled at him affectionately before resuming my role as Santa Claus.

The ejaculatory evening closed with a prayer to the Giver of all gifts; then a group singing of Christmas carols.

Mr. Dickinson and I were chatting together sometime later.

"Sir," he said, "please let me thank you now for the silver cup. I could not find any words on Christmas night."

"I brought the gift especially for you."

"For forty-three years I have been waiting for that silver cup! It is a long story, one I have kept hidden within me." Mr. Dickinson looked at me shyly. "The beginning was dramatic: I was drowning. My older brother had playfully pushed me into a fifteen-foot pool in a small town in Nebraska. I was only five years old then. As I was about to sink for the second time under the water, a dazzling multicolored light appeared, filling all space. In the midst was the figure of a man with tranquil eyes and a reassuring smile. My body was sinking for the third time when one of my brother's companions bent a tall slender willow tree in such a low dip that I could grasp it with my desperate fingers. The boys lifted me to the bank and successfully gave me first-aid treatment.

"Twelve years later, a youth of seventeen, I visited Chicago with my mother. It was 1893; the great World Parliament of Religions was in session. Mother and I were walking down a main street, when again I saw the mighty flash of light. A few paces away, strolling leisurely along, was the same man I had seen years before in vision. He approached a large auditorium and vanished within the door.

"'Mother,' I cried, 'that was the man who appeared at the time I was drowning!'

"She and I hastened into the building; the man was seated on a lecture platform. We soon learned that he was Swami Vivekananda of India. After he had given a soul-stirring talk, I went forward to meet him. He smiled on me graciously, as though we were old friends. I was so young that I did not know how to give expression to my feelings, but in my heart I was hoping that he would offer to be my teacher. He read my thought.

"'No, my son, I am not your guru.' Vivekananda gazed with his beautiful, piercing eyes deep into my own. 'Your teacher will come later. He will give you a silver cup.' After a little pause, he added, smiling, 'He will pour out to you more blessings than you are now able to hold.'

"I left Chicago in a few days," Mr. Dickinson went on, "and never saw the great Vivekananda again. But every word he had uttered was indelibly written on my inmost consciousness. Years passed; no teacher appeared. One night in 1925 I prayed deeply that the Lord would send me my guru.

"The next evening I attended, for the first time, one of your lectures here in Los Angeles, and knew then that my prayer had been granted."

We smiled at each other in silence.

48

At Encinitas in California

"A surprise, sir! During your absence abroad we have had this Encinitas hermitage built; it is a 'welcome-home' gift!" Sister Gyanamata smilingly led me through a gate and up a tree-shaded walk.

I saw a building jutting out like a great white ocean liner toward the blue brine. First speechlessly, then with "Oh's!" and "Ah's!", finally with man's insufficient vocabulary of joy and gratitude, I examined the ashram – sixteen unusually large rooms, each one charmingly appointed.

The stately central hall, with immense ceiling-high windows, looks out on a united altar of grass, ocean, sky-a symphony in emerald, opal, sapphire. A mantle over the hall's huge fireplace holds the framed likeness of Lahiri Mahasaya, smiling his blessing over this far Pacific heaven.

Directly below the hall, built into the very bluff, two solitary meditation caves confront the infinities of sky and sea. Verandahs, sun-bathing nooks, acres of orchard, a eucalypti grove, flagstone paths leading through roses and lilies to quiet arbors, a long flight of stairs ending on an isolated beach and the vast waters! Was dream ever more concrete?

This Self-Realization Fellowship ashram had been made possible through the generosity of a few American disciples,

American businessmen of endless responsibilities who yet find time daily for their KRIYA YOGA. Not a word of the hermitage construction had been allowed to reach me during my stay in India and Europe. Astonishment, delight!

During my earlier years in America I had combed the coast of California in quest of a small site for a seaside ashram; whenever I had found a suitable location, some obstacle had invariably arisen to thwart me. Gazing now over the broad acres of Encinitas, humbly I saw the effortless fulfillment of Sri Yukteswar's long-ago prophecy: "a hermitage by the ocean."

Many happy months sped by; in the peace of perfect beauty I was able to complete at the hermitage a long-projected work, COSMIC CHANTS. I set to English words and Western musical notation about forty songs, some original, others my adaptations of ancient melodies. Included were the Shankara chant, "No Birth, No Death"; two favorites of Sri Yukteswar's: "Wake, Yet Wake, O my Saint!" and "Desire, my Great Enemy"; the hoary Sanskrit "Hymn to Brahma"; old Bengali songs, "What Lightning Flash!" and "They Have Heard Thy Name"; Tagore's "Who is in my Temple?"; and a number of my compositions: "I Will be Thine Always," "In the Land Beyond my Dreams," "Come Out of the Silent Sky," "Listen to my Soul Call," "In the Temple of Silence," and "Thou Art my Life."

The secluded life of a literary minstrel was not my role for long. Soon I was dividing every fortnight between Los Angeles and Encinitas. Sunday services, classes, lectures before clubs and colleges, interviews with students, ceaseless streams of correspondence, articles for EAST-WEST, direction of activities in India and numerous small centers in American cities. Much time was given, also, to the arrangement of

KRIYA and other Self-Realization Fellowship teachings into a series of studies for the distant yoga seekers whose zeal recognized no limitation of space.

Joyous dedication of a Self-Realization Church of All Religions took place in 1938 at Washington, D.C. Set amidst landscaped grounds, the stately church stands in a section of the city aptly called "Friendship Heights." The Washington leader is Swami Premananda, educated at the Ranchi school and Calcutta University. I had summoned him in 1928 to assume leadership of the Washington Self-Realization Fellowship center.

Premananda accompanied me from Washington for a brief visit to the Self-Realization Fellowship center in Boston. What joy to see again the KRIYA YOGA band who had remained steadfast since 1920! The Boston leader, Dr. M. W. Lewis, lodged my companion and myself in a modern, artistically decorated suite.

The shadows of approaching carnage were lengthening over the world; already the acute ear might hear the frightful drums of war. During interviews with thousands in California, and through a world-wide correspondence, I found that men and women were deeply searching their hearts; the tragic outer insecurity had emphasized need for the Eternal Anchorage.

The war years brought a spiritual awakening among men whose diversions had never before included a study of the New Testament. One sweet distillment from the bitter herbs of war! To satisfy a growing need, an inspiring little Self-Realization Church of All Religions was built and dedicated in 1942 at Hollywood. The site faces Olive Hill and the distant Los Angeles Planetarium. The church, finished in blue, white, and gold, is reflected amidst the water hyacinths in a large pool. A universal benignity flows from small niches with statues of Lahiri Mahasaya and Sri Yukteswar, and of Krishna, Buddha, Confucius, St. Francis, and a beautiful mother-of-pearl reproduction of Christ at the Last Supper.

Another Self-Realization Church of All Religions was founded in 1943 at San Diego. A quiet hilltop temple, it stands in a sloping valley of eucalypti, overlooking sparkling San Diego Bay.

New Year's week of 1945 found me at work in my Encinitas study, revising the manuscript of this book.

"Paramhansaji, please come outdoors." Dr. Lewis, on a visit from Boston, smiled at me pleadingly from outside my window. Soon we were strolling in the sunshine. My companion pointed to new towers in process of construction along the edge of the Fellowship property adjoining the coast highway.

"Sir, I see many improvements here since my last visit." Dr. Lewis comes twice annually from Boston to Encinitas.

"Yes, Doctor, a project I have long considered is beginning to take definite form. In these beautiful surroundings I have started a miniature world colony. Brotherhood is an ideal better understood by example than precept! A small harmonious group here may inspire other ideal communities over the earth."

"A splendid idea, sir! The colony will surely be a success if everyone sincerely does his part!"

"'World' is a large term, but man must enlarge his allegiance, considering himself in the light of a world citizen," I continued. "A person who truly feels: 'The world is my homeland; it is my America, my India, my Philippines, my England, my Africa,' will never lack scope for a useful and happy life. His natural local pride will know limitless expansion; he will be in touch with creative universal currents."

Dr. Lewis and I halted above the lotus pool near the hermitage. Below us lay the illimitable Pacific.

"These same waters break equally on the coasts of West and East, in California and China." My companion threw a little stone into the first of the oceanic seventy million square miles. "Encinitas is a symbolic spot for a world colony."

"That is true, Doctor. We shall arrange here for many conferences and Congresses of Religion, inviting delegates from all lands. Flags of the nations will hang in our halls. Diminutive temples will be built over the grounds, dedicated to the world's principal religions.

"As soon as possible," I went on, "I plan to open a Yoga Institute here. The blessed role of KRIYA YOGA in the West has hardly more than just begun. May all men come to know that there is a definite, scientific technique of self-realization for the overcoming of all human misery!"

August 15, 1945, close of Global War II! End of a world; dawn of an enigmatic Atomic Age! The hermitage residents gathered in the main hall for a prayer of thanksgiving. "Heavenly Father, may never it be again! Thy children go henceforth as brothers!"

Gone was the tension of war years; our spirits purred in the sun of peace. I gazed happily at each of my American comrades.

"Lord," I thought gratefully, "Thou hast given this monk a large family!"

•••

PARAMAHANSA YOGANANDA

As I Knew Him

Roy Eugene Davis

Paramahansa Yogananda travelled from India to America in 1920 to teach the practical means by which people in all walks of life could nurture their spiritual growth and awaken to Self-and God-realization. He emphasized Kriya Yoga: intensive spiritual practices that can unify (*yoga*) one's attention and awareness with the infinite. During his thirty-two years of service he lectured to multitudes of people, initiated more than one hundred thousand students, wrote books and magazine articles, founded several ashrams and temples, and directed the activities of an organisation that continues to spred his teachings throughout the world.